Yellowstone Summers

Yellowstone Summers

Touring with the
Wylie Camping Company
in America's First National Park

JANE GALLOWAY DEMARAY

WSU
PRESS
Washington State University
Pullman, Washington

WSU PRESS
WASHINGTON STATE UNIVERSITY

Washington State University Press
PO Box 645910
Pullman, Washington 99164-5910
Phone: 800-354-7360
Fax: 509-335-8568
Email: wsupress@wsu.edu
Website: wsupress.wsu.edu

Library of Congress Cataloging-in-Publication Data

Demaray, Jane Galloway, 1957-
  Yellowstone summers : touring with the Wylie Camping Company in America's first national park / Jane Galloway Demaray.
     pages cm
  Includes bibliographical references and index.
  ISBN 978-0-87422-328-6 (alkaline paper) 1. Yellowstone National Park--Description and travel. 2. Camping—Yellowstone National Park—History. 3. Tourism—Yellowstone National Park--History. 4. Wylie Permanent Camping Co.—History. 5. Wylie, W. W. (William Wallace) 6. Frontier and pioneer life—Yellowstone National Park. 7. Yellowstone National Park—History. 8. Yellowstone National Park--Social life and customs. I. Title.
  F722.D46 2014
  338.7'619178752--dc23
                                                                    2014036205

In Memory of William Wallace
and Mary Ann Wilson Wylie

Contents

Illustrations

Acknowledgements

Will and Mary Ann Wylie's vision, perseverance, and love of Yellowstone National Park made this book possible. I am deeply grateful that Will wrote of his experiences and those of his family—family bound to him by blood and marriage, as well as his Park family. Although they are now in that peaceful place "where all languages are understood," two Wylie cousins deserve special recognition: Will and Mary Ann's granddaughter, Mary Lou Wardle, who saw Will's unpublished manuscript off on its journey from California to Montana, and Paul R. Wylie Sr., who helped the manuscript find its way to Montana State University's Burlingame Special Collections and the Yellowstone National Park Archives and Research Library. Now many years later, my work benefited greatly from the often humorous encouragement and sage advice I received from my cousin, Paul R. "Nick" Wylie Jr., an accomplished writer of western nonfiction who lives in Bozeman, Montana.

It was a privilege to work with the primary and secondary sources that are included in the book's bibliography. While working with those sources, I drew heavily upon the fine education and training I received in the public schools of Calgary, Alberta, and at the University of Puget Sound, the University of Montana, and Seattle Pacific University. Many, many thanks to the following professionals who modeled the importance of critical thinking and writing about life's big ideas for a general audience: Suzanne Barnett, Professor Emerita of History, University of Puget Sound; Terry Cooney, formerly at the University of Puget Sound, now dean at Towson University's College of Liberal Arts; the late Walter Lowrie, Professor Emeritus of History, University of Puget Sound; and Edward Kame'enui, previously at the University of Montana, now working as a professor of teaching and learning at the University of Oregon.

I would also like to recognize the dedicated support of reference historian Zoe Ann Stoltz, library manager Brian Shovers, and photo archives manager Delores Morrow, all working at the Montana

Historical Society; Kim Allen Scott, Montana State University Librar-
ies archivist; Jessica Gerdes, Yellowstone National Park research
librarian; Colleen Curry, Yellowstone National Park's museum curator; Steven Jackson, Museum of the Rockies' curator of art and photography; Greg Walz, research center manager at the Utah State Historical Society; and Quentin Kujala at Montana's Fish, Wildlife and
Parks office in Helena.

Martha Kohl, specialist at the Montana Historical Society, suggested that I work with Caroline Patterson of Missoula, a gifted writer,
editor, and teacher—an experience that I thoroughly enjoyed. Thank
you, Caroline, for your unwavering support and enthusiasm, and for
recommending Ann Seifert, a Helena-based copy editor. Construc-
tive criticism offered by Lee Whittlesey, Yellowstone National Park
historian; Karen Reinhart, author of *Yellowstone's Rebirth by Fire*; and
David Wrobel, professor of history at the University of Oklahoma,
also helped my work immensely. From our first email exchange
about the Wylie Camping Company, my editor at Washington State
University Press, Robert Clark, never wavered in his optimism about
Wylie's contribution to Yellowstone National Park history. Bob, I will
be forever grateful for your spirit of collaboration. I thank you and
the WSU Press staff.

I have a deep appreciation for my extended family and support
system. I am very grateful to my late grandparents and my parents, Susan and Dick, for insisting that my sisters—Patty, Carolyn,
and Katie—and I "go outside and don't cause trouble"; spend time
reading, writing, using our imagination, and laughing at ourselves;
put in our two cents during dinner-table conversations; satisfy our
curiosity; and work at our education. Thank you, Mom and Dad, for
being the extraordinary, loving role models that you are; and too,
for reading my early drafts and offering practical ideas about how
to improve. My in-laws, Joanne and Wendell, have also offered their
wholehearted support in so many ways. Two in particular come to
mind—the strength of their faith and telling me that they appreciated
my letters. To treasured friends and co-workers through the years
who have shared a little of their history, while patiently listening to
mine, I thank you. To my daughters, Elyse and Maria; my son-in-law,

Derek; and grandchildren, Sydney and Rally, I also dedicate this book—to your generations will come the eventual charge of caring for the national parks. And finally, to my husband, Kevin—for your patience, love, and understanding—I can never thank you enough.

No matter the genius of our civilization, the national parks remind us of our greater destiny.

—Alfred Runte

Introduction

I N 1896 WILLIAM WALLACE WYLIE printed stationary advertising his newly incorporated Wylie Camping Company. In the left-hand corner he promoted his "new method of caring for tourists." In a paragraph below his slogan he portrayed his vision of permanent camps spread throughout Yellowstone National Park—the nation's first national park, established in 1872. In the post-Civil War expansion of the railroad system throughout America,[1] Wylie discovered opportunities to encourage outdoor touring beyond "regional boundaries" and became a vital part of the "nationwide phenomenon" of vacationing.[2] From 1896 to 1905 the Wylie Camping Company would house, feed, and guide thousands of Victorian tourists during a six-and-a-half-day, unhurried tour of the park's natural wonders: the numerous geysers, hot pools, and waterfalls.

In her thesis about the Wylie Camping Company and its "important role in the establishment of Yellowstone as a legendary tourist destination," Elizabeth Ann Watry discussed the emergence, in the mid-nineteenth century, of an American "refined middle class...fostered by the growing prosperity of industrialization." As the country "shifted the production of wealth from agriculture to manufacturing," more Americans experienced an increase in both their financial resources and leisure time. "Even though this wealth was not distributed evenly throughout all levels of society," Watry wrote, "the rise in national wealth gave more people money to spend on material goods and cultural experiences, especially the emerging American middle class." Watry noted that "while the term *middle class* typically personified an economic classification, it also identified a social lifestyle that in time would include travel and leisure."[3]

Cindy S. Aron, in *Working at Play*, a history of vacations in the United States, observed: "The sorts of vacations that many of us are familiar with today took shape during the last four decades of the nineteenth century as middle-class men and women embarked on what, for many, was a new kind of experience."[4]

While the majority of the Wylie Camping Company's patrons were middle-class, the company also attracted many well-to-do patrons who were looking to break away from stuffy hotel rooms, overcrowded dining halls, and hotel employees with a perfunctory eye for tips. The Wylie Camping Company, with its tent camps, informative outings, fresh-air bonfires, and company credo that reflected this "democratization of the travel experience,"[5] treated their guests to a bold adventure in the distinctly American destination of Yellowstone, "something even Europe could not rival."[6]

Wylie lured travelers with promises of comfort, ease, and good food in the wilderness setting of Yellowstone National Park.[7] When he stated "no more moving of tents," he was appeasing his clients' fear of the unknown American West by providing them a sense of permanence in the wilderness: company camps that would stay put, and feature dining tents and partitioned sleeping tents with wire springs under fine mattress beds; no sleeping on the ground. The tents, Wylie promised, would be heated with stoves. Skilled cooks would while away the hours over a steel range cook stove with a spoon in one hand and a flyswatter in the other, turning "provisions best market affords" into appetizing meals.[8]

For the next nine years Wylie and his crew introduced Americans to Yellowstone National Park's "personality of place." At that time, "Yellowstone was being given an image; its character was being defined and institutionalized."[9] The Wylie Camping Company made the necessary introductions by bringing whole generations up close to the experience of Yellowstone's wondrous personality in "a natural theatre";[10] however soft the beds or well-prepared the meals, the company made the sights and sounds and smells of the Park real to its patrons.[11]

The Wylie Camping Company's six-and-a-half-day trip around the Park, by coach and boat, would be repeated again and again, acquainting generations of Americans with their first national park. Although every trip was unique in character, Wylie's route never varied: it circled Yellowstone from the Cinnabar railway station to Old Faithful, Yellowstone Lake, and back to Cinnabar.[12]

During the Yellowstone stagecoach era, the Wylie Camping Company earned a good reputation among tourists—teachers, college professors, politicians, artists, and church clergy among them—as it became synonymous with economy, ease of travel, unpretentious employees, comfortable lodgings, good food, and impromptu entertainment in camp. The entertainment often took the form of storytelling or straightforward commentary about Yellowstone's natural landscape—the origins of "formal park interpretation that began under the National Park Service."[13] At the time Wylie incorporated his camping company, many Americans were committed to a personal relationship with nature and the study of science as keystones on the path to a well-rounded education, self-improvement, and rejuvenation of the mind, body, and spirit.[14] The Wylies' policy of hiring honest, hard-working college students and teachers set an example for concessions throughout Yellowstone and in other national parks. In his emphasis on conducting informative, absorbing guided tours through the Park's wonders, Wylie remained true to his affinity for teaching. No matter the guests' reasons for visiting Yellowstone— from a search for pure enjoyment and respite from their daily routine to a curiosity about the western experience in an unparalleled outdoor classroom[15]—they were united in their respect for the Wylie Camping Company's approach to understanding nature and science through authentic and personal know-how.[16]

William Wallace Wylie's own curiosity about Yellowstone Park awoke when, as a student at Lenox College in Iowa, he read an article in *Scribner's Monthly*, "Thirty-Seven Days of Peril," by Truman Everts. Everts told of becoming separated from his party and surviving on his own—without food or weapons—in Yellowstone as part of the Washburn–Langford–Doane Expedition that left Helena, Montana, on August 17, 1870, to explore and map the area of northwestern Wyoming that later became Yellowstone National Park. General Henry D. Washburn, surveyor-general of Montana, and Nathaniel P. Langford led the expedition with Lieutenant Gustavus C. Doane as the military escort. Wylie recalled an exact passage in an account by Lieutenant Doane detailing the day that Truman Everts got lost from the Washburn Expedition. Doane wrote: "Mr Everts did not come in with the rest of the party, and the men sent back on the trail found no trace of him. We fired signal guns and kept watch fires during the night, but without success."[17] Wylie noted that the passage showed "how vividly my interest was awakened in this incident as well as in the locality where it occurred."[18]

In the *Scribner's Monthly* article Everts described how he left his horse untied and standing in a dark forest thick with trees south of Yellowstone Lake. When the horse spooked and ran away, Everts had only the clothes on his back, two knives, and a small pair of opera glasses. He had no matches or gun. He was nearsighted, had only limited backwoods experience, and was quickly lost. He meandered down to Heart Lake, then to Rustic Geyser's group of hot springs in the shadow of Mount Sheridan. He stayed there eight days, gathering thistle roots by day, which he ate raw or boiled in nearby hot springs. One night he slept in a tree to escape a mountain lion.

On September 19 Mr. Everts walked north, hoping to reach Yellowstone Lake at West Thumb. He was starving, weak, and cold, but the realization that sunshine and the lens of his opera glasses could produce fire saved him from despair. At present-day West Thumb Geyser Basin, Everts scrounged for food left behind by the expedition, but found only a dinner fork that he used for digging roots, and a yeast-powder can that served as a drinking cup and dinner pot.

From West Thumb Geyser Basin, Everts' exact route to the Yellowstone River is unknown. In a region noted for its abundance of birds and game animals and creeks, streams, and springs, Everts was without food for five days.

Finally, on October 16, 1870—Everts' thirty-seventh day of peril—he was found by Collins John H. "Jack" Baronett, a longtime scout, and George Pritchett, a prospector. They encountered Everts on the west slope of Crescent Hill, northwest of Tower Junction. He was nearly frozen, numb in mind and body, sustained by a diet of thistle roots, minnows, a snowbird, and broth made from the tip of a seagull's wing.

Years after the *Scribner's Monthly* article ignited the imagination of a dreamy, Iowa-bound college student, the paths of Wylie and Truman Everts actually crossed in Yellowstone National Park, when

Wylie witnessed Mr. Everts touring the Park with his daughter. At the sight of the elderly Everts helping his daughter see the park that had so dramatically affected his life, Wylie, too, would think of how Everts' account of his misadventures had profoundly changed his own life.

Wylie spent twenty-five years establishing his life in the Park, watching superintendents and soldiers come and go and regulations evolve, seeing tourists arrive first by railroad then by motorcar, and witnessing the parade of humanity from the untrustworthy to steadfast Park advocates. They were years that tesfed his dreams, his faith, and his hope; years that endowed him with a rich understanding of the power of family and friends.

Truman C. Everts, whose 1871 article "Thirty-Seven Days of Peril" about getting lost in Yellowstone National Park, published in *Scribner's Monthly*, ignited the imagination of young W.W. Wylie, an Iowa college student. *Courtesy, Yellowstone National Park Photo Archives. YELL 36596*

As the granddaughter of Frances Wylie Travis, Will Wylie's niece, I know one thing for certain: the Wylies love a good story—not unlike so many others who have contributed to or appreciated Yellowstone National Park's rich "history of storytelling, later called interpretation."[19] Sitting on my grandmother's couch in Bozeman, one Fourth of July afternoon in the late 1980s, Wylie's story immediately sparked my curiosity. My feeling at the time is best described by Patricia Nelson Limerick in her essay about tourism in the American West: "I would like to believe that at the heart of tourism is a very understandable human curiosity, a sympathetic impulse to go beyond the limits of one's own familiar world, and to see and to learn about new places and new people."[20]

While my grandmother and young daughters napped before the evening's fireworks, I sought hands-on knowledge about the logistics of how Wylie developed his Park business: how he handled the scheduling, gear, food, employees, horses, and the federal government's efforts to "keep Indians out of the park."[21] And, as a family member, I grew embroiled in his struggles against the federal government; an outcome of his company's competition with the Northern Pacific Railway for tourist dollars. His horseback rides alone from Bozeman to Mammoth took several days, a reality of years gone by that could imaginatively be tinged with the glamour of wildflowers, the smell of sagebrush, and quiet contemplation along the Yellowstone River through the Paradise Valley. Thanks to Will Wylie, I know better. Horseback riding aggravated his sciatica—and horses, even though he loved them dearly, ran away at the most inopportune times.

W.W. Wylie's parents, Moses II and Eliza Wylie, with their children circa 1890. Front row, from left: Belle, Moses II, Eliza, and W.W. Back row, from left: John, Oliver, Etta, Rob, and Cameron. *Courtesy, Museum of the Rockies.*

Mary Ann and W.W. Wylie with their family circa 1914. Mary Ann is seated in the back row, second from the left, next to one of their sons. W.W. is seated in the back row, far right, next to Elizabeth. *Courtesy, Museum of the Rockies.*

Mary Ann Wilson Wylie as a young girl in Independence, Iowa. Approximately a decade later, she would ride a horse into Yellowstone's Monument Geyser Basin with a friend—the first female tourists in the history of the Park to do so. *Courtesy, Museum of the Rockies.*

Mary Ann Wilson Wylie, Wylie's wife and resident of Bozeman, circa 1890s, who took an active role in the Wylie Camping Company's Yellowstone tours. *Courtesy, Museum of the Rockies.*

Whether he liked it or not, he chased those horses, a key component of his livelihood and customer service, without regard to the weather or time of day. For twenty-five years he tolerated the ride from Bozeman to Mammoth to spend his summers in Yellowstone, responding patiently to tourists' questions and needs, falling back on his sense of humor when Park adventurers disregarded common sense or the routine grew tedious. A man of strong convictions, Wylie refused to shut down his camping business when it threatened the interests of the Northern Pacific Railway. He believed in the value of his company's Yellowstone tour and encouraged his wife, daughters, and sons to be equal partners in his travel business. When he grew weary of the grind, he leaned heavily on his family, especially his wife, Mary Ann, and his daughter, Elizabeth.

From 1880 to 1905, Wylie embraced all aspects of the hard work—the good, the bad, and the ugly. Out of that acceptance emerged an authentic Park experience, a legacy of grace and wisdom, detailed in his 1926 memoir describing his camping company in that most magical of settings—Yellowstone National Park.

When my own persistence was in question, I drew inspiration from my great-great-uncle Will, who had so much fun writing his manuscript. I was also fueled by the belief that there is enormous significance in writing or "living over again"[22] the experiences of past generations of men and women like Will and Mary Ann Wylie. Their lives and struggles helped me understand the importance of family and the power of spirituality and courage in times of adversity. Will and Mary Ann moved west where they ultimately buried two children, developed a tourist business during the stagecoach years of a young national park, had an eventual misunderstanding about the transfer of goodwill inherent in the sale of their business, maintained a family life in the midst of lengthy separations of time and space, and dealt with dishonest Northern Pacific Railway officials and biased park superintendents. Their example of coping with patience, humor, and acceptance showed me the importance of setting realistic expectations for myself and others.

∾

In 1926 Wylie sat down and finished his ninety-eight page memoir detailing his association with Yellowstone National Park. He stated that the book did not need a preface, adding that "the few who may read it may think it needs more than that." He made no apology for the near constant use of first person pronoun, stating bluntly that his manuscript was "only a record of my own experiences and I can only tell it that way."

In the course of the memoir Wylie included observations that could be mistaken as scientific explanations for facts of nature, but cautioned that they were "not meant to be taken seriously." Finally, he concluded that "If the reader gets some interest and possible pleasure in perusing the book, I want to assure him it is little he will get compared with the pleasure I have had in writing it and living over again the maybe too many things told. Like they say over the radio, 'If you are interested sufficiently to make either criticism or commendation, drop me a postal card to station W.W.W.'"[23] With characteristic practicality, Wylie concluded by offering readers who might want to write to him his 1926 address of Emerson Street in Pasadena, California.

1

Fully Reimbursed for Any Hardships

EARLY IN 1878 WILLIAM WALLACE WYLIE was riding his horse near Lyons, Iowa, a small lumber community where he served as the school superintendent, when a stranger approached him. Wylie reined his horse to a stop. When the gentleman introduced himself as a merchant from Bozeman, Montana, Wylie remembered that the man's son attended Lyons' high school. In the middle of a road in southeastern Iowa the stranger asked a question that would change Wylie's life: "How would you like to go teach in the Rocky Mountain country?"[1]

The question, Wylie wrote, "arrested my attention."[2]

The man stated that the latest Bozeman newspaper had reported that the new school in Bozeman needed a principal. He promised that, if the position was still vacant when he returned to Montana, he would recommend Wylie to the school board.

Wylie agreed to seriously consider the offer. He told the man to expect a letter from him with his final decision.

Although there is no record of the letter, it was clear that Wylie's attention was more than arrested. It was captured. He took the principal's job in Bozeman, beginning in September 1878. His bride of four years, Mary Ann, stayed behind in Independence, Iowa, with the couple's two small children, Elizabeth, age three, and Fred, age one. We can only guess as to the reasoning for this decision, but it was common at the time "when the Far West was only Iowa,"[3] for the men to go ahead, evaluate the risks involved, and send for their families later.[4]

In the late nineteenth century the northern plains provided a backdrop for the armed conflict between Native Americans and the U.S. military. Reports of the brutal struggle for control of right-of-ways[5] and land out west filled newspapers in the Midwest and the East—including tales of the Bozeman Trail through Wyoming to Montana's gold mines and the 1876 death of George Armstrong Custer and more than two hundred members of the Seventh Cavalry on the banks of the Little Bighorn River in southeastern Montana.[6] In August 1877—just months before Wylie's serendipitous invitation to teach in Bozeman—the Cowan Party, a group of tourists from Montana, was captured by the Nez Perce Indians in Yellowstone National Park.[7]

A great distance stood between Iowa and the northern plains, and transportation costs to the Rocky Mountain country were expensive. A one-way fare from Council Bluffs, Iowa, to Virginia City, Montana, was $105 in a time when a family's average grocery bill was forty-nine cents for eggs, milk, and salt pork,[8] and a one-story cottage could be purchased for $600.[9] Will's salary for the 1878–79 school year was approximately $1,500, starting in September 1878 with a payment of $150. He was rehired in 1880 by Bozeman Public Schools at an annual salary of $1,600.[10]

Traveling to Bozeman from Lyons, Iowa, was not only expensive, it was, as Wylie would find out, quite an ordeal. He traveled out of Iowa on the Union Pacific Railway, stepping off the train in Ogden, Utah Territory. There he boarded another train, this time a narrow gauge railroad that proceeded north from Ogden to Onida in the Cache Valley on the forty miles of track allotted for passenger cars.

At that point, he had to board a stagecoach provided by the Gilmer and Salisbury Stageline. On the advice of his Bozeman acquaintance, Wylie had planned ahead and secured a seat with the driver.[11]

In his essay on early transportation and tourism in the West, Carlos A. Schwantes contends that "stagecoaches were strictly utilitarian vehicles. They did not normally advertise or attempt to cater to tourists." While this utility vehicle became the idealized representation of Wells Fargo Bank, even Louis McLane, Wells Fargo's general manager and eventual president, noted in 1865 that lithographers fell short of capturing an overland journey by stagecoach as "the devil in reality…crowding and intense jolting…aching bones and bruised flesh." Allegedly, most experienced stagecoach travelers packed their "twenty-five-pound allotment of personal luggage in bottles and flasks, the contents of which dulled the miseries of the journey."[12]

The Gilmer and Salisbury agent introduced the driver as Pete. Pete apparently shared the conclusion of one stagecoach traveler who wrote: "I had always considered the physical essentials to be food and drink, but soon I learned they were drink and food."[13] Pete was drunk.

"We expressed to the agent our concern because of this," Wylie wrote. "He assured us that Pete was a better driver drunk, than any others were sober."[14]

The agent, however, had a plan. As they had to change horses every ten to twenty miles depending on road conditions, he suggested another sober driver could take the lines for the initial twenty miles with Pete up front beside him. Wylie would ride in the stage with the other nine passengers, where one can only imagine the conversation. Pete, the agent argued, would be sober enough to take the lines after the first change. The sober driver could remain behind at that point and Wylie would then ride up front with Pete.

All went as planned, but at the twenty-mile stop, Pete ordered the coach wheels greased before he took over the lines. Although this was unnecessary because the wheels had been greased in Onida, the other driver relented and helped Pete finish the job. After Pete greased one wheel, the other driver told him to stop, that the other wheels were already greased. Wylie wrote that at that point, "Pete was still so unbalanced" that he believed the statement to be true.[15]

At approximately 2 A.M., the stagecoach gave a jerk. Wylie looked down and saw that the front wheel had sunk into a pothole. Convinced that the stage was going to topple over, Wylie looked over at Pete and realized that he had been sleeping and letting the team of four horses walk. Wylie recalled that he ordered the horses to stop. He then shook Pete and ventured that perhaps he should take the reins and allow Pete to nap. Pete disagreed. Instead, he jostled the reins to get the horses to straighten up and pull the stage out of the hole. Over went the stage, loaded with twenty-five hundred pounds of freight, mail, and two bags of coal for a Montana blacksmith. Not to mention ten passengers and all their belongings.

It was sheer chaos. As they extracted themselves from the overturned stagecoach, the passengers fumed at the Gilmer and Salisbury Stageline for carrying such a massive load on a passenger line, with a drunken driver no less. Flurries of anger arose when the driver proposed that the passengers stay put until the stage was reloaded. It meant, after all, missing their breakfast stop.

Wylie asked if they had to reload everything.

Pete said yes, it had to be done.

Two women and some of the men walked on ahead. Wylie and another passenger removed their coats and helped Pete reload the stagecoach. In order to right the stage, they had to cut the binding rope to free the load. When it came time to rebind the load to the stagecoach, they came up short of rope.

As they worked, Pete looked around anxiously. Wylie asked if Pete was missing something. Pete expressed concern about the whereabouts of a small keg. Wylie and the other gentleman knew that passenger James H. Mills, Montana's territorial secretary, had hauled the gallon whiskey keg away into the brush.

Wylie realized that Pete was not up to the drive, so he concocted a plan that would get them down the road, even though it was long after the other travelers arrived at the breakfast station.

"Pete, I have a flask of good brandy in my grip in the front boot of the coach, and if you will let me dole it out to you I will let you use it," Wylie told the anxious driver. Pete "promised to do so, and lived up to the promise."[16]

Two days later Wylie was called to action again, just out of Pleasant Valley Station near the Montana-Idaho border. This time there was a new driver driving six horses, instead of the standard four, because they were headed across the Continental Divide to Montana's high plains. The new horses out of Pleasant Valley, however, were green, or wild, because Indians had made off with the best stage stock.

The driver stopped the team and announced that a leather thorough brace had broken on his side. He passed the lines to Wylie and climbed down to investigate.

"Yes," the driver said, after examining the brace. "It is broken and the passengers will all have to get out."[17] All passengers except two women climbed down from the coach and stood with the driver examining the broken leather brace. Wylie gripped the reins, but the horses were nervous and nearly impossible to control. Although Wylie attempted to jimmy the foot brake, he found that the front boot of the stagecoach—a flexible leather storage compartment—had crumpled up between his seat and the driver's, preventing him from gripping the brake lever.

One of the wheel horses threw up his head and snorted. The driver lunged at the horse, trying to grab its bit, but the wild horses threw him back. All six horses streaked forward for the freedom of the sagebrush-covered plains.

From his perch atop the stagecoach that was now careening behind the thundering horses, Wylie heard the two women passengers screaming. Since he couldn't reach the brake, his only option was to try to guide the team back to the road where the speed of their galloping would be less risky to the disabled coach. Eventually he was able to calm the horses to a standstill, save for the wild pair at the wheel still trying to gallop. Wylie used every ounce of strength he had to work the wild pair until the driver caught up with the coach.

The driver exclaimed, "My God, you have more grit than any passenger who ever rode with me."[18]

At supper that night the other passengers raised a chorus of cheers for Wylie, thanking him for his efforts to save the lives of the two women. The driver most moved Wylie that evening, when he took him by the hand and expressed his gratitude. Later, in hindsight, Wylie wrote that he "cared more for the thanks of the driver as he held to my hand at our parting, saying, 'You have sure saved me my job today.'"[19]

The Bozeman that Wylie arrived in that summer of 1878 was still a wild western outpost. It had been platted just fourteen years earlier by John Bozeman, creator of the Bozeman Trail connecting the Oregon Trail with the Montana mines. He chose the Gallatin Valley as the site for the town because, he noted, it was in a good location to sell goods to the miners streaming toward Virginia City.

Raised on a farm in Iowa by his parents Moses and Elizabeth, Wylie was likely impressed with the Gallatin Valley's superior agricultural potential: fertile soil, the climate conducive to crop growth, and the ample sources of water. On his horseback rides he would have noticed more and more farms and ranches peppering the valley.[20]

In the foothills of the sweeping Gallatin Mountains, the craggy Spanish Peaks, and the high rugged Bridger Mountains ran a profusion of streams and rivers, and the area was dotted with meadows, plateaus, gulches, and vales; stands of pines, fir, cottonwood, and aspen; and thick serviceberry bushes. The Gallatin Valley and its surrounding mountain ranges fostered large wintering herds of ungulates: elk, white-tailed deer, mule deer, and antelope. All sorts of predators called the region home: bobcats, black and grizzly bears, coyotes, eagles, hawks, falcons, and owls.

Wylie arrived in Montana Territory during the extermination of the bison, which occurred across the West from 1872 to 1884.[21] Nevertheless, Wylie noted, it was a common sight in the Gallatin Valley to see native tribes from Idaho and points west journeying south to the lower Yellowstone region for the annual fall hunt "to procure new robes and meat for the comfort of the ensuing winter. They trekked through Bozeman to and from these hunts with wives and children."[22]

In fall 1878 Wylie settled into his office in Westside School, located in the hills just west of Bozeman, and threw himself into his work, taking on additional duties as the superintendent for the Bozeman public schools. Westside School, with its brick exterior, bell tower, and plastered walls, was initially a source of civic pride, but Wylie faced parental concerns about student safety amid the shoddy construction and poor design. He also participated in discussions about how to pay for an endless series of repairs and alterations with limited tax dollars.

He designed curriculum for the students in grades one through eight, followed by three years of high school. He made certain that teachers had adequate materials—good textbooks and curriculum— as well as supplies. Pens were expensive, so the children used slates or lead pencils and notebooks.

Wylie stayed in Bozeman until late June 1879, when he returned to Iowa to move his wife and three children back to Montana. Before he left, he crusaded for the computation examination, a novel method of hiring teachers that involved candidates completing a written test and the school board evaluating it. This would replace the common practice of a personality-based interview by school board members and "competent" members of the general public.

As he journeyed from Bozeman to Fort Benton, Montana, on a Gilmer and Salisbury stagecoach again, Wylie and the passengers encountered a downpour, causing "mud to so clutter the wheels" and the horses' hooves picked up "this mud matted with the short bunchgrass, so that they could not travel."[23] Freight outfits, plagued by the same conditions, camped along the roadway. The coach could not continue for twenty-four hours. The next day, however, the sun shone, oblivious.

Wylie, nonetheless, was worried. When he finally reached Fort Benton to board a steamboat returning downriver to Sioux City, his boat had already departed. The agent had no idea when another would arrive—dreadful news for Wylie who hadn't seen his family in almost a year and had yet to meet his newborn son.

In those days merchandise bound for Montana towns generally traveled by steamboat up the Missouri River to Fort Benton, and the best way out of the state was to catch a steamboat headed back east. Carlos A. Schwantes noted in his essay about early transportation and tourism that "in 1860 the first steamboat reached the head of navigation on the Missouri River at Fort Benton to offer commercial transportation between there and St. Louis. Again, few people who made the trip could recommend it to any but the most venturesome tourists."[24] Schwantes argues that the journey by steamboat—generally between sixteen and twenty days downriver to St. Louis—"could not be labeled a pleasure cruise, except perhaps by comparison to an overland stage journey." Plagued by boredom and fear of boiler explosions, fire, and the "ubiquitous snag…plying the muddy waters of the Missouri," some passengers spent evenings with a bottle of whiskey, "sleeping off their liquor-induced haze during the follow-ing day."[25]

If this darker side of steamboat travel added to Wylie's anxiety, he left no record of it. Wylie wrote that he and his fellow passengers checked into a hotel in Fort Benton, a rowdy gambling town. About the time he called it a night, a steamboat whistle sounded. He grabbed his belongings and headed for the docks on the Missouri River.

Everyone in Fort Benton—young and old, rich or poor—gathered at the sound of the whistle to see the great boat slowly ease its way around the bend. The steamboat, owned and operated by the federal government, had unloaded supplies for Fort Assiniboine, a new army outpost sixty miles downriver. Instead of returning empty, it docked at Fort Benton.

A few passengers disembarked. Wylie walked aboard and was immediately assigned a stateroom. He asked the clerk what his chances were of spotting bison on the trip along the Missouri as he hadn't seen any in his earlier travels. The gentleman replied that the boat would be in bison country early the next day. Wylie asked to be awakened at the first sighting. He was awakened—at 3 A.M.—to see two bulls running along the riverbank just beyond the boat. They were, Wylie wrote, "apparently trying to get into the river ahead of the boat. One or two passengers were shooting at them. When hit, they would shake their heads as though angered, but kept on running."

By eight in the morning, the river was so thick with bison that "the captain ordered the boat stopped and tied to shore. He said that without [a] load the steamer might be overturned plowing through the mass of animals filling the river."[26]

More shots rang out, then the captain ordered an end to the shooting, stating that there was enough fresh meat on board for the passengers' needs.

In later life Wylie characterized the sight of the bison crossing the Missouri as "hard to believe without seeing…the cows and bulls pair off as do geese and some other animals. At the water's edge a cow and a bull and a calf would maneuver until they got the calf between them, the bull always on the lower side, to hold the mother and calf against the stiff current of the rushing river, then with the calf's nose over the joined noses of the parents, would convey it safely across the river." Wylie observed "hundreds of such trios" throughout the day. It was "late in the evening before there was open water enough to risk navigating the boat."[27]

He continued with this commentary:

> This was the last great migration of buffalo from the winter feeding grounds in Canada to the summer ranges in Montana. Following this came the great slaughter of this noble animal in Montana during the hard winters of 1879 and 1880. Following these two winters the buffalo hides were piled along the new Northern Pacific Railway in eastern Montana, like cord wood used to be along the Missouri River for steamboat use. Following this, fur and hide buyers from St. Louis wintered in Bozeman, Montana, some of them boarding where I did in the winter of 1880, buying these hides for $1.25 each. A few years later good buffalo robes were sold for $300 each. During the slaughtering time of these herds it was unpleasant to listen to these fur merchants talk about how many skinners a good marksman could keep busy. Conversation about buffalo killing and skinning was then as common at table with these families as talk of operations is in Rochester, Minnesota, much later. I then wished such talk could be prevented in dining room[s] as operation talk is forbidden by signs posted in dining rooms in Rochester.[28]

In his memoir, Wylie lamented the passing of these great animals. "Like the poor Indian," he wrote, "these noble animals were forced to give way to so-called civilization."[29]

Back in Iowa Will's wife, Mary Ann, readied the children, Elizabeth, Fred, and baby Frank, born in February 1879, for the long trip back to Montana. Before the family's departure, Will spent four weeks in August teaching at a Normal Institute in Bedford, Iowa, for which he received $250 to help defray the expense of traveling to Montana.

When the Wylies arrived back in Bozeman, Will faced an 1879–80 school year marked by ongoing concerns about repairs to the Westside School. The entire town knew that Beall and Chestnut, the contractors, had procrastinated in making many of the numerous necessary repairs to the school. Rumors abounded about the company's conflicts, mounting bills, lack of cash flow, and faulty bookkeeping.

The school board requested a $2,000 levy to offset the cost of repairs and set an August date for this special school levy election. The opening day of the 1880–81 school year could not be set until after that election, so Wylie negotiated his new contract at an annual salary of $1,600, then left for Yellowstone National Park in late June 1880. He traveled with Richard "Dick" Lockey, a well-known citizen of Helena with mercantile interests in Bozeman. They were traveling to check on Lockey's mining claims in Cooke City—just over Yellowstone's northeast border.

Wylie took his own saddle horse and Lockey rode a horse that he borrowed from an army officer stationed at Fort Ellis, two miles east of Bozeman. The two men borrowed a third horse as a pack animal from Bozeman's Presbyterian minister. Wylie's horsepacking skills, learned in the Midwest, were a great help to him in this rugged country. "I learned the diamond hitch from old packers," he wrote, "which stood me in good stead for many years to follow."[30]

When Wylie and Lockey reached Mammoth Springs, they met Philetus W. Norris, the superintendent of Yellowstone National Park. Riding a large buckskin horse with an axe attached to the saddle, Wylie recalled, Norris was the Park's premier enthusiast. Carrying food in his saddlebags and a blanket behind his saddle, he was not particular about reaching road camps for a night's shelter. Norris blazed, built, and cleared trails and roads for travelers, cutting down trees with his axe and requiring his men to follow him faithfully. Because the pay for such hard labor was woefully inadequate, Norris often dipped into his annual salary of $1,500 to pay his crews.

Norris suggested that the two men visit the Lower Geyser Basin and assured them that they could travel to the Yellowstone River from there, then proceed to Cooke City. Wylie and Lockey accepted his advice. A young man named Jackson, a jeweler from Helena who had trailed Wylie and Lockey from Bozeman, asked if he could join them on the trip to Cooke City.

Years later Wylie recalled that the trip cost Lockey and himself $2.27 each. Lockey served as cook and Wylie recalled that he sliced the bacon very thin. Jackson had a horse and a saddle, but no provisions or blankets. He anticipated paying for his food as they went along and the other men agreed upon a sum of one dollar per day. For blankets, he was on his own, and he eventually bought a couple from a small supply store that was operated by a Park old-timer, Jim McCartney.

Throughout Norris' Park administration, there was no road from Upper Geyser Basin to Yellowstone Lake. Even horseback travelers trying to reach Yellowstone Lake were obliged to return to the Lower Geyser Basin and follow a trail that had been made by General Oliver Howard and the U.S. Army when they were pursuing Chief Joseph and the Nez Perce in the summer of 1877.[31]

In early July 1880 the men began their Yellowstone journey at the Firehole River and proceeded east along Nez Perce Creek and over Mary Mountain. As they traveled, Wylie saw the evidence of the struggles that Howard's army underwent trying to move machinery across the rugged terrain. Once over the mountain travelers ended up in open meadows, and from there they could easily find the Yellowstone River near Mud Geyser and follow it to the outlet of Yellowstone Lake.

From Yellowstone Lake they headed north past the Great Falls and Grand Canyon of the Yellowstone, across Dunraven Pass, and up to the 10,223-foot summit of Mount Washburn. When they reached Jack Baronett's bridge, approximately eight miles below Tower Falls where the Cooke City road crossed the Yellowstone River, the men's itinerary changed. Lockey said he would pack some grub and visit Cooke City as originally planned.

Wylie and Jackson, however, decided to traipse west toward Mammoth Springs. When they reached a locale known as Blacktail Deer Creek, Wylie and Jackson made camp. On the opposite side of the creek was a tepee. The tepee was in perfect shape, not a pole touched since the Indians took their belongings and moved on. Wylie concluded that the previous inhabitants were Sheepeater, or Tukudeka, Indians, a band of the Shoshone tribe. Living in small family groups with the constant companionship of dogs instead of horses, the Sheepeaters depended on mountain sheep for food and clothing. When David E. Folsom, C. W. Cook, and William Peterson explored the Park in 1869, the Sheepeaters lived in the Blacktail

Deer Creek area and moved to lower elevations in the depths of winter.[32]

To reach the tepee Wylie and Jackson's horses jumped the creek, which was narrow and very deep between grassy banks. The men camped on the opposite bank for the night. The next morning they looked for the narrowest point across the ice-cold stream for jumping the horses. A tall snag stood near the stream on the opposite bank. The saddle horses made the leap successfully, but the pack horse, when righting himself after the jump, struck his burden against the snag. This threw him off balance and he toppled into the creek, head upstream and pack acting as a highly effective dam.

Seeing the horse in the water and on the verge of drowning, Wylie drew the horse's head over to the riverbank and secured it to a tree. He cut the lash ropes, letting all the gear float downstream.

Jackson shook with laughter at the absurd scenario.

Wylie ordered Jackson quickly downstream to salvage what bedding and food he could as Wylie struggled to get the horse out of the water. He snubbed the horse's halter to his saddle and helped the animal to straighten out. Aided by the swift current, Wylie pulled the horse downstream as the animal struggled up on its feet and onto the riverbank. The horse was nearly frozen. Wylie lugged him behind his sturdy saddle horse, and with tremendous effort, they ran laps to warm the chilled horse.

Jackson was able to fish some of the party's gear from the creek. Flour, sugar, and dried fruit were all gone—soaked and ruined. Jackson laughed all the while, until he found his cigar box. When he opened it, he stopped laughing immediately. The cigar box was filled with fine jewelry—watches, lockets, and brooches—that was completely waterlogged. Friends in Helena had convinced him that he would find wealthy tourists in Yellowstone willing to purchase fine jewelry. His hopes were destroyed. Jackson immediately built a fire of sagebrush to try to salvage what he could.

The next afternoon the men repacked their remaining provisions and set off for Mammoth Springs, where they found Norris looking for more men to work on the roads. When Wylie expressed his desire to return to the Park later that season, bringing along his wife, Mary Ann, and a few friends, Norris encouraged him to do so.

Clearly, this early Park superintendent who literally shaped the Park with his hands—cutting trees to clear roads—impressed Wylie. "A hasty look over the park map will show many places or objects named 'Norris,'" Wylie wrote. "Many other points so named were later dropped out by his successors in authority. What Norris did in the early days in opening ways through park forests making accessible the various points of interest was simply wonderful, with almost no money to do it with. Great credit should ever be given to his memory."[33]

∾

Wylie returned to Bozeman in August to discover that the special school levy had been defeated, 134 to 51. A list of unfinished items at Westside School went to the contractors, Beall and Chestnut, with a threat to sue. In addition the school's foundation desperately needed repair. Beall and Chestnut started work under the supervision of a committee chaired by Nelson Story. Story, a former Texas longhorn drover and one of Montana Territory's foremost horsemen, contributed his own money to help the community move on toward an October 1880 levy revote and a subsequent start of the school year.

Wylie also returned to Bozeman with a vision: a wheeled-vehicle tour that he would lead into Yellowstone National Park. Fresh from his wondrous Yellowstone experiences, Wylie joined other visitors who "were vocal in their amazement"[34] about the Park's character. He wanted to share Yellowstone's sights, sounds, and smells with his family and friends, so while he had extra time and energy he launched into plans for his three-week tour. He assembled a party of nine in Bozeman—his first party of tourists. These included a young minister from San Francisco with the surname Wright, who had come to town and purchased a saddle horse, looking for the chance to join a party. Also in the party were a Presbyterian minister, two young men from Bozeman, and a friend of Wylie's wife. Will's family rounded out the total—wife, Mary Ann, now expecting Mary Grace, plus his three children: Elizabeth, Fred, and Frank.

To prepare himself for the trip, Wylie purchased the usual provisions and, in addition, a new lumber wagon manufactured by Wisconsin's Bain Wagon Company. An "emigrant cover," muslin stretched over wooden bows, topped the wagon. Wylie also purchased a new pair of harnesses.

As they began their Yellowstone tour, Wylie's Bozeman party encountered a family with a spring wagon. A husband, wife, and daughter named Thompson wished to join them. This proved to be an excellent arrangement, since it was often necessary to use all four horses on one rig to plod through the Park's difficult roads. In the morning, Wylie climbed over Mammoth Spring Mountain, a little west of Liberty Cap, to Swan Lake, the four horses pulling his wagon. In the afternoon, the same four brought Mr. Thompson's wagon to the edge of this tranquil lake.

The roads were rough, although Wylie, a great fan of Norris, was gentle in his description of them. He wrote that "it is not needful to expose Norris' 'Good Roads,'" but suffice it to say the tree stumps were not always "low enough" to allow wagons to "pass without the axle of wagon catching." At times, a team had to be hitched to the back of a wagon in order to "draw it back" so that the men could "cut the stump shorter."[35]

Wylie chose as a camping spot Willow Park, about six miles from Mammoth and across from Apollinaris Spring. The party spent their second night there, as it was ten miles to another decent spot. Leaving the nearby Obsidian Cliff, the party traveled up a very high hill, the summit of which offered breathtaking views of the Madison Range and Lake of the Woods, an enticing little lake set amidst towering pines.

The party continued on to Norris Geyser Basin. Along the Gibbon River, long stretches of the road were uncleared, so the party had to drive in the riverbed. Traveling south the wagons headed on to Gibbon Basin where they found some excellent camping.

Wylie was concerned, however, about continuing because he knew there was no grass for the livestock in the next seventeen miles. At the entrance to Gibbon Basin a one-mile trail rose to Monument Geyser Basin. This basin, a thousand feet higher than the Gibbon

The main road to Yellowstone National Park through the Lower Canyon of the Yellowstone River. This portion of the road south from the Paradise Valley to the Park's northern entrance offered occasional turnouts to keep traffic flowing. Photograph by F.J. Haynes, 1881. *Courtesy, Montana Historical Society Research Center.*

River, features perpendicular cones hard as granite, some of which have steam escaping through vents at the top. Wylie's wife, Mary Ann, and her friend rode horses to and from Monument Geyser

Travelers on this quarter-mile stretch of "main" Yellowstone National Park road navigated the bed of the Gibbon River—an example of one of Park Superintendent Philetus Norris' "good roads." Photograph by F.J. Haynes, 1884. *Courtesy, Montana Historical Society Research Center.*

Basin, the first female tourists in the history of Yellowstone National Park to do so.

The party journeyed for more than a week from Mammoth Springs to the Upper Geyser Basin. At Upper Geyser Basin the Wylies, Thompsons, and their traveling companions were fully reimbursed for any hardships with frequent geyser displays and unforgettable beauty.

When he returned to Bozeman, Wylie headed back to his desk and the lion's den at Westside School. The school levy had been put to a revote in early October. The revote passed, 182 to 112. School opened on October 11, 1880, with five teachers and Principal Will Wylie. Many of the parents, however, were still outraged over the crumbling state of Westside School. At a special board meeting the week before the school's opening, controversy dominated the agenda, and more than one taxpayer demanded that Westside be condemned and recommended building a safer, state-of-the-art facility on an available parcel of land east of Bozeman Creek. This school, they suggested, could be called Eastside School.

The board also adopted a resolution that addressed the ever-onerous issue of Bible reading in school. All of the board members were religious men, but after a great deal of debate, they voted against a motion to establish formal Bible instruction in Bozeman schools. They went on record stating that Bible reading was not within the parameters of public education.

If Wylie's mind wandered during board meetings, it might have rested on memories of the summer of 1880, filled as it was with the sights of the spectacular Upper Geyser Basin with its sprays of water, camping in the lodgepole forest at Gibbon Basin, or taking in the sublime views of the Madison Range. Wylie wrote: "I have always looked back upon the summer of 1880 with [our] two rather eventful tours of the park, with much interest and pleasure."[36]

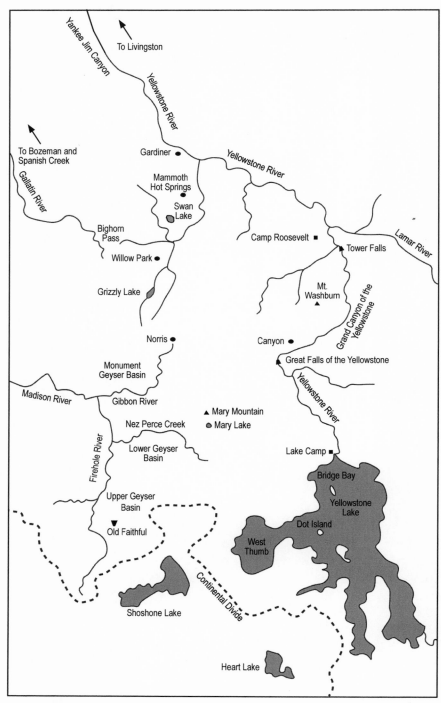

Yellowstone National Park. *Map by Edward Sala.*

2

Views of the Wonderland

I N THE SUMMER OF 1881 WYLIE was once again back in Yellow-stone National Park with Henry Bird Calfee, one of the Park's first photographers. Wylie and Calfee spent a majority of their time in the Upper Geyser Basin, followed by a lengthy stay at the Grand Canyon of the Yellowstone. Unless Calfee required assistance, Wylie occupied his hours on the sidelines, writing a guidebook geared for tourists. Together Wylie and Calfee positioned themselves near the front of a long line of writers and photographers who described the park's wonders in words and images, assembling some of the first promotional materials about this amazing "wonderland" to which Americans had just been introduced.[1]

Aubrey Haines cautions that "not all the scattered information on Calfee fits together." Nonetheless, there is agreement that Calfee, a native of Arkansas, was born in about 1847 and came to Montana in the early 1870s, settling near Bozeman. While working as a prospector and printer, Calfee developed an artistic pastime—photographing Yellowstone. By the summer of 1881, he owned a photography business in Bozeman with a catalog of no less than 295 photos of the Park's marvels. He marketed his images of the Park's geysers, rock formations, and waterways around the country, giving illustrated lectures with lantern slides and selling stereograph series with names like "View of the Wonderland" or "Wonder of the Yellowstone National Park."[2]

In about 1872, while on his earliest photographic expedition in the geyser basins, Calfee and his traveling companion endured unimaginable hardships in their "enthusiastic desire to make this land of wonders known to the world."[3] Although Wylie's reminiscence does not mention Calfee's companion by name, Calfee's account identifies the gentleman as Macon Josey, a shoemaker.[4] Calfee and Josey were two of "only a few hundred people"[5] who reached the Park that year and while their story captured Wylie's imagination like Truman Everts' account of his "Thirty-Seven Days of Peril," it also serves as a fine example of Paul Schullery's argument, outlined in his study of Yellowstone's early tourism, that the region's early travelers relied on "their own hunting skills to feed themselves...following their own judgment about where to go, how to acquire firewood, and how to treat the park's fragile thermal features."[6]

As Calfee and Josey prepared to leave the Lower Basin and head home, their provisions were so low that the choices were meat, meat, and meat. Calfee left camp in hopes of shooting a deer. He shot and wounded one, but the deer broke into a run across the basin. As the deer leapt across a pool, it caught its front feet on the far rim, and its hindquarters fell into the boiling water. Josey, who was in camp nearby, leaped up and grabbed the deer's front legs to pull it out of the water. The rim broke. Josey fell into the boiling pool, the water temperature approximately two hundred degrees.

Josey was severely burned. The men were miles from the nearest doctor or any sort of medical facility, much less a town. Calfee was able to cut the clothes off his friend's body and use the little flour that was left from their provisions to cover the burned areas. Bandages were minimal, at best. The two men headed immediately for the Madison River, riding cross-country without a trail of any kind. A saddle was not an option because of the severity of Josey's burns, so Josey had to be bound and carried on top of a pack.

That evening, after traveling nearly ten miles, Calfee laid Josey against a log and, for a second time that day, went to hunt for meat. After he walked a short distance away, he looked back to see Josey with a gun pointed to his head, his foot on the trigger.

"Put that gun down or I'll shoot you at once,"[7] Calfee shouted, aiming his gun at the unfortunate man, nearly out of his mind with pain.

Josey obeyed, taking his foot off the trigger and putting the gun at his side.

The trip with a critically burned companion, over rough terrain, must have been miserable, but Wylie leaves us to only imagine the horror: "The trip of several days over the untrodden Mountains with the man in great agony all the while, need not be detailed," he wrote. One afternoon, as they passed over a high ridge, they heard shots from the brush near the Madison River. They looked down and saw what Calfee deduced to be horse thieves "shooting at a mark, and near at hand a band of fine looking horses." Calfee and Josey "hastened on, trying to avoid being seen by the men in the valley."[8]

When the two men arrived in the Gallatin Valley, they encountered several farmers who were enraged about their stolen horses. Calfee reported what he had seen, and the farmers quickly formed a posse and headed to the Madison River valley. After securing medical aid for Josey, Calfee served as their guide. When the group arrived in the Madison River valley, they found the tree the thieves had used for target practice and followed the trail of horseshoes, some of which were familiar to the horses' owners. The posse tracked the thieves west from Henry's Lake to Red Rock Lake.[9] The tale had a happy ending for everyone except the horse thieves. A number of the horses were recovered. Macon Josey survived. And several of the robbers went, according to Wylie, to "where there are no horses to steal."[10]

Calfee's pictures were taken by the old "wet plate" photographic process, arduous work that involved carrying weighty glass plates; a heavy, cumbersome camera; a tent to serve as a darkroom; and a variety of chemicals "on pack horse from Bozeman."[11]

Wylie was amazed at the effort that Calfee put into each photograph: "this was tedious work, having to use a dark tent, sensitizing the plate before each and every exposure, then the care with which these exposed glass plates must be handled and transported on pack horse back to studio at Bozeman."[12]

Wylie also pointed out the patience the photographer took to capture the image that he wanted. Calfee, Wylie noted, had his

camera set on the [S]plendid geyser for thirteen days before a satisfactory exposure was obtained, although the geyser then operated every other day and often 12 or more times on that day. This was the difficulty, the artist must wait till the geyser was in action before going into dark tent to sensitize plate, then put it in camera, by this time the best of the display would be weakening, so it must be tried again. The Splendid, although the most excellent of all geysers at its best, gave no preliminary indication of its eruption."[13]

At the end of the Yellowstone season, Wylie noted, Calfee trotted away with "a very fine set of slides."[14]

Wylie, meanwhile, worked on what would become his guidebook with the title of *Yellowstone National Park or The Great American Wonderland.* The subtitle read: *A complete description of all the wonders of the park, together with distances, altitudes, and such other information as the tourist or general readers desires: a complete hand or guide book for tourists.* Published in 1882 by Ramsey, Millet & Hudson, Wylie's book provided a plain and straightforward guide for tourists. He kept his explanations simple and truthful, providing answers to only those queries most commonly asked. Compared with other literary productions on the Park that covered the geological formations or the history in greater depth, Wylie worried that his guidebook might fail to measure up, but because of its subject—the great Yellowstone National Park and its wonders—he hoped that his descriptions and practical advice would be appreciated.

Wylie and Calfee camped ten days in the location of the future Grand Canyon Hotel. They didn't see another soul until a group traveling on saddle with a pack train and military escort arrived. The party included Secretary of State John T. Sherman; the artist Albert Bierstadt, who became known for his dramatic paintings of the Park; then-Senator Benjamin Harrison, who would be elected president just seven years later; a Supreme Court judge; Montana Territory's Governor Potts; and a few others of merit.[15]

Before nightfall, the hunters for the party hung the carcasses of three deer, two elk, and one bear in camp. Wylie and Calfee shared willingly and abundantly from the wealth of fresh meat. In return, Wylie showed the group the Great Falls and the Grand Canyon of the Yellowstone, his "first party of distinguished personages."[16] He also escorted the artist, Bierstadt, to the Red Butte, well down in the Grand Canyon. Here, Bierstadt completed his well-known painting *Lower Yellowstone Falls,* an oil on paper, working quickly while keeping up a steady stream of conversation. Through landscapes, photographs, and descriptive writing, the fireside companions—Bierstadt,

W.W. Wylie and Carter Harrison (foreground) in a horse-drawn buggy. Harrison, mayor of Chicago and son of President Benjamin Harrison, toured the Park in about 1890. During the summer of 1881, Wylie escorted President Harrison to the rim of the Grand Canyon of the Yellowstone River. *Courtesy, Yellowstone National Park Photo Archives. YELL 38017*

Calfee, and Wylie—invited viewers and readers to experience the power of the West's "stunning scenery"[17] and thereby helped market an American "cultural heritage…apart from the European legacy."[18]

During the time he was in the Park with Calfee, writing his guidebook and accompanying travelers to the Park's wonders, Wylie undoubtedly tried to figure out how to turn his love of Yellowstone into a means of making a living or, at the very least, supplementing the income he made as an educator. Mr. G. Barnes, general passenger agent of the Northern Pacific, expressed interest in selling Wylie's guidebook on his trains.[19] At the conclusion of the summer season, Wylie and Calfee finalized plans for a lecture tour around the country—Wylie discussing Yellowstone National Park's many wonders and Calfee showing his fine set of slides. The two men anticipated starting out in the fall, which meant some big adjustments for the Wylie family. Wylie and Mary Ann felt there was potential for him to follow the lecture circuit indefinitely, so Mary Ann returned to Iowa with the couple's four children.

Calfee and Wylie went on the road in early fall 1881 to share the wonders of Yellowstone National Park with audiences around the country. In his memoir, Wylie stated that this was the pre-electric lantern era, but a more accurate description might be that the men were touring a region where electricity of the Thomas Edison variety was not yet widely available. Edison had formed the Edison Electric Company in 1878, and by January 1880 he had received a patent for the incandescent lamp he developed in his Menlo Park, New Jersey, laboratory. In order to project a magnified image of Calfee's slides on the wall or screen, a lantern was needed on the Calfee–Wylie tour. The stereopticon was a mono projector, so Calfee's pictures were not three-dimensional. At every lecture stop, Wylie and Calfee created limelight, or oxyhydrogen lighting, by manufacturing oxygen and hydrogen, then introducing it to a lump of lime, a risky task that was expensive, labor-intensive, and often produced a lot of smoke. "The experience proved more interesting than profitable," said Wylie.[20]

Calfee and Wylie gave lectures at stops in Colorado, Nebraska, Utah, Wyoming, and Minnesota. There was so little known about the Park that no amount of advertising could incite interest in the minds of the public. Even so, the audiences they did have would plead with them to stay on another night, promising another enthusiastic group. The men agreed to do so several times. The second night returned the same audience with new questions, and additional friends and family members. If a lecture did not draw a large audience the first night, Calfee and Wylie concluded that it made sense to move on. Even so, local newspapers from Omaha to Minneapolis, and host towns in between, praised the "grandeur and beauty" of Calfee's stereopticon views of "Wonderland," arguing that "a more interesting reservoir of natural wonders does not exist anywhere on the globe," and also commented that Wylie's remarks were "clear, explicit, and not too lengthy." The illustrated lecture was "in every way an admirable entertainment"[21] and a great benefit to children, more beneficial than reading about geography in a book.

Generally, there was enormous fascination with geyser activity and the wildlife of the Park. Of the innumerable questions posed, a major portion were variations on "How are geysers formed?" or "Are there bears in the Park?"

Wylie, assuming most folks lacked easy access to geological reference books, outlined the Bunsen theory as the cause of geyser activity in conjunction with Calfee's splendid slides. The Bunsen theory assumed that groundwater trickled down to the Earth's core, finding its journey extremely hot. Once the water heated to at least boiling point, "an explosion takes place which must find release… in the direction of least resistance which is through the fissure or vent reaching to the surface of the ground." The "quantity of water or size of tube [vent]" and the temperature of "the super heated steam" contributed to the determination of a geyser's height. The variables of water supply, sub-surface heat, and the behavior of neighboring geysers determined the length of rest periods.[22]

Wylie noted that snowfall influenced the geysers. Deep snows increased the amount of water seeping into the earth through seams or channels. This water accumulated in underground reservoirs, eventually creating spectacular geysers. When unusually high numbers of game were reported outside the Park's perimeters during the winter as a result of heavy snowfall, folks predicted an excellent year for geysers and it was thus.

When people from the audience asked him about the names of the geysers, Wylie reported that the geysers still bore the names "given them by the Washburn Party in 1870, the first party of men to visit the Upper Geyser Basin, if we except the Folsom–Cook party of the year before, who did not in reality see the geysers in this Basin since they came across from the Lake into the Lower Geyser Basin."[23] The Washburn Party lingered only a short time at the Upper Basin because of their distress about the missing Truman Everts, and their dwindling supplies. But Wylie told the audience that if the expedition's men revisited the Park to tour the region more thoroughly, they would note, likely with a twinge of pride, that the names inscribed

on boards next to each geyser were the ones they had originally proposed: Giant, Giantess, Grand, Splendid, Beehive, Old Faithful, Riverside, Castle, Fountain, and the Great Fountain.

He also described to the audiences that gathered in auditori-
ums, church basements, and school gymnasiums, the wildlife that
gathered in Yellowstone. The Park region, situated as it was on the
North American continent's highest plateau, supplied more than
sixty square miles of bountiful, nutritious bunchgrass, excellent feed
when it was brown and dry and even more so when it was green. For
fauna, ranging in size from beaver to bison, the Park offered forest
protection and plenty of clear, cold streams. Wylie explained that the
Park displayed "mute evidences"[24] in the form of skulls throughout
its forests and meadows, because it was originally a breeding ground
for American bison. During the summer, bison coexisted on the plateau with deer and elk. In the winter, the animals migrated to lower,
warmer regions outside the Park.

As more settlers ventured into these regions, Wylie warned his
audiences, this pattern would eventually be impossible. Between the
winter weather and the hunters, he added, the wildlife struggled to
survive.

> Elk, deer, [and] antelope are the only cloven footed animals that use
> their feet to uncover grass covered with snow, as does the horse.
> But in severe winters when snow is three or more feet deep this is
> too much to expect of them. Then too, there are frequent chinook
> winds in this locality, which thaw the snow rapidly, but which are
> always followed by severe freezing, which forms a crust that cannot
> be broken with the feet. The chief cause, however, of the diminishing
> of the numbers of these herds is more likely the fear of the hunter
> bred into their subconsciousness while seeking their winter feeding
> grounds.[25]

His hope, he told audiences, lay with the concept of game pre-
serves surrounding the Park and effective laws designed to protect
winter habitat and therefore, the noble animals.

Both young and old were interested in the habits of the bear
before, during, and after the long Yellowstone winters, which lasted,
Wylie estimated, approximately seven months. Squirrels, beavers,

chipmunks, and other fur-bearing animals horded food to sustain themselves over the winter. Bears, however, laid in a store of nutrients for the winter in the form of fat in their bodies. Following their instincts in fall, bears ate nearly all day long, accumulating enough stores of fat in their body to last the winter. During this time, he warned, bears functioned much like youngsters before a meal: irritable and easily provoked. Wylie advised his audiences to be very wary of bears at this time.

In early October, while prowling for food, Wylie observed that it was more likely for bears to hunker down and become buried in heavy snow than it was for them to lumber into a cave and sleep for the winter. Initially, the bear's body warmth melted the snow, opening the space around the bear, then the inside wall of snow froze as the temperatures outside dropped, encasing the bear in a cave as the snow outside continued to build up the walls. As the bear settled into hibernation, its body temperature dropped to a very low degree, circulation nearly ceased, and it often sucked on a forepaw, taking the pad behind the toes into its mouth.

In the spring, however, when it came out of hibernation, a bear was once again hungry and easily irritated. The bear's first meal, Wylie noted, was the inner bark, or cambium of the pine tree—a purgative. During the first tour of Yellowstone in the early summer, he pointed out that travelers could assess how deep the snows had been at the end of hibernation by the height of freshly stripped bark on the-pines. The bears, in a feeble state, lay on the snow's surface while barking a tree. These markings were often ten feet up—an indication of how deep the snowpack was in winter—and were especially conspicuous in the heavy forest to the west of Yellowstone Lake.

Wylie ended his discussion of the bear with the warning that no one should ever attempt to touch or handle a bear cub, no matter how tiny or vulnerable it might appear. Mother Bear, always within easy reach of the cub's utterance of "ma," was a force to be reckoned with.

Wylie and Calfee closed their lecture tour in St. Paul, Minnesota. There, at Wylie and Calfee's invitation, many of the officers and directors of the Northern Pacific Railway attended one of their lectures.

The next morning, Northern Pacific Railway officials, in business to break down "the barriers of distance and time"[26] while making a healthy return on their investment, invited Calfee and Wylie to a conference where they proposed sending the two men on a European tour to spread the word about the wonders of Yellowstone National Park. American perspectives about vacations, rooted in the merits of "work, discipline, and industry," needed more time to evolve from "problematic" to a middle-class "privilege," and eventually, an "entitlement."[27]

The chief legal counsel for the Northern Pacific argued that domestic audiences had been fairly small and that it was too early to mount a European tour.

While the "twenty-five years after the Civil War brought more than a fourfold increase in the number of railroad miles operating"[28] in America, the chief legal counsel was correct when he reminded all that railroad lines were a year or two away from the Park. Instead, he proposed providing Wylie and Calfee with an advance agent, transportation throughout Northern Pacific territory, and accommodations.

The two men took him up on his offer. Wylie and Calfee traveled on the Northern Pacific Railway to the major cities and towns in Minnesota and Dakota Territory. Their last stop—Glendive, Montana Territory—was end of the line in 1882 for westbound passenger trains. But the advance agent caught wind of an eager crowd in Miles City, a worksite for the railroad's construction department, so Calfee and Wylie ventured down there as well. Though hardy travelers by the tour's end, the two men paused to think about the single means of travel from Miles City to Bozeman: "buckboard stage…exposed to danger from hostile Indians."[29] Even though Montana Territory's Indian wars were over by 1882, thus minimizing the risk of traveling this way, Wylie decided to return to Iowa to fetch his wife, Mary Ann, and the children.

Soon after he returned to Bozeman with his family, Wylie was up to his elbows in the business of educating children. He also worked part-time as a bank cashier and dabbled in the real estate and insurance businesses. In addition, he visited rural schools on behalf of

Cornelius Hedges, the superintendent of public instruction for Montana Territory.

∾

In 1882, Wylie's guidebook, *Yellowstone National Park; or The Great American Wonderland*, complete with illustrations from photographs by H. B. Calfee, was introduced into the Office of the Librarian of Congress in Washington. Measuring approximately five by seven inches, the ninety-nine-page book was available for one dollar for a "stiff cover" or seventy-five cents for a "flexible cover." Payment could be sent directly to Wylie in Bozeman or to the publisher, Ramsey, Millet, and Hudson of Kansas City, Missouri, and a guidebook would be supplied by post.

The stiff-covered edition, with its leather binding decorated with a gold-embossed geyser and pine tree, must have pleased Wylie to no end—a guidebook he might purchase himself and keep handy in his saddlebag. He hoped others shared the same sentiment. Because of Wylie's responsibilities as an educator, many of his guidebooks initially fell into the hands of teachers.

In his book Wylie included background on scientist Ferdinand V. Hayden's 1871 exploration of the Yellowstone region. Dr. Hayden, a trained medical doctor with a passion for geology, served as head of the U.S. Geological Survey of the territories. On January 19, 1871, in Washington, D.C., Hayden attended Nathaniel Langford's lecture about Yellowstone country. Langford, a member of the Washburn Party and an employee of Jay Cooke and Company, agents for the Northern Pacific Railway, motivated Dr. Hayden to request congressional funding for an official exploration of Yellowstone. From July 15 to August 30, 1871, Hayden surveyed the park's geological features and initiated the beginning of an accurate map of the region. His party's notes, sketches, photographs, and specimen collections elaborated on existing descriptions of Yellowstone's remarkable geothermal features. In the winter of 1871–72 Dr. Hayden pushed hard to pass national legislation creating Yellowstone as a national park.[30] As Wylie wrote, "Too much credit cannot be given this remarkable man for his influence in bringing about so prompt action by congress in saving for 'The Benefit and Enjoyment of the People' forever, this peerless National Park."[31]

∾

In his guidebook Wylie added a poetic description of Yellowstone National Park formulated during the second session of the Forty-Second Congress (1871-72) by the U.S. House of Representatives, Committee on the Public Lands:

> The ranges of mountains that hem the valleys in on every side rise to the height of 10,000 and 12,000 feet, and are covered in snow all the year. These mountains are all of volcanic origin, and it is not probable that any mines or minerals of value will ever be found there. During the months of June, July and August, the climate is pure and most invigorating, with scarcely any rain or storms of any kind; but the thermometer frequently sinks as low as 26 [degrees]. There is frost every month of the year. This whole region was in comparatively modern geological times, the scene of the most wonderful volcanic activity of any portion of our country. The hot springs and geysers represent the last stages—the vents or escape pipes—of these remarkable volcanic manifestations of the internal forces. All these springs and hot pools are adorned with decorations more beautiful than human art ever conceived, and which have required thousands of years for the cunning hand of nature to form. Persons are now waiting for spring to open to enter in and take possession of these remarkable curiosities, to make merchandise of these beautiful specimens, to fence in these rare wonders, so as to charge visitors a fee as is now done at Niagara Falls, for the sight of that which ought to be as free as the air and water.[32]

Yellowstone National Park, or The Great American Wonderland was organized in the order of a tour. Readers could use the book, Wylie proposed, instead of a guide, or if they were unable to visit Yellowstone, they could read it as a travelogue and enjoy an armchair visit to the Park.

Wylie began his guidebook tour in Bozeman, eighty miles from the north entrance to Yellowstone National Park, and routed travelers and their animals over the seven-mile, steep, rocky grade of Yankee Jim Canyon on the Yellowstone River. He preferred this route, to the Virginia City route, ninety-eight miles west, because tourists struggled to crest the Virginia City Hill between Virginia City and Ennis. His idea was that travelers could enter the Park at Mammoth, go to the Geyser Basins, over to Yellowstone Lake, the Great Falls and the Grand Canyon of the Yellowstone, and back to Mammoth. Wylie arranged the tour by highlights—starting out with the less interesting sights at Mammoth and climaxing with the wonders at the Geyser Basins and the Great Falls of the Yellowstone River.[33]

Wylie expressed appreciation for Mammoth Springs. The time, effort, and expense he spent bringing travelers to "this marvelously beautiful wonder"[34] brought him great satisfaction. His guidebook also included information about Rustic Falls, Obsidian Cliff, Lake of the Woods, Norris Geyser Basin, the Paint Pots, and Monument Basin—including Mrs. Wylie's sidetrip, Gibbon Canyon and Falls, and the Lower Geyser Basin, where the Virginia City road entered the Park. By the time the traveler reached the Upper Geyser Basin with Old Faithful, Grand, and Castle Geysers, "the tourist experiences a full sense of satisfaction, so far as the *wonderful* is concerned."[35]

After the excitement and enchantment of the geysers, where many tourists whooped with joy and wonder at the sight of the gushing towers of steam, Yellowstone Lake was a peaceful respite. After the intense odors and the sight of so much hot water, Wylie wrote, many a tourist (himself included) stood in quiet admiration by Yellowstone Lake, listening to its peaceful waters lap upon the shore.

From Yellowstone Lake Wylie, ever the choreographer of the travel experience, directed travelers on to the massive falls and canyon of the Yellowstone River. People who wanted to adventure farther into the backcountry could establish a base camp at the canyon and follow a trail north to the area of Tower Fall and Specimen Ridge.

Wylie noted that Thomas Moran—the painter who accompanied the 1871 Hayden Expedition and painted lush landscapes of Yellowstone,[36] a painter known for his talents as a colorist—claimed that the Grand Canyon's remarkable tints were beyond the reach of human art.

North of the Grand Canyon, near 10,223-foot Mount Washburn, visitors were treated to fields of lush wildflowers—paintbrush, lupine, and shooting stars among the many species—as well as sweeping views of the entire Park. Visitors stopped to examine the wide variety of breccia—layers of rock formed when angular volcanic fragments are meshed roughly together—which formed Mount Washburn and its neighbors during the Cenozoic era (approximately 66 million years BP.)

From Mount Washburn, Wylie visited his favorite campsite at Tower Fall. In addition to the area's lovely scenery, the grass was thick and rich in hues of green. The water was cold and clear. At the mouth of Tower Creek, every grasshopper guaranteed a fish on the line. Will also mentioned the many curiosities in and around the Petrified Forest and Specimen Mountain.

Wylie devoted a large portion of his guidebook to general advice about the Yellowstone area. He noted that the region northwest of the Gibbon Basin was known to be elk habitat—the animals could often be seen there in early morning. He cautioned, however, that travelers should not assume that game was abundant, for the moment people accepted that, the animals moved into the backcountry or left the Park.

Tourists generally underestimated the amount of food they needed, so Wylie advised a stop at G.W. Marshall's supply store in the Lower Basin where flour was available at a cost of $2.50 for one hundred pounds, rice for fifteen cents per pound, and coffee for twenty-five cents per pound. Wylie advised estimating provisions—including ample bacon, flour, sugar, yeast powder, tea, coffee, and dried fruit—then doubling the amount. Of the many wonders in the Park, he noted, one of the greatest the tourist meets is "his or her own appetite." He also urged travelers to refrain from hastening to the Upper Basin at the cost of neglecting the Lower Basin: take time, he noted, for one can't always come back. He also advised travelers to take time for their hygiene: "Consider a stop at the Queen's Laundry, two miles south of the Lower Basin, where the Superintendent had arranged for bathing."

Wylie's guidebook included a geyser table specifying time of action and height and frequency of displays. He compared a calm, clear morning in the Upper Geyser Basin with its columns of steam rising to various heights to a vast manufacturing city with its many columns of smoke.[37]

Looking at Yellowstone as a single park, Wylie observed, was something of a misnomer. Wylie shared the view of fellow Park adventurers that the area was actually an expansive wonderland of many parks. Its dense forests of lofty symmetrical pines, primarily lodgepole pine, were a prime attraction. In localities where they grew intermittently, small groves sheltered lovely grassy clearings.

Temperatures, he observed, varied widely, from approximately seventy degrees during the heat of a July day to the nightly frosts that occurred throughout the summer. Yellowstone's plants and grasses had adapted to these wild fluctuations in temperature, which provided game an abundant and varied supply of fall and winter fare. For example, Wylie observed that a bouquet of wildflowers in a tent would have frozen petals, easily broken by touch, in the morning, and by evening the blossoms would once again be soft and fresh. Picket ropes, moved about the dewy grass by restless horses throughout the night, were heavy with ice in the morning.

Wylie inserted numerous practical observations in his guidebook. For example, because of the Park's hills, he encouraged tourists to consider traveling with pack animals instead of wagons. He noted that geyser water, if well below the point of scalding, might have a disagreeable taste, but it would not be harmful. He also pointed out that many a fish had been caught with grasshoppers in Yellowstone Lake. Fishermen could snag a fish and cook it without removing it from their line; Wylie and Calfee did so many times. They would catch a fish and drop it while still on the line into a small geyser a short distance south of the lake's Boiling Pool. As the water temperature was 220 degrees, the fish cooked in less than two minutes. The fish, however, were inedible. Long white worms, most likely tapeworms, were found in the flesh and intestine and the cause, Wylie believed, existed in the lake.

Wylie advised travelers to reserve a Pullman sleeping car, leave St. Paul mid-month, and plan on twenty days for the round-trip excursion, six to eight of which would be spent in the Park. He quoted a price of $200 per person from St. Paul to the Northern Pacific terminus, which by 1883 was in Cinnabar, just north of present-day Gardiner.

The tourist season in Yellowstone extended from July 1 to September 1. The Northern Pacific Railway offered one excursion a month from St. Paul. In Wylie's opinion, August was the best month to visit. In July one battled a multitude of flies and mosquitoes; in September it might be snowflakes.[38]

For the Park tour, Wylie listed for travelers the costs of packing into the Park. For a weeklong trip, saddle horses could be rented for $30 to $75, pack animals $30 to $50, and a new wagon $100 to $140. Guides and packers could be hired for $3 to $5 per day, although he added that "Guides are not essential, but packers are." If they advertised themselves as both, Wylie advised sticking with a guide. Guides could be contacted directly in Bozeman and could furnish both pack and saddle horses. He recommended a few, one being George Houston, who had been chief scout for General Howard.

What should travelers bring? Wylie had very definite recommendations, including a pair of smoked glasses to protect one's eyes from the glare of light reflected off geysers and springs. Lots of blankets, "as the nights are cool, one can never have enough blankets; make certain one is rubber to be placed between bedroll and ground."[39]

Finally, he added, "Leave your arms at home. Indians and animals are not a threat." Wylie's lack of "concern about Indian attack" typified guidebooks and "visitors' diaries" of the time. When not blazing trails or talking about Yellowstone with travelers, Superintendent Philetus Norris made a concerted effort to "keep Indians out of the park." Tourism, and "a conviction that Yellowstone held no real significance for the surrounding native communities" of Crow, Shoshone, Bannock, and Sheepeater, remained on Norris' mind throughout his tenure. Nonetheless, Indian bands "did not avoid Yellowstone...but simply abandoned the heavily visited areas along the northern stretches of the park." For hundreds of years, "this area had long served as the most important route between the plains and the western slope of the Rocky Mountains, but the near extinction of the bison rendered such travel obsolete." Even so, the native tribes returned to the park's "remote southern and western perimeters" to hunt "elk and other game animals," harvest plants, fast, and gather "medicinal herbs,"[40] well away from Norris' successor Patrick H. Conger, Wylie, and Wylie's traveling companions during the summer of 1882.

In late June 1882, when William Wallace Wylie was in Yellowstone leading a small group of tourists, his younger brothers—John, age twenty-four, and Robert, twenty-one—traveled to the Park with Jake Wilson. Low on travel funds, the three companions detoured for more than a day over steep, mountainous terrain to avoid paying James George's toll for crossing his claim to land in the vicinity of the rock-encrusted hill bearing the name "Yankee Jim."

Will, John, and Robert Wylie were part of the great westward progression of settlers and tourists from across the United States. In his essay, "Why I Love Tourists: Confessions of a Dharma Bum," Rudolfo Anaya writes:

> One description of the Anglo-American culture has been its mobility. Anglo-Americans, we are told, are a restless lot. They couldn't just stay over there in the thirteen colonies, no, they had to go West…So much a part of the history and mythology of this country is known from that western movement. Land, they smelled land, and gold and beaver pelts and gas and oil, all of which drew them west. So, Anglos are natural-born tourists…Maybe some people just take to touring better than others. Or perhaps there are times when mass migrations take place; need and adventure move entire populations.[41]

The seeds of the Will's Anglo-American roots began with the Wylie brothers' great-great-grandfather, who immigrated to Pennsylvania from Northern Ireland in the early half of the eighteenth century. The Wylie ancestry couldn't simply remain in Pennsylvania. The Wylies put down more roots in Ohio, Iowa, and Kansas. In 1881, John Wylie journeyed west to work as a carpenter during construction of the Northern Pacific tunnel through Bozeman Hill.

Will Wylie corresponded regularly with the parents he'd left behind in Kansas, Moses and Elizabeth, and convinced them to give their blessing to a plan for his youngest brother Cameron to quit his teaching job and come west to Montana, saying that it would improve young Cameron's marginal health. In an unpublished manuscript provided to family members, Cameron noted that a temperature of minus forty degrees greeted him upon his arrival in Bozeman. Eventually, economic need, love of family, a sense of adventure, and curiosity would bring Will and Mary Ann's extended families to the Bozeman area.

During the 1882 Park season, Dr. Renshawe, a topographer for the U.S. government, employed Cameron Wylie, age eighteen, as his assistant, and as his valet, he hired a young student from Harvard University. They were completing a topographical survey supervised by Renshawe. While working in the region east of Yellowstone Lake, the party moved camp and happened into a lovely little park. While all debated its merits as a potential campsite, an expedition member spotted a large grizzly sunning upon a breccia-strewn bluff a short distance to the east.

Although he had never handled a gun before the Yellowstone season, the nearsighted, bespectacled valet had developed a reputation as a superior marksman. He killed all game for the party's meat supply. He asked the doctor if he could shoot the bear. All understood the danger of a wounded grizzly. Dr. Renshawe responded that the valet must be certain he could kill the animal with the first shot. The young man said he could do it.

The doctor ordered other party members to safer ground with the pack animals and saddle horses. Then he instructed the eager marksman to steady his gun against a pine and take care with his aim. The valet did so. Then he fired. Dr. Renshawe, mounted on his horse, held tight to the reins of the marksman's mule. He observed the bear headed in their direction and shouted for his valet to run and mount the mule.

The young man bolted for the mule, gun in hand. But the mule would have none of that. It ran doughnuts around the doctor's horse, spinning the poor animal like a top. Renshawe, anxious that he could not hold the mule much longer, shouted at his valet to make haste. The confident marksman now withered. He ran for a tall tree, encircled it with his arms and sat down on the ground. The bear fell dead a few yards from the trembling student.

Later, as the party skinned the bear, they discovered that the ball had entered the bear's mouth and pierced the heart. Wylie commented in his manuscript that he had heard that bears wounded in the heart could chase down their assailants. Renshawe's party gave the student the bear's hide as a keepsake, but not before they "guyed" him relentlessly about embracing the tree.

ℳ

During the 1882 season, General Philip Sheridan toured the Park in the company of 150 men and 300 horses and mules.[42] At the visit's conclusion, he traveled to the mouth of the Clark's Fork of the Yellowstone River and then boarded a caboose of a Northern Pacific work train to travel another twelve miles east to Billings. In Billings, Sheridan received confirmation of negotiations between two of the founding members of the Yellowstone Park Improvement Company and Assistant Secretary M. L. Joslyn of the Interior Department for land on which to construct roads, hotels, and a rail line through the Park's northern entrance near Mammoth Springs to the geyser basins, likely Norris Geyser Basin and the Upper Basin. The negotiations spelled out rental fees of less than two dollars per acre for ground needed to facilitate construction and also included a square mile of ground at seven popular Park sites plus permission to cut timber for fuel and telegraph poles and use premier sites for raising vegetables and forage. This turn of events filled General Sheridan with worry. He commented: "I regretted exceedingly to learn that the national park had been rented out to private parties."[43]

Sheridan was not alone. These were precisely the negotiations Park superintendent Philetus Norris also argued against before he was replaced by Patrick H. Conger. Norris and Sheridan simply reminded Americans that the creation of Yellowstone National Park in 1872 was rooted in noble principles—in this case, the "desire to keep the region's scenic wonders out of the hands of private interests."[44]

The information available to the public about the negotiations were vague. An article in Bozeman's *Avant Courier* stated that "a couple of Dakota men are negotiating, with fair prospects of success, with Acting Assistant Secretary Joslyn of the Department of the Interior, for the necessary ground in…the Yellowstone National Park, upon which to construct roadways and erect hotels and other buildings for the accommodation and convenience of visitors."[45]

The "Dakota men," Henry Douglas and C. T. Hobart, represented interests far beyond Dakota Territory. Hobart served as primary negotiator for the twenty-five-member board of directors of a joint-stock company based in New York City that eventually incorporated as the Yellowstone Park Improvement Company. If the negotiations succeeded, the board of directors promised Hobart the positions of construction supervisor for the Northern Pacific feeder proposed for Yellowstone National Park and the vice presidency of the Yellowstone Park Improvement Company. They shared the optimism of retired banker and board member Rufus Hatch who, certain his $500,000 in seed money would bear fruit, delivered two steam mills and a shingle mill to the end of the track near the present-day town of Livingston.[46]

These men, wrote George Bird Grinnell, editor of *Forest and Stream,* would have the country believe that they "were working solely and simply for the interests of the people of this country… from philanthropic motives…that they wished in return for the benefits that they were going to confer upon the people, to have a monopoly of the hotel, stage, and telegraph privileges in the Park."[47] The ruse was, of course, that if trustworthy people gained control over the major points of interest, they would protect them out of sheer benevolence.[48] Grinnell pointed out, however, that acceptance of this subterfuge was pure folly.

General Sheridan joined Montana's Governor Benjamin Potts in making his views clear. After he visited the Park in 1882, he filed a report spelling out his concerns, calling for companies of cavalry or mounted police to protect the Park and its wildlife, and to enforce its rules and regulations. He also favored extending Park boundaries to allow more territory for game. These were issues that Superintendents Philetus Norris and Patrick Conger found particularly formidable. Norris and his successor, Conger, buckled under the weight of protecting the Park. No laws existed outlining specific offenses and consequences. Blatant vandalism, excessive hunting of game, and arson all drew the same end—ejection from the Park and/or confiscation of outfit.

Sheridan's powerful advocacy spelled out the threat to preservation in the country's first national park and was a wake-up call for sluggish Interior Secretary Henry Teller, who intentionally distracted himself with other matters to avoid confronting the influential Henry Douglas and Carroll Hobart. Sheridan finally convinced Teller to oppose the building of railroad tracks in Yellowstone National Park, and he enticed Senator George Graham Vest of Missouri to also champion the cause.[49]

General Sheridan also had success appealing directly to public convictions about Yellowstone, and because of his campaign, many were determined to name a geyser after him. Excelsior Geyser in the Midway Basin was targeted for an involuntary name change. First known to white men, women, and children in 1881, it resembled a water volcano. For that entire season, it erupted every two hours. Called the Sheridan Geyser for many years, Wylie expressed relief that the name did not last: "it would be unfortunate to have any geyser bear the name of a person, however noted that person might be. There are a few mountains that bear names of individuals, and one of these is Sheridan Mountain, south of Yellowstone Lake. This does not seem so inappropriate as it would to name a geyser thus."[50]

His bias stemmed from observations of others who, in viewing the geysers for the first time, would voice their amazement in the exact names of the geysers they were watching. One look at the marvel of Splendid and they would claim: "Isn't that splendid?"

"Yes, that is Splendid," Wylie would reply.

And at the Grand: "Isn't that grand?"

Using these words as a statement of fact, not query, Wylie would answer with "Yes, that is Grand." He recalled the old lady who did not think Adam deserved any credit for naming the hog, for anyone would know what to call it.

And so it was as well with other geysers: Old Faithful, Giant, Beehive, the Riverside, and the Castle.

The Wylie tent camp in the Upper Geyser Basin, circa 1885, along with two Wylie guests, Mr. and Mrs. Bayles. The Wylies offered a "sagebrushing" experience with moveable tents that year. *Courtesy, Yellowstone National Park Photo Archives. YELL 40326*

Sagebrushing It

I N AUGUST 1882 THE HAMLET OF CLARK CITY, located between Billings and Bozeman, was renamed Livingston, after Crawford Livingston, a Northern Pacific Railway board member. Confident that tourists would travel by train to Livingston and from there to Yellowstone National Park,[1] high-ranking officials of the railroad rescinded the agreement between their general passenger agent G. Barnes and Wylie to sell the guidebook, *Yellowstone National Park; or The Great American Wonderland*, on their trains. Instead, the railroad kept their contract with their official photographer, Frank J. ("F. Jay") Haynes, an entrepreneur from Moorhead, Minnesota, maintaining a relationship that began in 1879 when Haynes met with Charles Fee, secretary to the railroad's general manager. When Fee accepted a position as the railroad's general passenger and ticket agent, he nurtured Haynes' career by encouraging the photographer to visit Yellowstone. Haynes supplied publicity photographs for the Northern Pacific Railway as they expanded west. By 1882, Haynes held an Interior Department lease for a photographic studio in Yellowstone National Park.[2]

That summer many of Wylie's Yellowstone companions were teachers. Their purpose was to "sagebrush it,"[3] camping wherever the night fell. Wylie had provisions and equipment, such as tents, on hand. To provide his traveling parties with accommodations and a base of operations, Wylie bought a section of land at Spanish Creek in the Lower Gallatin Canyon, approximately twenty miles southwest of Bozeman—the Wylie Land and Livestock Company's first holding—used as a headquarters and to store an expanding inventory of camping equipment, horses, wagons, and rigs.

Wylie was a proponent of a wagon route using a trail from Spanish Creek along the Gallatin River that threaded its way past Sheep Rock to Castle Rock. The Gallatin Canyon's landscape was as stunning as it was intimidating: limestone spires worn sharp by wind and water shadowed the valley floor. Once a sketchy game trail, the route was described in a January 1883 article in Bozeman's *Avant Courier* as "a dizzy bridle path [that] led along the side of the mountain. The range rises abruptly some 1,500 feet above the path. An equal distance below flow the waters—boiling, seething—madly dashing in their course to the Gulf."[4]

The Gallatin County commissioners sent an engineer into the canyon to survey a wagon route that would save time and money for travelers headed to Yellowstone National Park. Wylie was eager to see the proposed wagon route go through, as it would allow his Park operation to leave Spanish Creek in June, journey through Gallatin Canyon, and come into Yellowstone at a western entrance. In addition to a small mileage savings, travel through the Gallatin Canyon avoided Yankee Jim Canyon's toll and laborious grade.

But without the route yet in place, Wylie and the help he likely hired—functioning as both drivers and guides—had to backtrack from Spanish Creek about twenty miles to Bozeman where tourists from various locales around the region assembled, eager to join the Yellowstone entourage. Wylie's party traveled for two days from Bozeman along Trail Creek Road, then ambled south along the Yellowstone River to the Park's entrance at Mammoth. Along the way, his party faced the arduous ascent of Yankee Jim's hill, very difficult for the horses that toiled and sweated as they pulled over the steep grade, cautiously picking their way among enormous stones and struggling with the weight of the wagons. In order to ease the horses' burdens, Wylie and his drivers left half of their camping equipment at the foot of Yankee Jim's hill. After unloading the first half, the men returned for the remainder. The contingent enjoyed the vista of the Gallatin Range to the west and the Absarokas to the east when they reached Mammoth the following day.

Another Wylie ritual along the Old Yellowstone Trail involved renting milk cows. Wylie paid a rental fee to Gallatin Valley farmers who did not want to milk cows at the expense of tending summer crops, agreeing on a fixed price in case the animal never returned from Yellowstone. As they journeyed south to the Park, milk cows in tow, Wylie traded milk for pasture with the farmers along the way.

Wylie believed that "camp life proves character,"[5] and in his guidebook he stated that a tour of Yellowstone demanded an ample stock of patience. Parties, he stated, should be limited to four to six people (excluding attendants), because he observed that the larger the group, the slower the travel and the greater the vulnerability to squabbling. Wylie suggested preparing a detailed itinerary beforehand, so as to prevent arguments and the dislocation of noses. Above all, it was important to choose party members with the utmost caution. Wylie recalled that many a camping party had been sliced up by quarrels—with some members joining other parties. He admitted to gaining a few tourists by those means. Other disgruntled campers simply cut their trips short and left the Park.

He illustrated his point with the story of his 1880 trip with Dick Lockey of Helena and Mr. Jackson, the Helena jeweler, when all the men camped near the edge of a dense forest, without water, halfway between Yellowstone Lake and Yellowstone Falls. As they were unloading their horses, Lockey spied fresh signs of bear and insisted that the party pack up again and move on. Exhausted and unwilling to move on, Wylie demanded that the group stay put, telling Lockey that bears never disturb a campsite on the first night. Wylie and Jackson set up their bedrolls and fell fast asleep, but Lockey remained awake the entire night.

At daybreak, the men packed their gear and started searching for water to prepare breakfast. When they reached the Great Falls of the Yellowstone River, they stopped on a hill beside Cascade Creek. Wylie unpacked the grub, Lockey made a fire, and Jackson slid down a steep incline, coffee pot in hand, to get water from the creek.

But as the coffee boiled, a log shifted on the fire, dumping the pot and spilling the coffee. Lockey cussed Jackson for the way he'd set the pot on the fire. Jackson told Lockey that he made inferior fires. The men faced off, ready to fight. Wylie quickly grabbed the coffee pot and navigated the slope for more water. He'd had nothing to eat for twenty-four hours. When he returned to the campsite, Jackson and Lockey were poking the fire and grumbling, as if the previous twenty minutes had never happened. The fire blazed, the coffee boiled, and everyone ate with gusto.

Wylie's belief that "camp life proves character" dovetails with the larger context found in Paul Schullery's essay about early tourism in the Park:

> Yellowstone required us to stretch our awareness in many ways, for the legislation creating the park did not tell people how to act. At every step along the way, the public, the park managers, and the resource itself would have to resolve what was and was not appropriate. The creation of the park in 1872 launched the American public, indeed the world public, on a search for Yellowstone in the grandest sense: not just to learn what was there and enjoy it, but to make sense of it in the context of their times.[6]

The nation's hopes for the Park "were not born out of necessity, but out of high ideals." The Act of Dedication that formally created Yellowstone National Park and was signed by President Ulysses S. Grant on March 1, 1872, was a "preemptive act"[7] that valued public land in a much different way than the Ordinance of 1785's emphasis on "sale and settlement."[8] Arguably of no value for lumber, ranching, mining, and agriculture, the Park's impressive landscape was allowed to "remain relatively untouched." Accepted as "nature for nature's sake,"[9] the dedication of the Park depended on congressional conciliation, national pride, and the development of a distinctly American education and culture.[10] The Act of Dedication, "AN ACT to set apart a certain tract of land lying near the headwaters of the Yellowstone River as a public park," proclaimed:

> *Be it enacted by the Senate and House of Representatives of the United States of America in Congress assembled,* That the tract of land in the Territories of Montana and Wyoming lying near the headwaters of the Yellowstone River, and described as follows, to wit: commencing at the junction of Gardiner's River with the Yellowstone River and running east of the meridian to the parallel of latitude, passing ten miles south of the most southern point of Yellowstone Lake; thence west along said parallel to the meridian, passing fifteen miles west of the most western point of Madison Lake; thence north along said meridian to the latitude of the junction of the Yellowstone and Gardiner's Rivers; thence east to the place of beginning, is hereby

reserved and withdrawn from settlement, occupancy, or sale under the laws of the United States, and dedicated and set apart as a public park or pleasuring ground for the benefit and enjoyment of the people; and all persons who shall locate, or settle upon, or occupy the same or any part thereof, except as hereinafter provided, shall be considered trespassers and removed there from.

Section 2 of the Act of Dedication stated that the "public park" was under the "exclusive control" of the Secretary of the Interior, who was responsible for developing and publishing rules and regulations that "provide for the preservation from injury or spoliation of all timber, mineral deposits, natural curiosities, or wonders within said park, and their retention in their natural condition." Section 2 also declared that the Secretary of the Interior was allowed to "grant leases for building purposes, for terms not exceeding ten years, of small parcels of ground, at such places in said park as shall require the erection of buildings for the accommodation of visitors."[11]

The phrase "accommodation of visitors" worried many. And their fears were well-founded as the railway and construction companies lined up, like bees to honey, attracted by the aroma of monopoly and hoping to gain exclusive contracts for railroad lines, hotel and road construction, and stage and telegraph services.[12] Even though "Yellowstone's creators set it *apart* from the civilization that inevitably shaped its future," the Park remained "an American paradox, born of oddly and unconsciously contending impulses." Described as worthless for sale and settlement, there was no debating with American business about the "economic potential and national pride"[13] evidenced in Yellowstone's geysers, waterfalls, rivers, lakes, meadows, and mountains. The days when "there were practically no comforts for tourists"[14] would soon be discussed in past tense at lunch stations, on hotel terraces, and in history books.

While Wylie's imagination was captured by stories told by travelers such as Truman Everts, Bird Calfee, and Macon Josey—all of whom vigorously participated in their own survival with considerable hardship while visiting the Park—Paul Schullery maintains in his study of early Yellowstone tourism that "Yellowstone could not long afford highly individual approaches to its enjoyment." As the number of visitors to Yellowstone National Park increased, "the only way to move large numbers of people through Yellowstone and allow them the opportunity to view the recognized geological and geothermal 'wonders' was through industrial tourism."[15]

Decent roads and transportation, safe places to stay, and dependable dining options were, and continue to be, hallmarks of Yellowstone's "industrial tourism," also labeled "vacationing infrastructure."[16] By developing his "sagebrushing" tourist business, William Wallace Wylie helped "to decide where people should stay, what they should eat, and how they should travel. Thus began the often uneasy but entirely necessary three-way relationship between the federal government, the public, and the park concessioners."[17]

Because camping was not for everyone, especially those wealthy customers who vacationed in European spas or at fashionable resorts in the Catskills,[18] the Yellowstone Park Improvement Company had plans for an eight-hundred-guest hotel at Mammoth. Designed by architect L. F. Buffington of St. Paul, the proposed National Hotel was a green building with a bright red roof—a color scheme quite at odds with its background of muted grays and browns—with a veranda that ran the length of the 414-foot-wide structure. Mr. Buffington drew inspiration from the Queen Anne style of architecture popularized during the 1880s and '90s, and he combined a turret, gables, balconies, and the hotel's many windows in unusual ways.[19]

Wylie went along with the hotels, rationalizing that Yellowstone travelers should have a variety of travel choices, and he wanted his own business to be one of those choices. If he wanted respect for his sagebrushing ways and movable tents, then he knew he had to tolerate the hotels with their fancy bellboys and European chefs.

∾

On March 3, 1883, Congress passed the Sundry Civil Bill, which in addition to establishing the Park's annual appropriation of funds, also included proposals by Missouri's Senator George Graham Vest and the Committee on Territories, allies of General Phil Sheridan. The Vest committee's provisions limited the Secretary of the Interior's authority over leases and privileges. The bill prohibited "exclusive privileges or monopolies"[20] and also prohibited leases of more than ten acres per tract, with no leases within one-quarter mile of the gey-sers or the Great Falls of the Yellowstone River. The bill also allowed the Secretary of the Interior to call in troops through the Secretary of War and detailed the employment of ten assistant superintendents to act as police.

Thus began a banner year—1883—in the evolution of the extraor-dinary "brand-name tourist attraction"[21] known as Yellowstone National Park.

In April 1883 construction began on the Northern Pacific Rail-way's branch line from Livingston to Cinnabar, just three miles from the Park's northern entrance at Gardiner. Completed on August 13, 1883, it operated as "the first rail line specifically to a tourist destina-tion in the western United States."[22]

During the summer of 1883 General Phil Sheridan returned to Yellowstone, hoping to combine his ongoing interest in the affairs of the Park, specifically an effort to protect more game, with the enjoy-ment of travel and camping in the West. Sheridan argued that the Park's boundaries should be extended to include more of the Absa-roka Mountains to the east and the Teton Range to the south—a notion that expanded on Park superintendent Philetus Norris' pro-posal to set apart the Park's northeast corner, specifically the Lamar Valley, as a game preserve. He traveled with a number of statesmen, military men, and businessmen who, in a long elaborate pack train accompanied by a troop of cavalrymen, covered the backbreaking terrain between Fort Washakie, Wyoming, and Cinnabar, Montana, in August and early September.

Sheridan was accompanied by President Chester Arthur, Secre-tary of War Robert Lincoln, Senator George Vest, Montana's Ter-ritorial Governor John Schuyler Crosby, and Sheridan's brother, Lieutenant Colonel Michael Sheridan. The expedition also included Anson Stager of Western Union, Captain William Philo Clark, Judge Daniel Rollins, Surgeon Major W. H. Forwood, and F. J. Haynes, official photographer of Yellowstone Park Improvement Company. News reporters were purposefully excluded from the party. Efferves-cent reporting about the Park and appeals to public sentiment were left to Lieutenant Colonel Michael Sheridan. Paul Schullery noted:

Until the 1880s, most visitors were from nearby states, but after about 1883, as the railroad's publicity campaign geared up, the park began to attract the attention of more and more long-distance visitors. President Chester A. Arthur's visit in 1883 is seen as something of a milestone in this process; the visit was exhaustively reported in the world press.[23]

On this trip President Arthur, General Sheridan, and their traveling companions likely discovered several small touring companies organized by the Northern Pacific and a few independent parties including Will Wylie and his movable tents. Beginning in 1883 Wylie offered ten-day tours from Bozeman twice a month. The Yellowstone Park Improvement Company was in the midst of constructing its big, green hotel at Mammoth Springs, even though the land lease with the Interior Department was not yet formalized. The Yellowstone Park Improvement Company also managed tent hotels at the Lower and Upper Basins and the Grand Canyon.

As Sheridan was voicing concerns about protecting wildlife, the Yellowstone Park Improvement Company, very likely influenced by the Northern Pacific Railway, touted the benefits of a narrow gauge railroad from Cinnabar through Yellowstone National Park to the Cooke City gold and silver mines. In 1883 Lieutenant Dan Kingman of the U.S. Army Corps of Engineers was appointed by the War Department as the Park's chief engineering officer at the behest of General Sheridan. Lieutenant Kingman arrived in Yellowstone on August 13, eager to work on the Park's roads and bridges. He shared General Sheridan's general views about Yellowstone and opposed the railroad's incursion into Park boundaries. Kingman expressed the gravity of his concerns in his annual report:

> in the earnest hope and upon the supposition that it [the Park] will be preserved as nearly as may be as the hand of nature left it—a source of pleasure to all who visit it, and a source of wealth to no one...if its valleys are scarred by railroads, and its hills pierced by tunnels, if its purity and quiet are destroyed and broken by the noise and smoke of the locomotive;...then it will cease to belong to the whole people, and will interest only those that it helps to enrich, and will be unworthy the care and protection of the National Government.[24]

Park superintendent Patrick Conger, his assistants, and independent operators such as Will Wylie increasingly relied on Sheridan and Kingman's Washington, D.C., connections as well as their willingness to inspire government officials and the public to both handle Yellowstone National Park with great care and behave themselves. However, as Wylie and Calfee found out on their fall 1881 lecture tour, there was so little known about the Park that only time and consistent advocacy helped federal legislators understand threats to Yellowstone preservation and public safety. Time and promotion in brochures, periodicals, and newspapers also helped potential tourists understand that while the Park "attracted visitors for its relative wildness,"[25] the adventure need not be inherently frightening and best suited to male travelers. Nor should it require a large measure of guilt as a companion because a traveler took time off work to enjoy a novel, middle-class experience.

ॐ

As the number of travelers and contractors and their employees increased, so did incidents caused by bad judgment. A shooting episode on St. Patrick's Day 1883 occurred at a boardinghouse in the National Hotel construction camp, home to the hotel framing crew. In addition to working on the hotel, the crew spent time gambling, drinking, and fighting. David Kennedy shot Jim Armstrong twice— above the heart and in the pelvic area. Assistant Superintendent George L. Henderson responded to the shooting by negotiating an agreement with the repentant Kennedy, who consented to give his wages, time, and energy to nurse Armstrong until the patient either recovered or died. Henderson also convinced a vigilante "court" to suspend its sentence of immediate hanging, since Armstrong clung to life, eventually recovering in Kennedy's care. In his annual report for 1883 Superintendent Conger mentioned this shooting incident, stating that he notified the Interior Department and the Governor of Wyoming, William Hale.

Park superintendent Conger's communication with Governor Hale motivated the Wyoming territorial legislature to pass an act, or session law, on March 6, 1884, providing greater legal protection for

Yellowstone National Park, since most of the Park was located within Wyoming's boundaries. Responding to perceived congressional inaction over the application of U.S. laws and Interior Department rules and regulations in Yellowstone, the act, which was designed to protect the Park's timber, fish, wildlife, and curiosities, stipulated that the governor of Wyoming Territory name two justices of the peace and two constables "to assist and aid the government of the United States in keeping and maintaining the said Park as a place of resort."[26] The act set fines for Park violations: one-half of each fine was to be paid to the official, prosecuting witness, or informer, the other half to Wyoming Territory's treasury.

The Yellowstone Park Improvement Company, despite the fact it now had a ten-year lease to help develop the "Park as a place of resort," could not pay its creditors or employees who were working to complete the National Hotel at Mammoth Springs. By March 1884, the carpenters had enough of working for the most minimum of wages—nothing—in harsh winter conditions. The company owed them $9,000 in back wages. When Carroll Hobart of the Yellowstone Park Improvement Company attempted to placate them by mortgaging lumber at the Cinnabar mill for $200, creditors slapped liens on everything in the hotel, including the piano and all of the liquor. The carpenters staged a sit-in while the company went into bankruptcy. The carpenters eventually received $10,000 in cash and sixteen tickets east on the Northern Pacific. Receiver George B. Hulme hired Carroll Hobart as manager of the hotel for the 1884 season, during which the hotel posted a $4,587 loss.

The following summer, in June 1884, Mary Ann gave birth to Clinton Wilson Wylie, who joined the other Wylie children: Elizabeth, nine; Fred, seven; Frank, five; and Grace, three. Needless to say, Will made no reference in his manuscript to Mary Ann's role in Yellowstone that summer.

∾

Yellowstone National Park barely survived the brute force of the winter of 1884–85. Inside the park, the mountains and valleys, bison and elk were buffeted by snow, ice, and piercing cold. Outside the Park wind of another kind was blowing through boardrooms and back rooms: a wind spreading the conviction that the Park and profit were synonymous.

Yellowstone National Park superintendent Robert E. Carpenter of Iowa, appointed in August 1884, headed to Washington during the winter season to lobby Congress for the segregation of land: to remove key tracts from Park jurisdiction and allow these tracts to be occupied by private parties. Segregation of land in Yellowstone was still of interest to many people, some of them true-blue Park defenders such as Senator George Graham Vest of Missouri, whose bill, SB 221, proposed eliminating the slivers of Montana and Idaho from Yellowstone as well as the Clarks Fork mining locale. He also favored, per General Sheridan's suggestion, extending Park boundaries eastward and southward. He strongly opposed Carpenter's lobby, however, to open the door for the Cinnabar to Cooke City rail line in Yellowstone, specifically saying that "allowing any railroad to enter 'would end in the destruction of the Park.'"[27]

The owners of the Great Northern Railway; Montana congressional delegate Martin Maginnis, whose HR 4363 authorized the Cinnabar and Clarks Fork Railway; and Robert E. Carpenter ignored Vest's comments and persevered with their lobby to remove land from Yellowstone National Park authority. They had visions of laying down tracks from Cinnabar to Cooke City in order to stake claim to Montana silver and gold. From there they intended to reach the Great Falls of the Yellowstone River, Yellowstone Lake, Old Faithful Geyser, and then, who knows how far they could go.

Park superintendent Carpenter was so confident about passage of the segregation bill that he promised to telegraph an ally, apparently his son, from Washington with the news that specific coal deposits and other prize real estate were no longer protected by the Yellowstone Park Act. On February 20, 1885, he sent the telegraph to his son in Livingston: "Secure that horse at once." It was code, of course, for "get ready for a land grab." Carpenter's son then telephoned their compatriots who were waiting in Hall's store in Gardiner.

The telephone message, however, was garbled. A loud discussion followed, overheard by others who happened to be in the store when the phone rang. An alternate telephone message arrived, which fueled further suspicions among the men who were gathered that day at Hall's store: "No wind in Livingston." When Carpenter's friends left Gardiner before dawn the next morning, they were joined by forty to fifty interested observers. After a lengthy ride over mountains and through valleys, nearly every man in Gardiner and Mammoth Springs had secured "a horse." Names appeared on claim posts, names such as C. E. (Carroll) Hobart and R. E. (Robert) Carpenter.[28]

Meanwhile, back in Washington, D.C., SB 221 failed to pass the Senate, despite its passage in the House and weeks of intense debate. Throughout the country citizens voiced their disgust with Superintendent Carpenter's lack of scruples. *Forest and Stream* demanded that Secretary of the Interior Lucius Lamar fire Carpenter. In Montana Territory newspapers in Livingston and Cooke City led a verbal rampage against the superintendent. On June 10, 1885, Carpenter's association with the Yellowstone Park Improvement Company became public knowledge, and ten days later, Colonel David W. Wear of Missouri replaced him as superintendent. Colonel Wear's admirers heralded his vigor, his reputation as a gentleman, and his intelligence. Recommended for the position by Senator Vest, Wear faced high expectations to reform the reservation's administration.

During the 1885 tourist season, Wylie faced disheartening circumstances because of the way the Yellowstone authorities interpreted the Park rules and regulations. In June 1885 he traveled with several prominent Bozeman merchants and townspeople, including banker Peter Koch and dry goods merchant Paul Kirschner. They journeyed from Wylie's ranch at Spanish Creek, along the Gallatin River to the Park's west entrance at what is now the thriving town of West Yellowstone. Because there was no easy trail along the Gallatin, they had to stop frequently to clear fallen trees to allow the pack and saddle animals to carry on. After a six-day journey, the expedition camped in the Lower Geyser Basin.

Superintendent Wear had assistants located at all major points of interest. They had the authority to initiate complaints about rule violations before a justice of the peace who upheld the laws of Wyoming in a courtroom located in the Lower Basin. It is worth noting that the assistants and the justice shared in penalties that were demanded from all convictions.

Lorenzo D. Godfrey, assistant superintendent, arrived at the campfire on the Wylie party's first evening in Yellowstone. After a brief speech during which he clarified several regulations, Assistant Godfrey moved about the group, shaking hands, asking for names and occupations, poking about the horses and the gear. After Godfrey's departure, Wylie was convinced that the assistant had made up his mind that this was an expedition of good pickings.

In the morning after coffee was made, Wylie supervised a careful dousing of the fire with water the men hauled in from a nearby brook, even though camp was situated in damp soil, as shown by the water-loving blue Gentian flowers that surrounded it. He knew that every ember qualified as a transgression of the rules. Later that afternoon, while viewing the geysers in the Upper Basin, the men were arrested for leaving a campfire. They knew they were not guilty as charged, but they returned to the Lower Basin anyway for trial the following morning.

There were a number of important men, in addition to the defendants, at the trial: Arnold Hague, geologist with the U.S. Geological Survey; W. Hallet Phillips, special agent with the Department of the Interior; and Samuel Langhorn, registrar with the Government Land Office in Helena. Hague and Phillips offered to act as witnesses for the Bozeman party.

Hague declared that in fifteen years of camping while fulfilling government duties as a geologist, he had never witnessed greater forethought in choking a fire. Mr. Phillips explained that he had been in the vicinity of the Geyser Basins for several days observing the execution of Wyoming laws, the treatment of tourists, the business of fines, and other issues. On behalf of the Interior Department, he stated that, in the case of the Bozeman party, they had adhered to the laws.

The justice of the peace, Judge Hall, previously self-employed as a woodcutter, wasted no time in levying a fine of fifty dollars plus costs of ten dollars against Mr. Wylie, the party's leader. The sentence, the justice indicated, could be appealed in Evanston, Wyoming.

Wylie refused to pay, and ordered the justice to put him in "the Bastille" and reinforce the door and windows with heavy bars. If witnesses went along for the ride to Evanston, Wylie estimated the price of an appeal at about $1,000. He left the judgment hall, trailed by witnesses and members of his party.

After thirty minutes of intense, angry discussion outside, Peter Koch, the banker in the party, slipped unnoticed into the courtroom and wrote out a check for sixty dollars. Wylie appreciated Koch's generosity, but he wasn't consoled until he had discussed the "unjust judge," with Superintendent Wear, who sent Justice Hall and Assistant Superintendent Godfrey out of Yellowstone "to find their way to Evanston, Wyoming, themselves."

Later that day, Wylie and his traveling companions reached the Upper Geyser Basin. The geysers performed spectacularly, as if, Wylie noted, to compensate for the indignities administered in the "hall of injustice."

They arrived at the Upper Geyser Basin at the same time as a group of congressmen and aides who were in the Park to gather information, input, and data because they wanted to formulate legislation to govern Yellowstone more effectively. As a result of Superintendent Robert E. Carpenter's misconduct, the House of Representatives had formed the Holman Select Committee. Judge W. S. Holman of Indiana, Congressman Joseph G. "Uncle Joe" Cannon of Illinois, and Congressman Thomas Ryan of Kansas were among its members.

Wylie and Koch were anxious to relate their experience of the "forenoon" and spoke with the men at length. Congressman Ryan told the two men that Hague and Phillips had already provided the committee with a detailed report of the Bozeman party's brush with Wyoming law. Ryan stated that the sooner the entire jurisdiction of the Park could be put under its own form of government, the better it would be for visitors. The congressional members used Wylie and Koch's story, as well as Hague and Phillips' written report of their treatment, to help formulate a report to Congress.

Several days later, the Bozeman expedition camped at Tower Fall. The best view was at the foot of the falls, but getting there was just shy of impossible. The route skirted the rim of Tower Creek to the Yellowstone River, then followed the creek to the falls. It was a hard trip, Wylie thought, but well worth the effort. He hiked with Peter Koch and a young man in his early twenties who had joined the party at the Grand Canyon. On the return trip, the young man shortened the hike back by scaling the canyon wall a short distance from the foot of the falls. Wylie insisted it could not be done; that the young man would give up from exhaustion, if he was lucky. Koch joined Wylie and plodded back to camp. As they walked, the two men became more agitated over the risks involved in such tomfoolery. As the young man passed from their sight, Wylie shouted that if he wished to reach camp it would be by return to the bottom of the canyon and taking the long way around.

After supper, as the party began making up their beds, the young man came dragging into camp. His clothes hung in tatters. His body was drenched in sweat. His shoulders were so hunched that his arms and knees seemed to bump into each other with every exhausted step.

Wylie insisted he lie down on a bison robe and take a few sips of coffee. The young man had no appetite. He insisted that it was his night to do the dishes and he must do them. Wylie ordered him to lie down and offered to do the dishes later. In spite of his experience the young man remained certain that he could scale the canyon.

The next morning, he ate a big breakfast and washed the dishes. But, Wylie noted, for the remainder of the journey, he took direction from the older gentlemen in the party.

Koch repeated the tale for years to come, Wylie said, citing it as a sublime kind of patience, the greatest he'd ever witnessed on Wylie's part. But Wylie maintained that he "deserved no credit. No one can successfully do a tourist business who is not made of patience."[29]

When the expedition arrived in the Gallatin Valley, the smoke was so dense—likely from regional forest fires—that it blocked the sun, and the day was cool and dark. Koch and Wylie bore the brunt of endless teasing for failing to douse the group's campfire in Yellowstone's Lower Geyser Basin.

Later that Yellowstone season of 1885, Lieutenant Daniel King-man of the U.S. Army Corps of Engineers received enough funds to put three twenty-five-man crews to work constructing roads and bridges in the Park. From Norris, one of the crews worked their way north to Obsidian Cliff near the Wylie camp at Willow Park. Human and bear interactions were frequent, as were conversations about them.

One evening, Wylie invited the boss of the Obsidian Cliff crew, a Mr. Somers, to have supper at the Willow Park campsite. The work near Obsidian Cliff was very involved, and the crew toiled long hours, leaving their cook alone in camp every day and some nights. Somers pointed to the location of the cook tent, under a tree across the meadow, and launched into a story about his former Chinese cook and a bear.

Somers told Wylie that one morning the cook informed him that a bear had pestered him frequently the two previous days. The cook asked him what would happen if the bear came to the cook tent while he was alone at camp.

Somers suggested that the cook nail some slats to the tent pole and cut a hole out of the top of the tent. That way, he reasoned, if the bear appeared, the cook could climb the slats up the pole, out the top of the tent, and onto the limb of an overhanging tree. Somers assured the cook he would be safe.

Later that morning, of course, a bear lumbered into the camp.

An extraordinary racket woke a night herder in a nearby tent. He looked out to see the cook, butcher knife in hand, peering out the top of the tent. The cook climbed out onto a large limb. It splintered and sent him crashing down upon the tent. The ridge pole collapsed and the tent covered the bear. Nevertheless, the critter stormed about the tent, engulfing the cook in billows of canvas. A mix of squeals, roars, grunts, and a great deal of shouting in Chinese filled the air.

After the cook and the bear sorted themselves out, the herder had trouble determining who was more frightened. The cook ran at top speed in one direction and the bear in another. When the cook arrived at the Obsidian Cliff, Somers could not convince him to return to camp. Somers agreed to drive him directly to Mammoth without clothing or bedding.

The bear was never seen again.

∾

Back in Bozeman, Wylie was contacted by Montana's Superintendent of Public Instruction Cornelius Hedges about assuming his position upon Hedges' impending retirement. Celebrated throughout the territory as the father of education, Hedges was respected for his four terms of service during which he lengthened the school year and encouraged the development of more schools and compulsory teacher institutes.

Wylie agreed to take the job. Beginning in 1885, he committed himself to extensive travel while representing education and balancing the needs of children, teachers, parents, taxpayers, and government.

The winter of 1885–86 brought little snow and unseasonably warm temperatures to Montana Territory, but it also brought sickness and death to the Wylie household. On February 25, 1886, Will and Mary Ann's third child, Frank Bozeman Wylie, died at the age of seven. Searches of both the Gallatin County Clerk and Recorder's Office in Bozeman and the Montana Office of Vital Statistics failed to find a record of Frank's death or any illness related to it, likely because there were no state requirements to file birth and death certificates until 1907. It is not difficult to imagine that the Wylies caught a glimpse of the coming Yellowstone season through the fog of melancholy.

Still, once March 1886 rolled around, tours were booked and names added to waiting lists. The Wylies likely drew great strength from their Presbyterian faith and family and friends, and also coped with their son's death by focusing their energies on their Yellowstone tours. Wylie trained his guides—schoolteachers, farmers, and college students—to provide patrons with factual and intriguing information about the Park's geology, history, and flora and fauna. He planned entertainment for nightly campfires, inspected camps, responded to company stage or wagon wrecks, and introduced himself and his guides to the Park administration. On top of all that, he personally greeted the three or four bears that visited camp nightly.

Even in 1886, the management of Yellowstone remained very tenuous. Railway companies and contractors anxious to accommodate Park visitors were still vying for the tourism dollar. State and federal rules governing the Park ranged from too strict to nonexistent.

Properties once belonging to the defunct Yellowstone Park Improvement Company were soaked up by a new company, the Yellowstone Park Association.[30] George W. Wakefield and Charles W. Hoffman retained the contract to haul Northern Pacific passengers from the end of the Northern Pacific line to association accommodations (the Mammoth Hotel, the hotel at Norris, and tent hotels in the Upper and Lower Basins and Canyon) and other park curiosities at twelve cents a passenger.

The stringent Wyoming legislation enacted in March 1884 was repealed on March 10, 1886, by Wyoming's territorial government. Some newspapers warned that the Park lacked an adequate legal umbrella. Other journalists focused on the recent report by the Holman Select Committee that mentioned the "Godfrey Incident" and in connection with such, W. W. Wylie of Bozeman. Holman Select Committee spokesman Thomas Ryan eventually became First Assistant Secretary of the Interior.

Congress failed to appropriate enough money to adequately protect Yellowstone National Park. The Sundry Civil Appropriation bill for the fiscal year 1887, which went into effect on July 1, 1886, budgeted the standard $40,000 for the Park. From this amount, the House subtracted $20,000 to pay Superintendent Wear and his ten assistants. Then Wear's assistants heard there was not enough money to fund their salaries, so some of them left the Park. In late July the Senate added $20,000, but negotiators from the House and Senate had abandoned any middle ground. Public sentiment about the Park ran the gamut from disgust with the Park's civilian administrations to moving toward the adoption of a policy of state administration of the park (in this case, Wyoming).

Secretary of the Interior Lucius Lamar turned to William Endicott, the Secretary of War, for assistance. By Special Orders No.

79, Headquarters, Department of Dakota, disseminated from Fort Snelling, Minnesota, Captain Moses Harris of the First U.S. Cavalry led fifty soldiers from Fort Custer, Montana Territory, to Mammoth Springs. They arrived on August 17, 1886, and immediately set up camp at the base of the Mammoth terraces in a locale known as Camp Sheridan in honor of the general, who had recommended Captain Harris for the assignment to Yellowstone.

When Captain Harris and his troops arrived, forest fires raged in the Park, set deliberately by visitors, employees, and other people living near Yellowstone to protest rules and regulations—fires probably set to embarrass Superintendent Wear and his assistants. Many of the blazes, Harris reported, had burned for the entire summer season with the exception of the devastating fire that ignited on August 14, 1886, near the east fork of the Gardner River. Approximately eleven miles long and four miles wide, the fire afforded the nearby National Hotel at Mammoth Springs a round-the-clock campfire. Crews were sent out to fight the fires. Jack Baronett, one of Truman Everts' rescuers, assisted the Park administration by scouting in the back country for rule violations, and the soldiers were given no-nonsense training in the enforcement of Park regulations. Captain Harris took over as Park superintendent on August 20, 1886.

Former Superintendent Wear guided Captain Harris quickly through the Park. Several of Harris' men, each with a small squad of military personnel, were assigned to posts occupied by former assistant superintendents: Norris Geyser Basin, the Lower and Upper Basins, Riverside on the Madison, Canyon, and Soda Butte.

Wylie, who was saddened by Colonel Wear's shabby treatment, expressed regret that with the appointment of Captain Harris he now worked under military instead of civilian administration. He wasn't, however, disappointed for long. Captain Moses Harris soon earned respect from individuals as diverse as the Secretary of the Interior to George Bird Grinnell, the editor of *Forest and Stream*, and on down to Will Wylie, for his consistent application of Park laws, fairness of judgment, and energetic advocacy of the public's interest in the Park.

∞

During the school year Wylie's responsibilities as superintendent of public instruction kept him on the road visiting larger urban centers and rural schools in less-populated counties to understand the needs of Montana schoolchildren, parents, teachers, and administrators. In his annual reports he discussed school funding, which at the time was acquired by direct taxation as there was no territorial or federal aid, and the schools' need to acquire revenue from "school lands"—sections 16 and 36 of each township. He also discussed how it was impossible to garner this funding until Montana attained statehood. In an effort to improve academic standards, Wylie encouraged county superintendents to design and grade their own tests for student promotion. He supported Montana teachers by calling for a raise in salaries.

During his superintendency Wylie once journeyed from Helena to Boulder to facilitate a teachers' institute. As he changed from train to stagecoach at Jefferson City, he thought the stagecoach driver looked very familiar. Wylie approached him, intending to ask if he could keep him company in the box, but a lady climbed up instead. At a Boulder hotel, the driver sat opposite Wylie during dinner at the community dining table.

The waitress addressed the driver as Pete and asked what he would like to order.

When she disappeared with the order, Wylie asked, "Pete, did you drive for Gilmer and Salisbury in Idaho at one time?"

Pete responded that indeed he had.

Wylie asked if he recalled upsetting a coach in Portneuf Canyon one night, a coach full of passengers and weighted down with freight. Pete paused to scrutinize Wylie's face, then extended his hand across the table and recollected that Wylie was the gentleman who gave him brandy. After dinner, the two men retired to the hotel barn for a thorough rehash of years gone by. Wylie wrote: "I was anxious to learn if he had been discharged because of that affair, because several of the passengers vowed that they would report him for drunkenness. He said he did not believe they did because he had been driving for Gilmer and Salisbury ever since."[31]

Wylie noted that teachers responded with enthusiasm about Yellowstone National Park. It was Wylie's "preferred classroom."[32] The number of teachers who not only owned his guidebook to the great American wonderland but were eager to tour the Park themselves astonished him. When he revealed that his upcoming tours were almost fully booked, he shared his disappointment with many of them, but he could also see the potential for being fully employed in the tourist business with a safety net, courtesy of Wylie Land and Livestock.

∽

During the mid-1880s, Wylie suffered periodic annoyance due to a discomfort in his thighs, buttocks, hips, and lower back that soon developed into debilitating pain. When this flared up, he had no choice but to go to bed until the affliction subsided.

Now closing in on his forties, Wylie attributed his pain to chasing horses during inclement weather. He felt that he was the only one of his staff well enough acquainted with the forests and the feeding grounds of company horses to do the chasing. The more horses Wylie brought into the Park, the more his responsibility expanded. In early July, he chased down a herd of company horses foraging west of Willow Park in an area near the base of Three Rivers Peak. Long after nightfall, he drove them through the forest. While fording rapids in an icy stream, Wylie's head caught a tree limb. He tumbled out of his saddle and into the creek. His horse continued on. Once upright, he realized he'd lost his hat and also his eyeglasses, for it had long been his habit to tuck them under the inside band when riding at night. He gave the hat a second thought only because he could not function without spectacles. Wading in waist-deep water, Wylie met up with a tree reclining across the stream. His hat rested against a limb, but his anxious hands failed to locate the glasses. Thrusting his face and hands into the frigid waters, he explored the creek bottom directly below where his hat tarried and scored a large quantity of gravel and the eyeglasses.

"Only those who are slaves to eyeglasses can understand my feelings at this moment," observed Wylie. "Was it not more than 'good luck'?"[33]

∽

By the summer of 1887 the Wylie Camping Company's business had increased nearly 25 percent. Recent rate wars reminded the railway companies of "the possibilities of selling Western travel on a large scale."[34] At the same time Wylie experienced greater interest in his camping approach that allowed middle-class men and woman to enjoy each other's company while adding to "their stock of knowledge, experience, and information,"—and provided just enough work to remain "safe from the potential dangers of idleness."[35] The Santa Fe Railway also reached Los Angeles and "the price of a ticket from Missouri River points fell for a year to twenty-five dollars or less." The railway companies transported "more settlers, speculators, and adventurers than tourists in the ordinary sense."[36] However, the broadening appeal of the West and shifting American notions about wilderness required that the country turn its back on the "carnage of the Civil War,"[37] and encouraged growth of the tourist economy as a "common, national experience."[38] In order to take advantage of these developments, Wylie hired more employees from the Gallatin and lower Yellowstone valleys to drive and guide tourists around the Park.

Minnie Stevenson Hughes, whose father served as the minister at Bozeman's Presbyterian Church from June 1883 to October 1889, reminisced about the Wylies in a letter written in 1969 to Max Goodsill of the Yellowstone Park Company. Minnie wrote that she and her family enjoyed the Wylies both as neighbors and friends. She remembered "as one of the small fry" watching as the Wylies readied a buckboard, a simple wagon for the tourist excursions, plus wagons loaded with tents and equipment. The drivers, Minnie stated, looked to be about eighteen years old. As the Wylies' business grew, many people in Bozeman joked that the entire "Presbyterian Church moved to Yellowstone Park for the summer."[39] Friends and acquaintances of Mary Ann and Minnie's mother served as camp supervisors. Their sons drove freight wagons and their daughters worked as waitresses.

All employees of the Wylies' company gathered at Mammoth before proceeding to Willow Park to prepare for the first tour. But flooding of the Willow Park road that led to pasture distracted the company from their usual preseason business.

Beaver! thought Wylie. Close scrutiny of nearby streams proved the beaver theory correct. After swimming the stock to pasture, Wylie instructed his blacksmith to create a hook. Hoping to discourage dam building and encourage the beavers to move on, Wylie dismantled several dams with the new gadget. After breaking up the dams in the late morning, Wylie discovered that to know the beaver is to witness persistence in action. Several camp employees reported at supper that repair work was well under way at the Willow Park dams.

Because of the beaver's tenacity, Wylie thought it the most fascinating animal in the Park's menagerie. A large and prolific population dwelt in Yellowstone's streams and cold-water lakes. During the initial stages of road building in the Park, a road that had been built twelve miles east of Mary Mountain to join the Lower Geyser Basin and the Grand Canyon was eventually abandoned to beavers. Wylie spoke often of his desire to travel to that locale to study the beavers in action.

Of chief interest to Wylie was the beavers' organizational hierarchy. At Willow Park, one very big beaver supervised the repair work. For many years, Wylie thought beavers used their tail as a trowel; not so, he learned at Willow Park. The boss beaver's tail aided its swimming, diving, and punishment of the noncompliant or slacker underlings.

Sharp teeth function as the beaver's primary tool, well suited as they are for a variety of work. When a beaver gnaws down a tree, it will fall in the direction the animal wishes. Limbs of trees are cut to size and stored in the cellar of the beaver's home for winter food.

The entrance to the beaver's home is always under water. The two-story dwelling has upper living quarters and lower storage for food, preferably wood with bark. By instinct, beavers know how high a lake or stream's water will rise. Even in high water, their living quarters remain dry. Imagine—a cozy, dry place to call home and plenty of work.

Wylie never forgot his hours sitting on a grassy bank watching a beaver repair a leak in a dam—observations that were almost certainly shared with his guides, customers, family, and friends in hopes of providing a more authentic visit to Yellowstone and transforming their perceptions of nature and science. The beaver employed many willow rods of exactly the same length. Using his front paws, he set one end of a rod a third of the way into the existing structure. Taking the middle of the rod in his teeth, he leaned backward and pushed the opposite end of the rod into the dam. The middle part of the rod took on a bow shape and remained in his teeth. Satisfied each end of the rod was secure and in position, the beaver pushed the bow toward the dam, a paw on each end and his mouth making minor adjustments. The first rod fastened parallel to the surface of the water, he placed a second in perpendicular fashion and the third diagonally across the leak. Wylie spent an entire afternoon watching the beaver's accomplishments with the greatest respect. Not only did the leak stop, but the beaver used all the rods in his stockpile to complete his handiwork and never left on a supply run.

With this experience in mind, plus the realization that he could not ask his stockmen to swim horses to and from pasture, Wylie conceded defeat in the furry face of buck-toothed persistence. The company built a new road some distance from the stream.

4

Natural and Unnatural Curiosities

WILLIAM WALLACE WYLIE SERVED AS Montana Territory's superintendent of public instruction until 1887. After leaving that position, he helped to plan and organize a new Presbyterian school called Bozeman Academy. Wylie assisted the principal with curriculum development and supervision during the building of the log school. Eighty-four students attended the academy during the 1887-88 school year.

Wylie continued his tradition of leading summer tours in Yellowstone National Park. In her thesis about the Wylie Camping Company, Elizabeth A. Watry mentions that "one of the first known newspaper advertisements for Wylie's camping operation appeared in the *Helena Daily Independent* in 1889," specifically "on consecutive Saturdays beginning on May 25, 1889 through June 29, 1889."[1] The advertisement named the Wylie & Wilson Camping Company, and Watry notes that Sam Wilson, Mary Ann Wylie's brother, was probably Wylie's business partner. Wylie and Wilson provided tents, food, cooking staff, and transportation by carriage or horse for the twelve-day tours of Wonderland. Patrons were expected to bring their own bedding.

At first glance it is possible to conclude that early in the 1890s, Will Wylie's Park business development was tinged with the same kind of providence he experienced when the stranger approached him in Lyons, Iowa, and asked: "How would you like to go teach in the Rocky Mountain country?" From 1883 to the early 1890s, he and Mary Ann spent a modest amount of time and energy in serious deliberations about designing a tourist business. As often happens in busy households, there was only so much time and energy to go around after the parents' day was done, and their children fed and tucked in for the night. In 1926 when Wylie recorded his reminiscences, he concluded that the business "just growed" and "it was at least ten years after this work began, before Mrs. Wylie and I realized that we were drifting into a tourist business."[2] Let us consider this conclusion from other angles.

Another shift in America's thinking about wilderness occurred: from an early perspective based on the "value system of primitive man," in others words, gratitude for "what contributed to his well-being" and trepidation about "what he did not control or understand," to the frontier as place of opportunity, and now, in the early 1890s, to a "sadness at its disappearance from the American scene." The 1890 census upheld the nation's guess that "civilization had largely subdued the continent." Roderick Frazier Nash comments that "the qualities of solitude and hardship that had intimidated many pioneers were likely to be magnetically attractive to their city-dwelling grandchildren." What were the alternatives to a wistful, collective hand-wringing about the 1890s as the "first decade without a frontier ?"[3]

Yellowstone National Park offered limitless possibilities; "as Wonderland, the experience of tourism as discovery and exploration remained a continual process and promise, rather than accomplished fact or feat. As Wonderland, Yellowstone always remained just on the edge of civilization…." and Americans, especially the "expanding middle class with time and money to spend on leisure," searching for "personal experience, an escape…where the self could be temporarily reimagined, an opportunity for physical, mental, and spiritual reinvigoration," and "a glimpse of 'the good life'" found that very appealing.

Wylie's camping experience offered a safe, "personal experience… on the edge of civilization."[4] Wylie was an educator to his core, with an intense curiosity about Yellowstone National Park's landscape—its plants, animals, geology, and geography. His guidebook, his speaking tour with H.B. Calfee, the fact-based Park tours that he organized, and his unpublished memoir—all reflected Wylie's sensibility as a teacher. He and his family appreciated an authentic Wonderland experience, which included exposing their guests to the Park's curiosities. They enjoyed sharing the experience with others, notably the increasing numbers of middle-class tourists seeking knowledge as a path to self-improvement, in an invigorating and natural setting like Yellowstone. The housing, transporting, and feeding of tourists, while not minor details, were of secondary interest to Will and Mary Ann. Even so, the growth in the Wylies' business can be partially attributed to their adequate consideration of those particulars, as well as their patrons' acceptance of the benefits and economic and cultural value of a Wylie camping tour.

While Wylie lived to tell about his own travel experiences by stagecoach and steamboat, travel by railroad to the Yellowstone region minimized the risk to tourists' sanity and safety, and generally made it possible to transport more travelers with a greater frequency of Park arrivals and departures. Beginning with the completion of the branch line from Livingston to Cinnabar in 1883 and over the next ten years, Wylie hosted many tourists who found a trip by train more appealing than by stagecoach; for example, female teachers on summer break or middle-class citizens who needed to return to work. Carlos A. Schwantes points out in his essay about early transportation and tourism in the northern West that "the tourist trade quickly formed an important part" of the railroads' business.[5]

While the railroads and concessioners such as Wylie vigorously promoted Park travel, it is important to consider Paul Schullery's argument in his essay about early tourism in Yellowstone. He writes:

> If the place had not lived up to its unofficial name of Wonderland, and if these people had not carried home such lively stories of its marvels, no amount of commercial promotion could have succeeded in making it the goal of one of American's foremost pilgrimages. If Yellowstone had not been an authentic global wonder, it would have settled into the role of a regional attraction, more on the scale of the New York's Catskills or the Wisconsin Dells.[6]

As more people heard the "lively stories" of Yellowstone's wonders and sought that experience themselves, the Park's tourist industry developed to meet the needs of visitors. By the early 1890s, members of the Wylie household probably passionately debated the merits of permanent versus movable camps. Thinking about the sheer work involved in organizing and moving camps—taking care with the increasing number of humans, animals, structures, and provisions involved as business grew—made the transition to permanent camps very appealing. The men who were employed as drivers could help with the preseason setup and postseason takedown and inventory of permanent camps. Mary Ann could work alongside her husband and assist him in inspecting the camps. And, finally, Will and Mary Ann would be freed up to pitch in—to drive or guide—where they were needed. No matter how much sense it made, however, the change to permanent camps was something that happened only after struggles with McMaster Camping Cars and ongoing struggles with a man Wylie termed the "subservient Army Superintendent."

During the preseason trip from Bozeman to Yellowstone, Wylie and his drivers and guides, now including his son Fred, most likely discussed the ins, outs, ups, and downs of operating a tourist business in a region filled with unusual wonders—most of them mysterious and inconceivable to the company's guests. Wylie's discussion included the warning: The geysers might not "play" when the military guards said they would and tourists might blame their driver for the geysers' failure. To ward off possible tension, Wylie recommended the drivers and guides politely remind their guests that the Park and its natural features were created long before the Wylies had anything to do with it.[7]

During the late 1800s, when Wylie, his family, and his employees drove tourists around Yellowstone, the geysers became less active. When Wylie first arrived in Yellowstone in 1880, the Giant performed every third day, but over the years it gradually lengthened its rest period until by 1925 it was erupting only once a month. In the early 1880s, Giantess erupted every two weeks and several times on that particular day. By 1925, it was classed as an exceptionally lovely pool. From 1880 to 1885, Grand erupted every twenty-four hours, but its eruptions diminished to the point where they arrived on no regular schedule at all. In the 1880s, Splendid "played" every other day, twelve eruptions per day. By 1925 it was dormant. Beehive Geyser, which had once operated every twenty-four hours and was, in Will's opinion, "the finest geyser of all in point of symetery [sic]"[8] also lay dormant.

Plenty of natural wonders, however, remained. While Old Faithful kept up its hourly schedule throughout the years of Yellowstone history, the Riverside Geyser erupted irregularly. In his guidebook, *The Great American Wonderland*, Wylie included a geyser table detailing information on various geysers, including length of display, height, and frequency. The height the water reaches and length of display, he noted, are related to the quantity of water or size of vent and the temperature of the steam. Frequency depended on how long it took a new water supply to smother the steam phase. His table, compiled in 1881, stated that Old Faithful "played" every sixty-five minutes, erupting for four minutes to a height of 160 feet.

Old Faithful's neighbor in the Upper Geyser Basin, the Castle, blasted steam and minimal water on a daily basis. In his guide-book, Wylie noted that Castle performed for thirty minutes, reaching heights of 150 feet. This display occurred once every two days. The Castle's impressive eruptions of hot water were documented in a painting titled *Castle Geyser, Firehole Basin* by Thomas Moran. However, Walter Trumbull, member of the Washburn–Langford–Doane Expedition of 1870 and Truman C. Everts' assistant, was disappointed in Castle's water display, which he described:

> The water did not retain the shape of a column, like that thrown out by "Old Faithful," but rather splashed up and slopped over. This gey-ser did not appear to be doing its best, but only spouted a little in a patronizing way, thinking to surprise us novices sufficiently without any undue exertion on its part.[9]

Perhaps, Wylie surmised, water piped into Castle Geyser would help control the water supply and regulate its cycle—an idea that would be anathema today. Wylie was also struck by the unique structure of Castle Geyser's cone, which was remarkable in size and age and resembled a medieval stronghold.

Wylie was unwavering in his belief that the wonder of the Park lay in its variation and unpredictability. While Old Faithful was the most reliable, Excelsior Geyser, the world's largest geyser in the 1880s, received a lot of attention during that time period, when the geyser was unusually active. Eventually, its repeated eruptions damaged the siliceous sinter lining and it became dormant. Even though it was technically a geyser, Wylie felt it should be metaphorically called a water volcano, for it exploded instead of erupting. It was dangerous for a person to stand next to it while it erupted. Prior to the eruption, the earth shook, then there was a resounding *boom!* as water rose from the cone 200 feet into the air; stones, 300 feet. During the 1880s, tourists viewed at least one performance. Even if it was the only geyser they saw while in Yellowstone, they felt compensated for their journey, regardless of the expense. Its last dazzling eruption was in late July 1890. After that, the limelight shifted to Excelsior's very large crater from which nearly 4,000 gallons of hot water per minute churned into the Firehole River.

Wylie also counted tourists and the unpredictability of their experiences as one of the many wonders of the Park. Put easterners face-to-face with western wildlife, Wylie knew, and anything could happen. Tourists were fascinated by the bears, elk, and bison—but they were also frightened, so such encounters were a double-edged sword for a guide trying to lead a group safely through the Park. Their encounters with the animals—ranging from bears to chipmunks— were the source of many of Wylie's best stories.

Wylie's favorite bear story, which he called a "man story," happened one summer night when Wylie was eating in the dining tent with a large group of tourists fresh off the train. A driver sought out Wylie to report a fine-looking bear at the edge of camp. He asked Wylie if he could have permission to tell the guests.

Wylie asked that the driver let the group finish supper and then tell them about the bear. Most tourists, he knew, were more interested in bears than geysers, but Wylie tried to keep them from seeing a bear the first day or two, because so many of them feared tent walls were insufficient protection against big teeth and sharp claws.

The driver rallied the other drivers—approximately thirty were in camp that night—and they circled their wagons around the bear to contain it until supper was over. The visitors ate their meal, then eagerly accepted an invitation to view the bear. Sixty tourists joined the drivers in the circle. The driver who initially spotted the bear instructed all to shout when he gave the signal, the hope being that the bear would climb a tree.

When he gave the signal, a shout rose up from the crowd and reverberated through the forest.

The bear looked over the circle of horses, wagons, and eager-faced tourists, swinging his heavy head slowly from side to side. Then, spying daylight between the legs of a male visitor, the bear charged.

The gentleman's legs buckled and he was thrown atop the bear's back, his face buried in its rump. Clutching the bear's heavy black fur, the man rode the bear for what Wylie described as a respectable distance. When the animal finally threw him off, sympathetic bystanders-helped him back to camp. His face was ashen; his mumbling, unintelligible. It was several hours before he could fully appreciate the hearty congratulations that were bestowed upon him by his fellow tourists, the Wylies, and their employees.

At the end of his tour with the Wylies, the man returned to the campsite, removed the aluminum nameplate from inside his hat, and secured it to a tree. He told Wylie that when folks asked about the nameplate, he should tell them it belonged to the man who "rode the bear."

Wylie's clients were also crazy about the chipmunks that scampered up and down the lodgepole pines in the Park's dense forests. All tourists noticed the chipmunks perched on logs along the road, yapping as vehicles passed, their tails snapping with each chirping bark. Taking notice of this oddity, one woman asked Herman, one of the Wylies' most engaging drivers, if the "little creature" made the chattering noise by moving its tail.

Herman replied that it was so. By summer's end, he elaborated, the tail would be worn off. But not to worry, he added, during the long winter a new tail would sprout and by next Park season, the chipmunk would be ready to charm all who passed its way. The Wylies' employees later overheard the woman explaining this information about the chipmunk as one of the interesting natural history "facts" about the Park.

Another story that Will loved to tell was about a gentleman who, as they rode from Cinnabar to Willow Park, peppered Will with questions about the flow of water in a roadside canal near Gardiner—a spot that puzzled many passersby. To appreciate this tale, it is important to understand that water can be deceptive—especially if it flows in a canal in an area where the road leads quickly up a grade. The water will appear to be flowing uphill.

As he and the gentleman headed uphill toward the Gardner River, Wylie asked if the gentleman noticed that the water in the canal flowed uphill.

The man eyed the water carefully and agreed with Wylie.

"Do you see the team crossing the bridge ahead?" Wylie asked him. "The water flows under the bridge and makes its way right here to us."

The gentleman was amazed, then added, "What energy it must receive from its source!"

When he tried this ploy on another man, the gentleman scrutinized the water and commented, "Well it looks that way, but water will not run up hill in Missouri and dam'd if I believe it will in any other country."[10]

❧

Wylie's memoir included stories about runaway horses for the "many people [who] think all kinds of park work is only fun."[11] Wylie loved horses; however, when one went missing someone had to chase it. That someone was Wylie. He knew the habits of horses and where to find them, but the chases, while they made amusing stories later, were arduous. For example, there was the horse that robbed him of a good night's sleep. By the time his night herder told him that a pair of his horses was missing one morning, several people had already begun searching for the two missing steeds, to no satisfaction. Wylie ordered saddle horses harnessed as substitutes and sent his patrons off on their tour of the Park.

Assuming the team had headed for Bozeman, Wylie saddled up his favorite stallion and streaked for Mammoth Springs. Passersby indicated they had spotted the horses galloping across the flat in front of the Mammoth Hotel. Wylie knew these horses were too intelligent to pass the registering station, so he checked the cedar grove behind Fort Yellowstone. He found nothing. He pushed on to Gardiner and then Cinnabar, where he knew they would be sighted between the railway station and the store. No one had seen them. He rode back over the hills to Mammoth Springs, still convinced those fool horses were in the grove behind Fort Yellowstone. He climbed a hill to keep watch, hoping the horses would show their long, sorry faces at dusk. Just past sundown, they bolted from the cedar grove and onto the road—running for Gardiner. Wylie hurried down to the road and attempted to pass them on the Gardner River Bridge.

When his watch chain caught on his saddle horn, he slowed down and let them take the lead. After he untangled his watch, Wylie urged his saddle horse on until the three horses were neck, neck, and neck. Then the errant team veered off into the sage-covered hills. Wylie readied his lariat and roped the leader of the pair. Furious, he dismounted, stomped over to the horse, and slapped his saddle on it, certain the mate would follow and the saddled horse, sufficiently exhausted, could be easily led. Wylie mounted the lead horse and it wasted little time in bucking for all it was worth on the steep incline.

At Mammoth, Wylie sought out George Wakefield, who had been appointed the Yellowstone Park Association's Master of Transportation for the 1891 season. Wakefield took Wylie's horses to the association's transportation barn with the directive that they be well fed and watered, then he took Wylie to the hotel to be well fed and watered over a thorough rehash of Park business. After supper, Wylie rode the bucking horse and led the other team horse and his saddle horse back to Willow Park, the entire distance under pouring rain mixed with thunder and lightning. Wearing a corduroy suit but no raingear or overcoat, he stopped at the previous night's camping spot, only to find it abandoned. This discovery was underscored by bright flashes of lightning, and with each flash the team horse neighed for the horses up ahead and bolted for the woods. Wylie pressed on to Norris.

Six miles farther, he stumbled on three freight wagons parked on the edge of the road. On the opposite side of Obsidian Creek, Wylie noticed a smoldering campfire with the dark forms of sleeping men lying around it. A flash of lightning momentarily robbed him of his sight and he fell neck-deep into the creek. Once out of the icy waters and on the other side of the creek, Wylie approached the men.

"Pardon me," he shivered. "May I lie down or at least rebuild your fire? I am very cold and wet."

"This is a hard night, pardner," said the first gentleman. "We have no more covers."

"What is your name, sir?" asked a second gentleman.

"Wylie," said Wylie through chattering teeth.

"Here. Take this overcoat," insisted the gentleman. "I came into one of your camps one night and was treated decently."

Raising his head to look Wylie over, another man pulled out a blanket and suggested taking cover in one of the wagons.

"Thank you," said Wylie. "I'm much obliged." He sat wrapped in the coat and blanket until dawn, then prepared his saddle horse for the ride back to Willow Park to check on the whereabouts of the loose horse. As Wylie approached the former campsite, the horse ran to him and Wylie quickly switched his saddle to its back, letting his saddle horse follow. When Wylie returned to the freight wagons to collect the feisty, bucking bronc of a horse, the men invited him to breakfast and fed his horses as well. After breakfast, forecasting that he could meet up with his patrons in the Grand Canyon, he mounted his saddle horse, with one team horse tied to his saddler's tail and the other team horse tied to the tail of the second. He reached the campsite at the Great Falls and discovered that all the rigs were there when they should have been five miles away, along the rim of the Grand Canyon with the tourists. "Ahn, where are all the horses?" Wylie inquired of the Chinese cook.

Ahn was in the middle of preparing a batch of doughnuts. He paused, with a cluck of disgust. "When you go away, every thing go wrong. Horses all lost, no find them, people have to walk."

"Load me up with doughnuts, Ahn. I will go find them," Wylie said. Half a mile from camp, Wylie met up with his best horse man, but no horses. He asked the man where he'd been looking and mentioned one place specifically.

"I just came from there, but did not see them," the man said.

Wylie rode for almost an hour, looking for the horses. His last resort was the area he'd mentioned to his horse handler. When he arrived there, he found the entire band of horses, asleep, and content to stay that way. This, however, was not what Wylie had in mind. The horses were herded back to camp at a dead run, hitched to the rigs, and aimed in the direction of the Grand Canyon to pick up the famished, plodding patrons.

∾

Another time, in late August, the Wylies' superintendent of transportation approached Wylie at Willow Park and informed him that six company horses had been missing for six weeks and they'd be left to starve over the winter unless Wylie found them. Wylie left camp before daylight the following day with provisions and an extra blanket tucked under his saddle. He told Mary Ann to send out a search party if he didn't return in three days.

In the early morning Wylie came upon a bear in a grassy park lunching on a freshly killed bull elk. He drove the bear away and, while still astride his horse, studied the elk's massive antlers. Then he rode on for another half mile on his search for the missing horses. He stopped again. He decided he'd been a fool to leave the remarkable antlers behind and turned back. Unable to relocate the grassy park, he rode into another and found all six lost horses—chubby from grazing on the tall grass. Wylie forgot about those antlers, for the battle to head the horses to Willow Park began in earnest.

The fight raged on—one man determined to get his horses home and six horses who were certain they preferred life on the graze. Wylie characterized his ordeal as the "hardest riding ever experienced."[12] For five hours, Wylie pushed his distracted horses through pine forests that sheltered 80 percent of Yellowstone and small parks of the finest grass known to beasts. Wylie reached Willow Park at 9 P.M., the end of a long day.

∾

Wylie had to draw on that well of determination again when his relationship with the federal government became more strained in 1891. The politics over park leases reached new intensity after the arrival of a new superintendent, Captain George Anderson. Anderson replaced Captain F. A. Boutelle on February 15, 1891, and was charged with the expansion of Fort Yellowstone. Wylie's relationship with Anderson was characterized by periodic outbursts and misunderstandings. While Anderson acknowledged camping as an inexpensive and "delightful" way to tour the Park, he also argued in reports to the Secretary of the Interior, John Noble, that camping parties were prone to leaving fires unattended. He was also concerned that camps fell short of policing their patrons and lacked the authority, manpower, or will to prevent campers from littering, gathering Park specimens, or writing their names on the Park's wonders.

Because of Yellowstone National Park's expansive and varied geography as well as the limited numbers of experienced personnel and relatively slow systems of transportation and communication, Anderson wanted travelers controlled. Faced with those realities, it was no surprise that Anderson laid his goodwill on the doorstep of the hotels, where guests could be contained and supervised. He also favored an official registry of tourists who traveled on their own or with camping outfits, something that was initiated three years later, in 1894.

When Wylie first met Anderson during the 1891 season—Anderson's first in Yellowstone—Wylie did not need a license to operate in the Park. He most likely felt he could take his time developing a relationship with Anderson.

Acting on a request from a newspaper, Wylie prepared an article on Park accommodations, management, and other issues "of public concern," specifically "drunken men on every hand."[13] Instead of consulting with Anderson, Wylie wrote Secretary of the Interior John Noble and asked for clarification about the laws that related to selling liquor in the Park. He informed Secretary Noble that he'd been asked to write a newspaper article and he wished to be just in his opinions. Wylie asked if the open bars in the Park's hotels violated the law or "how the rule is set aside."[14]

When he replied on September 26, 1891, Secretary Noble stated that "no one has a license to sell intoxicating liquors within the park, or to set aside or violate the published rules on that subject."[15]

Nearly one year later, Anderson acknowledged the "sale of intoxicating liquors" in an August 1892 letter, but he advised Wylie to keep to himself his "peculiar notions on the people who think differently," for the sale of liquor was "properly supervised and controlled."[16]

It is worth noting that the bar receipts for Yellowstone Park Association's 1893 season totaled $22,461.47.

∾

When Anderson detailed Park transportation highlights for the 1891 season, he made specific mention of "the Wiley [sic] tours" and stated his belief that "such established institutions" should not be permitted. Businesses such as the Wylies' "originate and advertise their business outside the park, but the conduct of the business is wholly within it." Anderson argued that "to the greatest extent possible"[17] these businesses operated beyond his control or supervision.

The Yellowstone Park Association's transportation privileges were revoked in November 1891, after the Interior Department investigated the death of a tourist on one of their tours: Guy Pelton, who died in July 1890. Sixty-four years of age, weak of heart but willing in spirit, Pelton died on a sweltering day in late July as he attempted to climb Devil's Stairway. Drivers of heavily loaded tourist outfits who dreaded the steep grade from Nez Perce Creek up Mary Mountain known as Devil's Stairway often asked tourists to walk the grade to save their horses, though it was not a well-publicized practice.

When the Yellowstone Park Association lost its transportation privileges, the association's transportation manager, George Wakefield, handed over the reins to the Yellowstone National Park Transportation Company, incorporated in May 1892 by Silas Huntley (friend of President Benjamin Harrison's son, Russell Harrison), Aaron Hershfield, L. H. Hershfield, Harry W. Child, and E. W. Bach.[18]

While the Department of the Interior may have changed the lease for the 1892 transportation privileges to S. S. Huntley's Yellowstone National Park Transportation Company, complaints about the company's "lack of stop-over privileges" were received soon after the Park's 1892 opening. Wylie, of course, benefited from these complaints.

Anderson thought seriously about this dilemma. A perfect Yellowstone tour offered as much time as an individual desired at any number of the Park's wonders. Yet, for the sake of customer service and to avoid overcrowding, Huntley's transportation company also depended on some level of predictability and organization. Despite his reservations, Anderson recommended camping parties due to their flexibility: "It is proper that these parties be given the greatest latitude consistent with proper park management."[19]

∾

Wylie inaugurated two McMaster Camping Cars for the 1892 Yellowstone season. The camping car, "slightly wider and longer than an omnibus"[20] (a horse-drawn vehicle designed for mass transit that combined elements of a stagecoach with elements of a carriage), had a high price tag and intriguing results. Built to accommodate four patrons and equipped for a twelve-day trip, each car had upper and lower upholstered berths and was pulled by four Clydesdale horses, which made a breathtaking and genteel presentation. For five dollars per day per person, Wylie's guests could take their time at all natural wonders and spend their evenings casting at first-rate fishing spots, a fine deal when compared to the ten dollars hotel patrons had to pay for a hotel and stage ride. Will supervised the camping cars; Mary Ann managed the movable tents.

On Wylie's second tour of the Park during the 1892 season with the McMaster Camping Cars, he was arrested in the Grand Canyon by an army officer who refused to state what Wylie was being charged with. Wylie was forced to abandon his patrons and accompany the officer to the army post at Mammoth. The other transportation companies were quick to make the "subservient Army Superintendent" aware that the camping cars frightened coach horses.

Wylie denied observing any such fright. "I do not know what would have happened had coach horses seen an automobile in those days," Wylie observed in his memoir. "The whole trouble was that it dazzled the eyes of my competitors. But I was held under arrest" and taken to Fort Yellowstone. Wylie's guests were "set afoot at Grand Canyon."[21] Wylie's movements at the army outpost were without restriction, so he took full advantage of his access to Mammoth's telegraph office and wired Montana's Senator Wilbur Fisk Sanders in

Washington, D.C. He telegraphed friends to do the same. The next morning, Wylie was released.

Who was this "subservient Army Superintendent?" In Wylie's memoir, the gentleman remains nameless. A reasonable hypothesis would name Superintendent Captain George Anderson, who would have been administering the Park when Senator Sanders was in Washington.

Because he realized he didn't have the support of Superintendent Anderson, Wylie knew he had to lobby the Interior Department directly. Wylie packed his bags in March 1893 and headed to Washington, D.C., to seek permission to establish permanent camps and lunch stations in Yellowstone National Park. When new Interior Secretary Michael "Hoke" Smith took office in early March 1893, a commission comprised of Captain Anderson and two bureaucrats who had never visited Yellowstone National Park expressed their concerns about Wylie's application, noting the "unsightly appearance of the structures usually incident to such camps" to the "unsanitary arrangements and conditions into which such places are apt to fall." The commission recommended an "experiment of permanent camps."[22] Wylie was granted a permit for one year only, based on the appeal of camping to a large number of Park tourists.

Wylie declined their offer. For him, a one-year experiment would not justify the hefty expense of purchasing the equipment and manpower necessary to establish the permanent camps. Yet he remained hopeful that he would eventually obtain a permit for a longer tenure, so he made a request to secure one-acre sites at nine of the Park's points of interest.

Captain Anderson did not support Wylie's request and he set forth his disagreement in a letter to the Secretary of the Interior. Anderson attempted to balance the heavy hand of his worry, that the camps would be unattractive and challenging to oversee, with a willingness to take direction from Washington and assign Wylie the nine one-acre sites. In his 1893 *Report of the Superintendent*, Captain Anderson again outlined his objections to the permanent camps, concerned that such structures in Yellowstone National Park would be a sacrilege.

In all fairness, the context of Captain Anderson's resistance cannot be separated from another beloved tourist attraction, Niagara Falls. Unless he was raised in a remote cave, Anderson would have grown up hearing about what Elizabeth A. Watry describes as "the despoliation of one of America's most iconic natural attraction, Niagara Falls," which "captured the attention of nearly everyone." Watry noted that "Niagara had developed into a dizzying world of trinket shops, photographers' studios, hawking tour guides, and boat tours." In addition, "ladders and stone stairways to the bottom of the American Falls and a wooden walkway to the brink of Horseshoe Falls... provided some tourists with a heightened sense of the falls, but for others those developments obscured the scenic panorama of the natural landscape." Captain Anderson denied many "petitions for commercial development in Yellowstone, including an application to build an elevator to the bottom of the Lower Falls. While his resistance to the establishment of permanent camps was by no means an exceptional occurrence of Anderson's dealings with concessioners, it nonetheless presented a problem for Wylie."[23]

Wylie's visit to Washington coincided with a national economic crisis. By 1893, after eight years of steady economic growth, the country's gold reserves fell below the $100 million level when silver was overvalued relative to gold. Farm prices were declining and the Philadelphia and Reading Railway and countless other businesses filed for bankruptcy. The stock market went into a tailspin.

However, the economic uncertainties of 1893 had few repercussions in the Gallatin Valley. Bozeman was heralded by the Montana legislature as one of "several ambitious cities,"[24] and it provided funds to found an agricultural college there. East of Bozeman, coal mines were expanded to provide fuel for the railroads and the copper industry in Anaconda, Butte, and Great Falls. The Farmers' and Merchants' Elevator Co., with a capital of $25,000, incorporated and built facilities for the storing and handling of grain. "This enterprise is one of far more than ordinary importance not only to the hundreds of industrious and enterprising farmers within a radius of a dozen miles of Bozeman, but to the business interests of the city generally."[25] The Bozeman Presbyterian Society saw growth on the horizon and was on a mission for land within two blocks of Main Street on which to build a new church edifice and parsonage. "The society has 154 active members and the present church will now more than seat them comfortably, should they all attend at once,"[26] stated Bozeman's *Avant Courier* in 1893. To show the $20,000 project to its best advantage, the site needed to include enough ground for a spacious lawn. Among the Presbyterian Church's active membership who could count on a comfortable seat were Mary Ann Wylie, also active in the Bozeman Missionary Society, and Will Wylie, church elder.

For the 1893 season, Wylie forsook the camping cars, not because of his arrest or pressure from the "subservient Army Superintendent," but because the cars were not economically viable. The cars accommodated only four patrons, which did not offset the cost and effort of moving them around the Park. In addition, the cars were too heavy for existing Park roads.

For his camping company, Wylie dreamed of driving his guests in covered rigs with matched teams of horses to permanent compartment tents with fine mattress beds. Selecting and purchasing horses in matching breeds and colors brought Wylie more satisfaction and pleasure than anything else in the camping business. The four-horse coach teams were eventually at the center of many arguments about the merits of eleven-passenger carriages versus motor coaches. Despite a large number of rarely publicized wrecks and a smaller number of hold-ups, Wylie preferred the horse and coach, especially his six four-horse teams that met the trains and transported patrons to the first station at Willow Park. Each of his teams was distinctive. One had four light-colored sorrels (yellow-brown) sporting white manes and tails. Another was black as coal in contrast to another team of snow-white horses. The Wylies owned a team of dark bays (brown coats with black points on the legs, mane, and tail), another team of dappled grays, and a third team of dappled bays. These four-horse teams—in their various shades of white, black, gray, and brown—were the show teams of the Park, Wylie recalled, often convincing an indecisive tourist to sign up for a ride.

The team drivers displayed great regard for their charges. The tackies (horses) and coaches were washed each day, and the driver of the snow-white team rinsed his steeds with a blueing solution. A pail hung on the back of the rig for watering the horses several times a day. Each team worked a six-day shift, walking or trotting steadily during the daylight hours, pulling a full coach or rig. A feed bag filled with oats could be strapped to a horse's head, which allowed the horse to eat without being unhitched.

In his memoir, Wylie doubted that passengers in the motor bus of the 1920s experienced any more pleasure than passengers in a rig or Concord coach. One or two seats could be removed from the rig to create more space and canvas curtains drawn around the sides to offer protection from the rain. By the time he was writing his memoirs, however, Wylie refrained from arguing for a return to team-drawn coaches. The horse-drawn coaches were a pleasing memory, but, Wylie concluded, they "are gone forever."[27]

The 1893 tourist season in the Park was, according to Yellowstone Park's Superintendent Captain Anderson, "the most peculiar of any in the history of the Park."[28] In spite of the West's best efforts—by local chambers of commerce—to invite Americans to counter "the slack in immigration and travel"[29] that characterized the country's depressed economy, the number of tourists traveling in Yellowstone with the Yellowstone National Park Transportation Company was down: 3,076 compared with 3,645 the year before. Anderson expressed certainty that the decrease in numbers could be explained by the national economic downturn and the World's Columbian Exposition—Chicago World's Fair—of 1893, which opened on the shores of Lake Michigan on May 1, 1893, and had received 27 million visitors by October 30, 1893.

Anderson credited travelers from afar with saving Park business from ruin, as it was commonplace for hotel registers to document the arrival of patrons from ten to twelve foreign countries on a single day. The gravest financial wounds, Anderson noted, were suffered by camping parties and outfits that contracted irregularly with individuals, and he wondered if most ended the season with a negative balance.

ॐ

Beginning with the first session of the Fifty-third Congress, convened in August 1893, the Wylies had a year's worth of topics to discuss with family, friends, and employees. Lawmakers introduced bills to provide Yellowstone National Park with adequate legal protection, a step that had been taken with little success for approximately twenty years. In 1893 the only herd of bison, wandering in their native habitat on U.S. soil, lived in Yellowstone National Park. In his Yellowstone National Park history, Lieutenant Hiram Martin Chittenden, of the U.S. Army Corps of Engineers, described the national sentiment about the bison herd: "There has always been a lively interest in the preservation of this herd, and its extinction would be regarded as a deplorable calamity. With proper protection, it will undoubtedly flourish, but there is no margin for carelessness or neglect."[30]

Chittenden worried about the "wanton recklessness of those who seek special privileges in the Park, and are unwilling that any measure for its welfare shall pass unless coupled with their own private schemes." This inclination of politicians to protect self-interests jeopardized any hope of passing a bill to protect the Park. Nevertheless, as Chittenden wrote so eloquently, "the prompt manner in which a great misfortune was changed into a lasting benefit"[31] in the last days of winter 1894, reversed this course of neglect.

In March 1894 two expeditions traveled in the Park. One group, which included scout Felix Burgess, was intent on hunting down Ed Howell, a notorious poacher. The other party, sponsored by *Forest and Stream*—the Yellowstone National Park Game Expedition—focused on the Park's wildlife. Included in the second party were photographer F. Jay Haynes, seeking to expand his photography portfolio of game and winter scenes, and Emerson Hough, writer for *Forest and Stream*.

Based on information he had received from the field, Captain Anderson concluded that poacher Ed Howell was headed to Cooke City for supplies and that he'd return to the Park. He ordered Burgess to thoroughly search the country east of the Yellowstone River for clues of Howell's whereabouts.[32]

Early in the morning on March 12, Burgess and Sergeant Troike of the Sixth Cavalry left Lake Hotel for the wilds east of the Yellowstone River. The next morning they picked up an obscure trail cut by snowshoes in the Astringent Creek valley and followed it to a canvas tepee outfitted with a sleeping bag, provisions, and a smoldering fire. A toboggan leaned against a tree. From the tree dangled six bison heads.

Burgess and Troike set out once again, determined to end such ghastly lawlessness. They soon heard a succession of rifle shots pierce the air. Shoeing wildly through a timber stand, the men spied Howell, surrounded by five bison he had herded into deep snow and shot, his rifle leaning against one of the sorry animals.

Dense snow flurries, a strong wind blowing from the poacher toward Burgess, and his absorption in skinning a bison's head, prevented Howell and his dog from noticing Burgess' approach across four hundred yards without cover. Howell surrendered without resistance, and the party, with Howell in tow, made a challenging ten-hour march to Lake Hotel.

At 9:30 P.M., Superintendent Anderson received word of Howell's capture. He shared the news with Emerson Hough of *Forest and Stream,* part of the Yellowstone National Park Game Expedition and his guest at Fort Yellowstone. Within twenty-four hours of Howell's capture, Hough wrote a detailed account of this threat to Yellowstone's wildlife and telegraphed it to the magazine.

Outrage over Ed Howell's attacks on Yellowstone's bison made legislation for protection of Yellowstone National Park a congressional priority.[33] The public had refused to allow railroads in the Park and also refused a change of the park's boundaries to the valleys, because poachers would hide in the mountains. Now the public spoke out again, pressuring Congress to put teeth into the preservation of Yellowstone National Park's natural curiosities, forests, and game.

Representative John Fletcher Lacey, eight-term Republican from Iowa, introduced a bill in the House less than two weeks after Howell's capture. Captain Anderson's unwavering commitment to protect the Park and his summary of Burgess and Troike's bravery; Hough's report in *Forest and Stream* along with pressure from his editor,

George Bird Grinnell; and dramatic black-and-white photographs by F. Jay Haynes that emphasized the pristine nature of the Park combined with public and private pressure to force congressional action.

Congress passed H.R. 6442, which became known as the National Park Protective Act, or the Lacey Act, to protect the Park's birds and animals and to assign punishment for violations. It was signed into law on May 7, 1894, and "established the framework for future wildlife protection policy in all national parks."[34] Poaching was punishable by imprisonment, a fine, or a combination, replacing the prior practice of confiscating outfits and depositing the violator and his gear at the Park exit. It established the full-time position of U.S. Commissioner for Yellowstone National Park, a position first filled by Judge John Meldrum, the "grand old man of Yellowstone," who took a liking to his job and served from June 1894 to July 1935.

Interior Department officials initiated discussion about previous legislation—the Sundry Civil Bill of March 3, 1883—that prohibited hotel construction within one-quarter mile of a geyser or curiosity for fear those holding such a lease would charge the public for a look at such wonders. Time had erased such anxiety and the Interior Department called for its repeal, stating that the potential hotel site at the Upper Basin—within a quarter mile of Old Faithful—was prime. The Interior Department also requested repeal of the rule that barred any one person or corporation from leasing more than ten acres in total.

On August 3, 1894, Congress passed the Hayes Act in an attempt to modify specifics in the Sundry Civil Bill and address leases in Yellowstone National Park:

> *Be it enacted by the Senate and House of Representatives of the United States of America in Congress assembled*, That the Secretary of the Interior is hereby authorized and empowered to lease to any person, corporation, or company, for a period not exceeding ten years, at such annual rental as the Secretary of the Interior may determine, parcels of land in the Yellowstone National Park, of not more than ten acres in extent for each tract and not in excess of twenty acres in all to any one person, corporation, or company on which may be erected hotels and necessary outbuildings: *Provided*, That such lease or lease shall not include any of the geysers or other objects of

curiosity and interest in said park, or exclude the public from free and convenient approach thereto or include any ground within one-eighth of a mile of any of the geysers or the Yellowstone Falls, the Grand Canyon, or the Yellowstone River, Mammoth Hot Springs, or any object of curiosity in the park.[35]

The act also stipulated that exclusive privileges were tied simply to a specific tract and for a time period outlined in the lease. Lease holders were expected to abide by provisions in congressional acts and Interior Department regulations related to Yellowstone National Park. The Secretary of the Interior could, at his discretion, change those regulations, placing the burden on lease holders to keep abreast of Interior Department publications about "the use, care, management, or government of the park…under penalty of forfeiture of such lease." Independent operators or companies that held leases prior to August 3, 1894, could, if they wished, "surrender" those leases and negotiate a new one with the Interior Department. The Hayes Act was not "to be construed as mandatory upon the Secretary of the Interior, but the authority herein given is to be exercised in his sound discretion."[36]

In an article published in Bozeman's *Avant Courier*, the Interior Department passed along good news about Yellowstone Park Association hotels at Mammoth, Fountain, Lake, and Canyon, calling them satisfactory operations. The Cottage Hotel at Mammoth and lunch stations at Norris, Upper Basin, and Thumb were also noted as competently managed by the association. Notably absent in print was any mention of Wylie and his camping operation, a slight that may have been no surprise to Will and Mary Ann.

Hotel construction was an Interior Department priority. Norris needed decent accommodations, as did the Upper Basin. Before the existence of the Old Faithful Inn, association patrons left their hotel at Lower Basin and traveled to Upper Basin for a half-day tour of its curiosities before they returned to their hotel for the evening. Fine print on the patron coupon allowed for a longer "stopover," but the Yellowstone National Park Transportation Company despised empty seats and agreed to stopovers only if the entire load of eleven people insisted upon it.

A Yellowstone Park Association hotel at Upper Basin would quell complaints about the "stopover" policy. In addition, promotion of an association hotel gave camping operators a run for their money.

At several army posts the Interior Department added men to the forces to help combat poaching, forest fires, and vandalism. Two additional scouts were needed to track poachers and an agent from the Department of the Interior could aid investigations. The U.S. Fish Commissioner planted eastern brook trout in Moose and Shoshone Creeks to replace large quantities of fish removed from the Park's lakes and rivers.

Despite all of the new protections for fish and wildlife in place, the 1894 tourist season showed little recovery from the struggles of the previous season. During the month of June, most of Yellowstone's guests traveled from points west. But many other Westerners, whose summer plans included a June trip to Yellowstone National Park, were kept away by railroad washouts caused by the quick melt of heavy snow. Railroad strikes from June 26 to July 20 brought train traffic to a standstill. Tourists booked for later in the season probably crossed Yellowstone off their list of summer plans, preferring destinations free of strikes.

Captain Anderson concluded that the 1894 "season continued to the end the poorest ever known in the history of the Park."[37] If reflection is limited solely to the 1,635 tourists accommodated by the hotels, then yes, the season could be deemed bleak. On the other hand, 1,470 guests toured with camping parties, according to Anderson's official registry.

Anderson must have laid awake nights wrestling with the overall decrease in travel that plagued Yellowstone National Park, "where there are so many wonders and beauties to be seen and where so much is done for the accommodation and comfort of the traveler." Confounded by the increase in the numbers of Americans traveling overseas, Anderson expressed frustration that the Park's wonders were included in the German public school curriculum, yet nothing like this existed on any consistent basis in American schools.

"We are constantly informed by visitors that they had no idea of what there was to be seen here; how many attractions the Park trip presented, or how many superior accommodations were offered them," he wrote. He believed that something had to be done to help "the mass of the people...realize what a store of wonders and beauties they have within their boundaries. It would be valuable to them as part of an education, even if they should not be able to see the Park for themselves."[38]

5

A New Method of Caring for Tourists

P ARK ADMINISTRATORS AND OFFICIALS of the Interior Department insisted that they were always looking for dependable
individuals and outfits to do business in Yellowstone; however, they
were dogged by the perception that "dependable individuals and
outfits" were a matter of interpretation—their interpretation. Even
though the Hayes Act stipulated that leases were not to exceed twenty
acres total to any one person, company, or corporation, the tight and
symbiotic nature of the relationship between the Yellowstone Park
Association, the Yellowstone National Park Transportation Company, and the Northern Pacific resulted in accusations by competitors that the companies monopolized Park leases by combining their
efforts to transport and accommodate tourists, thereby controlling
more than the twenty-acre limit.[1]

The effect of the Hayes Act on the Wylie Camping Company
seemed unpredictable. The Interior Department favored a system in
which a vast majority of leases would be for one year only. While
he praised Park businesses in his report to Interior Secretary Hoke
Smith, Superintendent Captain George Anderson declared that he
was in favor of merging "all the interests in the park…under a single management." Anderson feared the difficulties of managing "so
many operators with different objectives."[2]

Camping tours began unusually early in 1895 because of the unseasonably warm weather. At this point, several companies competed
for the tourist dollar. The Yellowstone Park Association cut its
camping tour rates from $5 to $4 per day, hoping to appeal to more
patrons. The Yellowstone National Park Transportation Company
offered vacationers greater choice in routes and schedules around the
Park. The hotel and transportation companies booked approximately

Wylie Camping Company coaches and teams stand waiting, at an unidentified location, to begin a new day of Park adventures, circa 1895. The Park was blessed with unseasonably warm weather that year, so camping tours began unusually early. *Courtesy, Yellowstone National Park Photo Archives.* YELL 713

one thousand more tourists during the season of 1895, although the overall numbers of Park visitors had declined from the peak of more than seven thousand visitors who toured in the early 1890s.

When his lease expired in 1895 Wylie had to submit an application through Anderson, who might or might not endorse it to Secretary of the Interior Smith. The fact that Smith had granted Wylie's camping business a permit for the two previous years, and that Wylie had operated honorably during that period, did not entitle him to special consideration for continuing that agreement, or any other for that matter. Wylie planned to vigorously lobby to lease land for the upcoming 1896 season for permanent camps or stations.[3]

Wylie envisioned submitting his application through Anderson, then boarding a train to Washington to fight for his lease through his Washington, D.C., attorney, George H. Lamar, who specialized in Interior Department matters. Before Wylie departed for Washington, D.C., the Wylies invited all of their employees to a reunion at their home in Bozeman, which had become an annual January affair of storytelling and an opportunity for Wylie to share his plans for the upcoming season with his "park family."

As would become his habit in subsequent years, Wylie departed for Washington in January 1896. Colonel E. C. Waters, owner of a Yellowstone Lake boat franchise, either accompanied Wylie or met him in Washington.

Waters, who had worked at the Yellowstone Park Association for a number of years, was bedeviled by controversy.[4] It was alleged that he soaped Beehive Geyser—a practice used by impatient humans to "trigger" balky thermal features—and he had conflicts with the Park administration. In 1889 Waters purchased the *Zillah*, transported it from the Great Lakes in pieces, and had it reassembled at Yellowstone Lake by a crew that carried guns, traps, and poison. Since they were wintering in Yellowstone to reassemble a steamboat, Park superintendent F. A. Boutelle found their selection of tools most interesting. When he accused Waters and several association employees of poaching, Waters went to Russell Harrison, the son of President Benjamin Harrison, demanding Superintendent Boutelle's suspension. Harrison did not act on that demand.

Waters later faced allegations that he suggested that Charles Gibson, president of the Yellowstone Park Association, issue one hundred shares of association stock in Harrison's name with the intent to expose Harrison's business relationships. Harrison refused the shares and accused the association of trying to disgrace him. Waters was dismissed in 1890 as general manager of the association when he was charged with extorting large amounts of money from a meat contractor.

Despised by many and susceptible to what Wylie described as "ugly flings" of temper, Waters was also, in Wylie's estimation, an efficient, hardworking, and straightforward man when it came to their business dealings. He wrote: "Any true history of Yellowstone park development should give large credit to Col. Waters for the part he had in popularizing Yellowstone Park travel."[5]

In 1896 Waters traveled to Washington, D.C., to confer with the Interior Department about his plan to build a larger steamer. The

Yellowstone Park Association wanted Waters' Yellowstone Lake boat franchise and had filed two complaints with the Interior Department, protesting the fact that Wylie Camping Company clients received free boat rides and that Waters' steamship, the *Zillah*, was too small to easily accommodate the increasing number of Park tourists. Despite this criticism, the Interior Department recognized the fact that Waters was the sole person who had stepped up to offer tourists rides around the blue-green waters of Yellowstone Lake. Waters also sought permission to stock Dot Island in Yellowstone Lake with bison, elk, and deer in hopes of adding interest to the tourists' ride on the *Zillah*.

After countless long days of waiting for a hearing with Secretary of the Interior Hoke Smith, Wylie finally met with Assistant Secretary of Interior William H. Sims, which helped his case. They discussed a number of issues, including the fact that Wylie was eager to accommodate bicyclists, who were uncomfortable in the hotels in their dusty clothing and were opposed to paying $4 a night when the Wylies offered them lodging for $2.50. Wylie initially refused to accept a one-year license, as he was determined to obtain a longer, ten-year lease to justify his investment in the permanent camps. Sims could only offer a one-year license, but assured Wylie that it would renewed. Wylie agreed to the terms. He received a one-year license for permanent camps, with a promise of renewal presented in writing.

In 1896 Wylie incorporated as the Wylie Camping Company and appointed extended family members, likely his brothers and perhaps Mary Ann's brother, Sam, to the company's board. He sold to the corporation all the equipment he and Mary Ann used to operate during the Park's tourist season. He also ordered new stationary, which heralded in its top left-hand corner:

A New Method of Caring for Tourists

In copy below this headline, Wylie described his new vision of a permanent camp, designed for the comfort and ease of both travelers and the Wylie Camping Company:

Our camps are permanent; no more moving of tents. Excellent cooks at all camps; steel range cook stoves; dining and other tents heated with stoves. Large compartment tents. Woven wire springs under fine mattress beds; no sleeping on the ground. Provisions best market affords. Our ticket includes the steamer trip on Yellowstone Lake. Meet train every day. Fine covered buggies to ride in. Longer time at points of interest than any other method gives.

Address,
W.W. WYLIE
Gardiner, Montana
(During Park Season)
Bozeman, Montana
Balance of Year[6]

The Wylie Camping Company's permanent stations were established throughout the Park at locations that were spread far enough apart to allow an unhurried, but nevertheless active, six-and-a-half-day tour of its wonders.[7] After meeting patrons at Cinnabar's rail station, Wylie and his drivers transported them to Gardiner for lunch, then on to Willow Park's camp across from Apollinaris Spring for dinner and overnight, with a brief stop at Mammoth Springs. Willow Park also served as the company's Park headquarters; the station where the Park superintendent or his staff could contact Will or Mary Ann about their permit, discuss concerns and Park scuttlebutt, enjoy a meal, or leave a message for them to call at Fort Yellowstone. When nasty windstorms occasionally strafed the campsites at Willow Park, guests were summoned from tents left damaged by a barrage of tree tops and limbs. While the crew cleared the debris, the guests gathered around a campfire to listen to stories and interpretation about the Park's wonders, or sing songs, accompanied by a small organ, and watch wildlife.

After breakfast on the second day, tourists went to Old Faithful, with lunch served en route at Gibbon Canyon; the third day was also spent at Old Faithful with a jaunt to the Black Sand Basin. The Old Faithful camp was located near Daisy Geyser. Hot water from the Punch Bowl Spring was piped into the camp kitchen. The camp was large by Wylie Camping Company standards, serving one hundred and forty tourists compared to their other camps, which could serve sixty people at full capacity. A piano adorned the camp's reception tent, and according to camp lore, one night a patron, a certain college professor, ambled into the tent and noticed a sign announcing: Daisy Will Play at _____. Seeing that the time chalked in was just minutes away, the professor sat down to await this piano-playing Daisy. Daisy, of course, was not a talented employee tinkling the ivories, but Daisy Geyser, located less than one hundred feet away.[8]

On the fourth day, tourists traveled southeast from Old Faithful to Yellowstone Lake on the road from the Upper Basin to the West Thumb of Yellowstone Lake, eliminating the need to approach the lake via Devil's Stairway. Lieutenant Hiram Martin Chittenden of the U.S. Army Corps of Engineers—a graduate of West Point, civil engineer, and respected historian—supervised the construction of the road, which proved extremely challenging. On top of constructing and maintaining the Park's roads and bridges and overseeing other improvements, the lieutenant supervised the Lone Star Geyser to West Thumb segment of the road, directing work over Craig Pass and the Continental Divide at an elevation of more than 8,000 feet. The road from the Upper Basin to the West Thumb of Yellowstone Lake opened in 1892 to the joy of all Park admirers.

Park roads were extremely dusty. To protect themselves, patrons draped themselves in mosquito netting and brought along linen dusters from home or rented them from the Wylie Camping Company. Park officials tried to help settle the dust by sending water wagons to sprinkle the roads and mandating that stages keep one hundred feet apart.[9]

Wylie Camping Company patrons were served lunch at West Thumb, where they boarded the steamer *Zillah*. The breezy boat ride across the open, turquoise lake replaced a grimy, half-day ride through the Knotted Forest and over the Natural Bridge. The boat ride was respite for the company horses as well, giving them a rest after the strenuous crossing of the Continental Divide.

The Wylie Camping Company included the price of the *Zillah* excursion in the cost of its tour. The boat company collected a coupon attached to the camping company ticket and Wylie settled up with the steamboat operator, E.C. Waters, at a later date. All other tourists, including those served by the Yellowstone Park Association, paid three dollars for the ride, and the opportunity to complain about Wylie patrons getting theirs for free.

The *Zillah* navigated the waters of the lake from the West Thumb to the outlet, where the Association's Lake Hotel and Wylie's Lake camp were located. Waters also offered a coach trip to the Natural Bridge. To enhance the boat ride, Waters had acted on Interior Department permission to stock Dot Island with bison, elk, and deer. When the boat docked there, the tourists disembarked and wandered about the island, viewing the "wildlife." Waters provided hay for the animals year-round, at great expense.

At the boat dock on the lake's north shore, coaches stood waiting. The guests were driven down to the Lake camp, where they spent the night in tents that were arranged in a large semicircle with a campfire at the center. Here there were only quiet ways to pass time—walking on the lakeshore, breathing the fresh air, or staring across rippling blue waters at distant wooded shores and the Absaroka Range dominated by Grizzly Peak, Mount Doane, and Mount Langford. The tranquility of the location made it a favorite of many guests, and not simply lovebirds on the beach. On the nights when a full moon spilled its light across the chop of the lake water, stopping just shy of the camp, Yellowstone Lake was a spectacular sight for many.

Canyon camp was the fifth-day stop on the Wylie Camping Company tour, by way of the Mud Geyser and Sulphur Mountain, and included lunch. Many of Wylie's employees felt that the Canyon camp's location was poor. They had to haul water from Cascade Creek by way of a pail that moved along a windlass, a sturdy wire line running from the bank to the creek. The pail traveled to the creek, was filled with water, then was cranked back up the wire some one hundred feet. Pail by pail, the employees spent hours filling the camp barrels with water.

Nevertheless, the Cascade Creek site did not diminish the thrill visitors experienced on the sixth day, when they made the excursion to Inspiration Point and the Great Falls of the Yellowstone. There, travelers never failed to stand in awe, water droplets moistening their faces, before the roar of the 308-foot Lower Falls, taller than Niagara Falls, and 109-foot Upper Falls beyond.

On the tour's final day, travelers lunched at Norris on the way back to Willow Park. (The Norris cut-off road was completed in 1886, but six years passed before it completely replaced Nez Perce Creek/Mary Mountain road as the route of choice.) They dined in Gardiner before climbing aboard the train at Cinnabar and heading home, all the while chattering about the wonders of Yellowstone and the experience of roughing it with the Wylie Camping Company.

∾

The Wylie Camping Company's accommodations were simple. They consisted of two sizes of canvas tents clustered around a huge fire pit. Single tents had gabled roofs, double beds, and sheets of burlap, tacked down with wooden pegs, that functioned as wall-to-wall broadloom carpets. The larger tents were square and featured a hip roof and four double beds, one in each corner. The beds were set on the ground, but a board floor ran across the center of the tent. A separate bed per person was a rarity; strangers often doubled up for the night, usually women with women and men with men. Canvas curtains divided each bed in half so that two strangers would not be able to see one another; other curtains screened off each bed from the others in the tent. There were a few complaints about this arrangement.[10]

Although Wylie's camps usually passed government inspections as neat and clean, patrons did fuss about bathing. One guest stated that he could not travel without bathing nightly. To accommodate him, Wylie asked a Willow Park employee to heat water in wash boilers on the kitchen range and haul it to the gentleman's tent. The guest offered a five-cent tip, but the employee turned him down.

Inside each tent, Sibley tent stoves, which were wood stoves made of sheet iron that resembled inverted funnels, rested on a two-by six-foot board and heated each tent. They drew poorly, however, and offered no space to heat water. Wooden boxes stacked on top of one another served as washstands, each with its own supply of ceramic bowls and pitchers. Candles provided light.

Each camp or station had a twelve-by-sixteen-foot kitchen built of log slabs with sawdust floors and good, wood ranges. The guests dined in a fourteen-by-thirty-foot tent that had a sawdust floor as well. Lined up on benches that would be scooted underneath the tables at night, guests dined at long, linen-covered tables laden with stainless steel utensils and heavy-duty white china while Wylie's wife and children—Mary Ann, Elizabeth, and Grace—walked among them with primitive flyswatters, trying to prevent them from accidentally wolfing down flies with their meal.

Wylie and Mary Ann made a point of hiring spirited staff with a keen interest in Yellowstone National Park to work in the camps, drive the wagonloads of patrons, and work as guides—all were expected to be conversant about the Park's major points of interest. Many of Wylie's employees were from middle-class backgrounds; teachers, college students, ranchers, and cowboys, who often assisted patrons. Employees were taught that respect held the company reins for all clientele, even "ugly customers."

Wylie drew on his background as a teacher to advocate the importance of accurate, interesting information about Yellowstone National Park. He staffed all thermal areas with knowledgeable guides who conducted fact-packed tours about each of the site's wonders. Wylie's information-based touring, educating visitors about the Park's flora, fauna, geology, and geography, set a new standard for guiding. The Yellowstone Park Association, in contrast, preferred to require their porters to double as guides.

In early April 1897 Wylie learned that Captain George Anderson would be replaced as Yellowstone's superintendent by Colonel Samuel Baldwin Marks (S. B. M.) Young. Wylie's elation spilled over into his letter to Colonel Young dated April 4, 1897.[11]

Before Colonel Young took over as Park superintendent, Wylie and Captain Anderson found themselves embroiled in another distressing example of "the often uneasy but entirely necessary three-way relationship between the federal government, the public, and the park concessioners."[12] Both Wylie and Anderson demonstrated how difficult it was to maintain a working relationship, even though they shared a deep commitment to Yellowstone National Park.

At approximately the same time Wylie wrote to Colonel Young, the Society of Christian Endeavor, a three million-member organization of young people devoted to good lives and good works rooted in their commitment to God, were planning a July convention in San Francisco. Edward Swift, a member of the Society's New Haven, Connecticut, chapter, worked with James Williams, railroad manager for the state's Christian Endeavor Union, arranging travel to and from the convention with a side trip to Yellowstone National Park.[13] A party of approximately one hundred members wished to specifically camp with the Wylie Camping Company, perhaps because the Wylies adhered to Park regulations and offered an alcohol-free experience. When Williams and Swift met in a Bristol, Connecticut, home to finalize plans for the trip west, Williams shared a letter addressed to Frank Gross, district passenger agent for the Northern Pacific Railway, from the railway's assistant general passenger agent, B. N. Austin.

Austin wrote that the Wylie Camping Company was "entirely irresponsible," stating that "nobody has any control over" Wylie's operations, and he knew of tourists who paid Wylie in advance, grew unhappy with the accommodations once they were in the Park, and booked a room at a Yellowstone Park Association hotel. "Mr. Wylie never refunds anything," wrote Austin, concluding that Wylie's customer service policy was simple: be happy or "go elsewhere." He recommended confirmation of "these facts" with Superintendent Anderson, as he was "a government official and entirely independent." At a later point, Austin wrote that the Wylie Camping Company's permanent camps were nothing more than "rude huts built of logs." These camps, he stated, could not accommodate a large party and in the end, many in the group would have to sleep outdoors.

In his dire warnings, Austin also accused Wylie of lack of sanitation:

these mountain camps are always infested with vermin. Wylie has two or three camping wagons capable of accommodating about four people each and the balance of his outfit is of a very inferior order. For a party as large as that it will necessitate the employment of outside conveyances which are very poor.[14]

Swift read Austin's letter vigilantly and then copied down a summary of his allegations. When Superintendent Anderson wrote to Swift, he reported that Wylie could not accommodate more than twenty or thirty tourists. Anderson also mentioned that "It is not my intention to approve for this summer his license for permanent camps, or for probably more than five wagons."[15]

Anderson's intent contradicted the Interior Department's written promise to renew Wylie's license for permanent camps in 1897. Anderson's confidence may have stemmed from changes in Interior Department leadership. David Francis had succeeded Hoke Smith and served briefly from September 3, 1896, to March 5, 1897. Portions of Austin and Captain Anderson's letters made their way by mail from Swift's home in New Haven to Wylie's home in Bozeman, each portion copied in pen on a separate piece of "notepaper size" paper. Unfortunately, three pages were "pinned together" in such an order that the part of Mr. Austin's letter where he describes Wylie's permanent camps as "rude huts built of logs...incapable of satisfying a large party" and "infested with vermin" were mistakenly ascribed to Anderson. This section also included references to the limited capabilities of Wylie's transportation services.

On May 7, 1897, Wylie wrote to Charles S. Fee, the Northern Pacific's general passenger agent. He enclosed a copy of Austin and Anderson's letters. Wylie pleaded for the agent to consider the twin causes of the independent businessman and permanent camping as an alternative to hotel stays in the Park.

He went on to argue that if any one of the statements in Anderson's letter was accurate, Park officials would have had grounds to deny him privileges to operate in the Park. "I beg pardon for annoying you, Mr. Fee," he wrote, "but I am being grossly wronged and it is human to resent base misrepresentations." Before he took further action, he added, he would wait to hear from Fee. He asked Fee to do him the justice of enclosing "the copy of his letter accompanying this"[16] if Fee decided to write Anderson.

On May 12, 1897, Charles Fee wrote Wylie and Anderson each a letter. In his letter to Wylie, Fee expressed disbelief that Anderson had written "such a letter," but if so, Fee thought Anderson's statements were simple reiterations of his "official" position, which disapproved of Wylie's permanent camps.

In his letter to Anderson, Fee told the captain about Wylie's letter of May 7, 1897, notifying him that B. N. Austin had denied writing the statements about Wylie's camps. Fee included a paragraph from Wylie's May letter. Wylie's heated response to Captain Anderson's letter stated:

> His letter enclosed is a composition of lies that will astonish the hundreds who know the truth. I have always been obliged to get my privileges in the Park over Capt. Anderson's head, hence his statement that he does not intend to approve my application means very little. You very well know that both these letters are unfair and untruthful.[17]

When Wylie received a letter dated May 18, 1897, from Captain Anderson, it contained two enclosures: Captain Anderson's full letter and a "full extract" of B. N. Austin's letter to Mr. Swift. Realizing the gravity of his blunder, Wylie wrote to Anderson four days later, apologizing "that this mistake occurred."[18]

Between Charles Fee's letter of May 12, in which he also asked Anderson about Wylie's "standing" for the upcoming 1897 season, and Superintendent Anderson's letter of June 10, 1897, to new Secretary of the Interior Cornelius Bliss, Wylie received permission to operate his permanent camps.

In protest, Anderson wrote to Secretary Bliss "most respectfully and earnestly" about "the issue of license to Mr. W. W. Wylie with authority to establish permanent camps." He noted that Wylie received "a license for more wagons than are allowed to others." Anderson enclosed "copies of two letters written by Mr. Wylie." In Anderson's opinion, these letters, one to Mr. Fee and one to Colonel Young, "should forever disqualify him from conducting business of any kind within the park...by these he is proven to be a liar...a fawning sycophant…a pretentious Pharisee." Anderson closed his letter with an expression of deep humiliation, reminding Secretary Bliss that after "six and one-half years' hard, faithful, and honest service in the Yellowstone Park," he was "being scorned by the Department in the interest of a man of this character."[19]

Ironically, in their separate interactions with others, Captain Anderson and Wylie proved themselves to be men of decent character but together, their relationship hobbled along—once again crippled by a war of words. Wylie's Park permit included the words "personally conduct" in reference to Wylie's tours. Wylie interpreted the phrase "personally conduct" to mean that he, Will Wylie, would personally supervise the permanent camps; not that he should travel with every single coach. Captain Anderson interpreted the phrase more literally.

When Wylie entered Yellowstone with his first tourists in early June of the 1897 season, the park registrar at Mammoth told him that Superintendent Anderson wished to see him. Wylie left his patrons at the registering station and walked to Anderson's quarters at Fort Yellowstone. In his memoir, Wylie recounts that upon arriving at Anderson's home, he removed his hat, whereupon a barrage of the most vulgar language he'd ever heard greeted him as he stepped into Anderson's presence. Anderson called him one crude name after another, keeping up a steady stream of profanity about Wylie going behind his back to the Interior Department. Anderson paced back and forth in front of Wylie, who perched quietly on a chair in front of him. He expected at any moment to be punched or shot. Finally, Anderson stopped to catch his breath, worn out. Wylie asked if he was finished. Anderson said he was and he hoped to never see Wylie's "damn carcass" ever again.

Wylie put his hat back on his head and left. Even though Anderson had done everything he possibly could to assist the Wylie Camping Company's competition, Wylie refused to give up his license. He decided to call Captain Anderson's bluff. The captain called after Wylie, asking where he was going. Wylie responded that he was headed to the telegraph office. As he finished composing his message to the

Interior Department, Anderson walked in. In a hushed tone, Anderson politely asked if Wylie was sending a wire to Washington, D.C.

Wylie showed him a copy of the message, which informed the Interior Department that Anderson had demanded he "personally conduct" each tourist coach into the Park, and that this being an impossibility, Wylie would abandon his permanent stations and leave Yellowstone. Anderson acknowledged that he didn't want Wylie to have use of the permanent camps; however, he begged him to withdraw the message. If Wylie did so, Anderson said, he would never trouble him again.

Wylie asked Anderson to accompany him to the registrar's office near the Mammoth park entrance and order the officer in charge to allow free passage of Wylie Camping Company coaches to and from the Park. The captain agreed to do so. Wylie placed a hold on the message, telling the telegraph operator that it should be canceled if he did not return within the hour. The two men proceeded to the registrar's office, where the captain gave the order.

Captain Anderson stayed true to his word for the remainder of his very active duty in Yellowstone National Park. During Wylie's years in Yellowstone, Captain George Anderson, Sixth Cavalry, served as Park superintendent longer than any other officer detailed to that position.

Mr. Wylie Goes to Washington

F AR AWAY FROM THE BUBBLING MUD POTS and steaming geysers of Yellowstone, there was a struggle afoot in the white marble halls of Congress for control of the Park. In 1886 politicians passed an appropriations bill that neglected to fund salaries for the Park superintendent and his staff. The U.S. Army assumed control of the Park from August 1886 to October 1916, and a number of distinguished military men served brief stints as acting park superintendents before they were called to serve in various military conflicts, including the Spanish–American War and World War I.

A military transfer to Yellowstone National Park, described as "a continual series of astonishments" by Salt Lake City's *Daily Tribune*, was considered a significant assignment by politicians, the public, and the commanding officers detailed to the "Wonderland." Those officers were charged with protecting this "great storehouse of nature's wonderful work."[1] Safeguarding the Park's geysers, forests, and wildlife in a remote and great expanse of wilderness while developing a handbook of best practices was formidable enough; add in humanity—who, like the landscape, were also "a continual series of astonishments"—traveling from all corners of the globe or operating Park businesses, and these energetic, conscientious, and determined military men deserve to be treated with empathy.

Captain George Anderson, Sixth Cavalry, who served as Park superintendent longer than any other officer during the years Wylie operated his business, left his post on June 23, 1897. During that same month, Wylie "took his cause directly to those who would be most affected by his exclusion from the park—the people."[2] A newspaper article about Yellowstone National Park tourist camps was published in June 1897 in the *New York Tribune* and the *Chicago Tribune*. The *Salt Lake Herald* carried the article as well. The commentary provided the fine points about Wylie's conflict with Secretary of the Interior

Cornelius Bliss, Yellowstone National Park superintendents, and the Northern Pacific Railroad. It also noted that Wylie received broad support for his permanent-camps crusade—a pursuit rooted in his hope that more middle-class travelers might enjoy a safe Yellowstone vacation on a realistic budget. Elizabeth Watry stated that the article "apparently caught the attention of hundreds of teachers, students, artists, doctors, ministers, lawyers, dentists, school superintendents and principals, judges, piano dealers, druggists, and even senators, who not only traveled with Wylie in the summer of 1897, but also wrote letters to Secretary Bliss in support of Wylie's application."[3]

Captain Anderson was replaced by Colonel Samuel Baldwin Marks (S. B. M.) Young, who served in the Park for two brief stints, the first from June to November 1897 and the second from June 1907 to November 1908. Described by Wylie as an "exacting" man, Young seemed to get along with most of the business operators in the Park, as his expectations of them aligned with the government privileges defined in their licenses.

Shortly after he became Park superintendent in 1897, Young issued an order that no horses would be allowed to graze in the Park. Wylie did not know of the regulation until he reached Willow Park one evening and his camp manager and livestock foreman greeted him with the bad news.

Soldiers had arrived at Willow Park earlier in the day, the manager fumed, to tell him about the order. He stated that all camp managers had been informed.

Wylie consoled the foreman, who was beside himself with frustration and worry because the guests' teams were due in at any moment. What, he asked Wylie, should he do? There was no hay in camp as the Wylie Camping Company never fed their livestock hay, and the order forbade him to turn the horses out for the night.

Wylie told him to fetch a fresh team of horses. He told the foreman that he would drive to Mammoth and sort the matter out with Young. "Do the best you can with the horses," he told him.

Wylie traveled the six miles to Mammoth as fast as the horses could carry him. When he found Young at Fort Yellowstone, Wylie explained his concerns about the order.

Young told him that the order "was absolute" and "must be obeyed."

Wylie explained how grazing rights to the Park's grasses related to the details of his business, which he argued, depended on receiving Park permission to graze his horses. Wylie's prices, which had been authorized by the federal government, were also rooted in that policy. The Park order to feed the livestock hay meant that his original prices would be impossible to maintain. In addition, Wylie explained, the hay in Livingston or the Gallatin Valley was approximately three weeks away, if harvest and transport were considered. Wylie declared that he would cease operations immediately, at the height of the tourist season, telling Young that although he spoke only for himself, he knew that his situation reflected that of other men who were in the movable camp business: "I came to speak only for myself, but that there were a number of other men who had leases for movable camp business who would be obliged to quit and move out of the Park at once. [I] told him I had seen none of them and did not believe any of them yet knew of the order."[4]

Young insisted that Wylie feed his stock hay, just as the Yellowstone National Park Transportation Company fed their stock. Wylie bid Young good day and announced that he would take down his camps and cease operations at once. He stated that he "would wire my Washington attorney to this effect."

Young called Wylie back and asked him to further discuss the matter. A back-and-forth discussion ensued. Wylie said the two of them had talked and he had nothing more to say.

Young then asked Wylie where he liked to graze his horses. This, of course, was the discussion's turning point. Wylie indicated that the animals grazed on familiar range, away from all roads.

Young called for his secretary and issued an order that all guard stations be informed by telephone that the grazing order was rescinded. Then he asked Wylie to stay awhile.

With the grazing issue resolved, Young turned to Wylie and said he understood Wylie knew the whereabouts of the Park's only wild bison herd. Several of Young's friends would be visiting him soon and Young wondered if Wylie would take them to see the bison.

Wylie agreed to do so as long as all were capable of "a pretty tough horseback trip."

From that point on, Wylie and Young maintained a congenial relationship. Wylie later learned that his competition had taken advantage of Young's transition to the Yellowstone post and invented the "no grazing order," which they convinced Young to institute.

During the 1897 season H. F. "Tom" Richardson, Wylie's manager of the Grand Canyon camp who became known as "Uncle Tom," led folks on horseback across a relatively calm portion of the Yellowstone River above the present-day Chittenden Memorial Bridge to provide them a remarkable close-up of the Great, or Upper, Falls. The crossing was nonetheless a very risky venture because of the Yellowstone River's powerful current and the variation in water depth. Before Young left his Yellowstone post in November 1897, Richardson asked Wylie to request a permit for the 1898 season that would allow use of a rowboat or skiff to ferry tourists across the river. Giving Wylie and

"Uncle Tom" Richardson (center) flanked by two military men. Richardson managed the Wylies' Canyon camp, then developed a lucrative business guiding tourists on a path still known as "Uncle Tom's Trail." It leads to the foot of the Lower Falls on the Artist Point side of the Yellowstone River. *Courtesy, Yellowstone National Park Photo Archives. YELL 7976*

Richardson's application serious thought, Young insisted that a cable or rope span the river within easy reach of tourists' hands, which the gentlemen agreed to provide.

In his memoir, Wylie confessed that his hesitant approach to introducing himself to new superintendents and his own backwoods hospitality most likely contributed to some of his difficulties with a few of the Park administrators. The lavish entertaining in a Park hotel, with waiters and linen-covered tables, versus the rough-hewn dinners on the long board tables of his camps seemed worlds apart to Wylie. Eventually, however, he discovered that most superintendents relished a rowdy meal in a Wylie camp's dining tent.

On October 26, 1897, Young wrote to Secretary of the Interior Cornelius Bliss, stating that he had the "honor to submit the following report in the case of the application of William W. Wylie for a ten-year lease of certain parcels of ground in Yellowstone National Park, with the privilege of conducting a camping business for the accommodation of tourists." Young reviewed Wylie's 1897 season during which Wylie operated permanent camps under an Interior Department license. Twelve vehicles, wrote Young, transported 352 patrons to Wylie camps.

But even Young could not save himself from expressing an apparent bias, for he was critical of Wylie's operation in contrast to his remarks about the Yellowstone Park Association and the Yellowstone National Park Transportation Company.[5] Young regarded the Wylie Camping Company's transportation, food, and accommodations as "inferior in quality and quantity." He also argued legitimately that Wylie paid "no rental for the lands occupied by him; he is under no bond for the faithful observance of the conditions of his license and for the performance of his obligations towards his patrons, and he can not give that constant personal supervision to the parties under his charge which is required of other persons licensed to conduct camping parties through the park." Young worried that Wylie was under no formal obligation to start the Camping Company's season "early…when travelers are few." He believed that Wylie could shut down operations "as soon as the travel diminishes to the point at which it ceases to be profitable to him."[6]

Young went on to claim that "Mr. Wylie is not the real party in interest in this business, and the investment in the corporation for which he acts is so small as to insure no responsibility on the part of the real owners for the continuance of the business during an unprofitable season or for its proper conduct at any time." He worried that a ten-year lease would leave tourists without a guarantee that Wylie Camping Company services would be accessible when desired. Young stated that he preferred the Wylies hire a resident manager in the Park who would be available to problem-solve with the Park superintendent as needed. He also recommended greater flexibility in Wylie's operations, as well as better response to medical emergencies or illnesses, citing an example from the previous tourist season when "appeals were made to this office and to the Transportation Company to take aid to the sufferer or bring him to a place where medical and surgical assistance could be had."[7]

Young stated: "In marked contrast with the position which Mr. Wylie occupies and which he seeks to assure to himself for a term of years is the position of the Transportation Company and the Park Association in the conduct of their business." He mentioned that each of these companies paid an annual rent on parcels of land essential to their business operation and purchased bonds to ensure that the terms of their franchises or leases were followed. Young liked the Transportation Company and Park Association practices of hiring a residential manager he could contact at any time. He seemed convinced, in his report to Secretary Bliss, that large corporate investment ensured corporate responsibility. Young noted the vast amount of capital supplied by "these corporations" and contended that all obligations "to the people and to the authorities of the Department" will be met to avoid "the forfeiture of their franchises and the loss of a great part, at least, of their investments." He was sympathetic to the cost of maintaining "expensive establishments during the entire season, during certain parts of which the expense far exceeds the returns," and the age-old challenge that the hotel and transportation companies "must be prepared at all times to accommodate travelers who may ask for their services."

Young got to the heart of the matter when he pronounced that an Interior Department grant of a ten-year lease to Wylie would "create in him a powerful competitor of these companies without any of the restrictions and responsibilities by which the companies are bound." Superintendent Young did not recommend granting such a lease to Wylie. He noted that while there continued to be demand for camping tours, he suggested that camping services be provided by the hotel and transportation companies. "Such unity of control," Young believed, bred "unity of responsibility." He also believed that "a favorable consideration of Mr. Wylie's application" would hinder his ability and the ability of his staff to monitor the conformity of Park businesses to the conditions of their licenses or franchises.[8]

Young's letter underscored the conflict between matters such as Park business, which was primarily civilian in nature, and on-site Park management, which was rooted deep in the military. It also cast light on the overwhelming nature of the Park superintendent's duties. Young's argument (and that of his predecessor, Captain Anderson) was flawed by an incomplete understanding of business ownership and its relationship to ethical behavior, the value of competition, and the fight against monopolies. The argument also pitted large corporate investment against small business capital in a democratic nation that recognized the value of both entities in its quest for economic growth. The federal government and park superintendents, park businesses, and the public all struggled with the issues noted by Chris J. Magoc: "preserving cultural integrity while promoting it, selling history and nature without compromise. Alas, the contradictions that living brings."[9] Young's notion of Wylie as a "powerful competitor" who should be excluded and his fixation on "unity of control" and compliance were examples of simple solutions to the "contradictions that living brings." In the end, Wylie refused to quietly conform.

∾

On December 11, 1897, James A. Blanchard of New York City and George H. Lamar of Washington, D.C.—Wylie's attorneys—filed an amended application with the Department of the Interior. The brief cited B. N. Austin's correspondence with Edward Swift and contained testimonials and resolutions by members of the New Haven chapter of the Society of Christian Endeavor who toured the Park with the Wylie Camping Company that summer. The Wylie Camping Company's eye-catching striped house tents, divided by partitions with private sleeping quarters and hallways, provided the New Haven party of 116 with all essential amenities. Although the size of the party was larger than those the Wylies usually cared for, all patrons were "transported, sheltered and fed to their satisfaction." The group made specific mention of the camp at the Upper Geyser Basin, expressing gratitude for time spent lingering to watch the geysers instead of returning to the Fountain Hotel. While transportation was less stylish than the Concords, the Wylie wagons allowed tourists to admire the Park's wonders in all directions.

The group resolved to thank Mr. and Mrs. Wylie for their "kind and courteous treatment." The Wylies' efforts made the visit to Yellowstone unforgettable, leaving the guests from New Haven feeling like they were cared for as friends—it was a "privilege to be numbered among those whom they regard as their truest friends."[10]

In January 1898 the Wylies and their "Park family" again gathered at the Wylies' Bozeman home to celebrate the new year, look ahead to the upcoming Park season, and share tales of the "Wonderland." The Wylies' employees were routinely asked by Yellowstone visitors if their continuous rounds about the Park grew tiresome. Some replied that the change of patrons and their pleasure in the park relieved all monotony. Employees seldom worried about entertainment—nature provided that in the form of natural wonders ranging from geysers to mudpots, from chipmunks to black bears, as well as the guests, whose naiveté never failed to amuse.

Herman, the driver who was the chipmunk expert, loved to respond to tourists' bizarre questions. He told the tale of a woman who rode in the front seat with him as he drove a four-horse Concord coach through the lovely, wildlife-rich Hayden Valley. A man with a mower in a nearby field was cutting hay for E. C. Waters' bison.

As she watched, the woman asked Herman incessant questions about the hay-cutter. "What is he doing? Why is he doing that? What is it for?"

The more Herman tried to explain, the more the questions continued.

Finally, Herman stopped the horses, set the brake, turned the reins over to the woman, and jumped down to the ground.

Shocked, the woman asked him, "Where are you going?"

He turned back. "To talk to the fellow and find out what he is doing," Herman responded, looking off to the man and mower half a mile distant.

The woman and the other patrons pleaded with Herman to stay with the coach. Herman climbed on board and drove on.

The questions ceased.

"It had not occurred to Herman that possibly the woman had never seen nor heard of a mowing machine before, so he might not have been voluble enough in answering her first questions," Wylie recalled later. "I don't like to have the reader blame the driver too much….The help then, and ever since, have been called 'Savages.'"[11]

At this reunion of his "savages," Wylie unveiled a proposed private mailing or post card imprinted with a photograph of Yellowstone Lake and the steamer dock. Wylie chose the Detroit Publishing Company to produce the card.

Later that month, Wylie departed for Washington, D.C., to fight for his Yellowstone operation and lobby for a ten-year lease or franchise at the U.S. Department of the Interior. He arrived in the nation's capital on January 30, 1898. During his month-long absence from Montana, Wylie wrote letters from his hotel room to Mary Ann and his children. He wrote a letter once, sometimes twice a day, many of which presently survive, and posted them in the morning or the evening from the hotel lobby.

Much of the correspondence was addressed to his wife of almost twenty-four years, "My dear Mary" or "My dearest," and closed with "Most affectionately yours," "Lovingly yours" or "With <u>very very much love</u>." To his children, he wrote, "My dear ones at Home," signing off with "I am yours only—Papa." Wylie wrote on a variety of letterhead—some courtesy of his attorney, George H. Lamar, or on stationery from hotels including The St. James European and The Helena in Helena, Montana. When he used Wylie Camping Company stationery, Wylie crossed out the place name—"Bozeman, Montana"—on the address line and replaced it with "Washington, D.C." (in case there was any question as to his whereabouts).

Because the new Park hotels were not yet completed and the Yellowstone Park Association wanted permits for permanent camps, attorney George Lamar, Resident Counsel, felt that Secretary of the Interior Cornelius Bliss and his department, the Yellowstone Park Association, and the Yellowstone National Park Transportation Company would discourage Wylie's operations. Wylie, on the other hand, felt confident his business would continue to grow. Indeed, Park tourism was increasing, as indicated in Superintendent Young's annual report: 6,226 people toured the park during the 1897 season, an increase from 2,862 guests in 1896.

Colonel Young, the federal government, Yellowstone patrons, and Park concessioners, such as Wylie, were locked in what Hal K. Rothman has described as the "embrace of tourism" that "triggers a contest for the soul of a place."[12]

To prepare, yet again, for that contest, Wylie spent his first few days in Washington meeting with his attorney to fine-tune another brief in reply to Anderson's angry letter of the previous June and a "discussion of park combinations." In briefs filed with the Department of the Interior in 1897, Lamar called attention to the Northern Pacific Railway as majority stockholder in the Yellowstone Park Association, and its control of the Association and the Yellowstone National Park Transportation Company. Once again, in February 1898, Lamar and Wylie discussed this relationship that had begun approximately fifteen years before with the incorporation of the Yellowstone Park Company, in Minnesota, in alliance with the Northern Pacific. Over the years Wylie and Lamar had become very familiar with a number of associated company names: the Yellowstone Park Association, the Yellowstone National Park Transportation Company, and later the Yellowstone Park Hotel Company. These companies—lumped together informally as the "Hotel-Transportation Companies" by concessioners and their legal counsel, Park superintendents, government officials, and the touring public—operated under the auspices of the Yellowstone Park Company. When they needed operating capital, the Northern Pacific Railway often stepped forward. Wylie described the time spent with Lamar as the hardest work he'd ever done. When finished, the papers were sent to the co-counsel, James Blanchard in New York, for his approval and signature.

On February 7, 1898, a twenty-eight-page brief and a bound volume of letters from patrons supportive of Wylie's operations were filed with the Department of the Interior in preparation for a hearing before the assistant secretary of the Interior. Lamar said he felt "much pleased" about the case, but Wylie could not "feel happy" until he had results—until he knew "how helpful" his stay in Washington had proved to be. His letters to Mary Ann expressed his uneasiness, his dread that the brief would anger his adversaries. Anderson, Wylie wrote, has said "awful mean things about me." Through the Washington grapevine, Wylie heard that Anderson was in town, and he fretted that the brief would make Anderson "crazy mad," though he hoped Anderson would review the brief.

In its opening, Lamar's brief quoted word for word Captain Anderson's letter that described Wylie as a "liar," "fawning sycophant," and "pretentious Pharisee." It revisited the concern expressed in previous briefs about one entity holding a monopoly in the Park, in particular the "powerful combination held together by and conducted principally in the interest of the Northern Pacific Railway, which combination exercises the almost exclusive hotel, stage, and railroad privileges in and about the Yellowstone National Park."[13]

Lamar took issue with Anderson's statement that he "recommended his license year after year" even though the captain considered Wylie a self-serving flatterer, liar, and hypocrite. Anderson only recommended him year after year, Lamar contended, because, Anderson stated, Wylie "catered to a class of tourists who preferred to go with such a man, and whom others did not care to take."

Lamar also identified the travelers that had booked with the Wylie Camping Company. There were testimonial letters from "teachers, artists, scientists, College Professors, and Ministers of the Gospel, and from persons who had known him [Wylie] at home and in business relations." He also mentioned judges, well-known religious journalists, and authors "whose wisdom and virtues have endeared them to the people of all civilized lands." Background information about the Society of Christian Endeavor—over one hundred of whom had been served by the Wylie Camping Company—was also included in the brief. Lamar noted that there were tourists who preferred camping in the Park to staying in the hotels and who liked the permanent camps, coupled with Wylie's low-key style and generosity.[14]

Lamar also asked the question: "But why should the hotels 'not care to take' such tourists?" He wondered why the hotel association did not acknowledge these tourists as a "part of the people for whom the park was dedicated." He expressed doubt and wondered aloud about the hotel association's poor reception of "these Christian ladies and gentlemen." He invited the Secretary of the Interior to draw his own conclusions based on public record, but hypothesized that Wylie's 1891 correspondence with Secretary Noble about the sale of liquor in the Park was a contributing factor.

Lamar also reviewed Anderson's lack of "regard for Wylie's financial welfare," noting that Anderson ignored the Interior Department's 1896 written promise of renewal for permanent camps. Based on the potency of that promise, Lamar pointed out, Wylie incorporated and made "large additional expenditures." Finally, Lamar said, Anderson could not accept Wylie's permanent camps in the same way he accepted the interests of the Northern Pacific Railway, in particular the Yellowstone Park Association and the Yellowstone National Park Transportation Company.

In the brief, Lamar referred to the Swift–Fee correspondence and Wylie's May 22, 1897, letter of apology for his part in the whole debacle. Anderson made no mention, Lamar noted, in his June 10, 1897, letter of protest of the Wylie May 22 apology, nor did he send the Interior Department a copy of the letter. Lamar also mentioned Wylie's letter of greeting to the new superintendent, S. B. M. Young, saying that it illustrated "an honest, proper expression of his true feelings when he heard the welcome news of a change."

Lamar's final argument in the brief focused on former Interior secretary John W. Noble's testimony before the First Session of the 52nd Congress (December 7, 1891 to August 5, 1892) that the relationship between the Northern Pacific Railway, the Yellowstone Park Association, and the Yellowstone National Park Transportation Company constituted a monopoly. When the Yellowstone Park Association's transportation privileges were canceled in November 1891, the hotel business and transportation operation were administered as separate entities. Noble believed that the Northern Pacific Railway wanted to take control of the Yellowstone Park Association and the Yellowstone National Park Transportation Company, but if such a combination occurred, he stated, "the park would become a monopoly...whatever I may put in the lease." Noble was an unwavering advocate for separate concessioners to operate the Park's hotels, transportation, and boats. "If I did not stop the combination then embracing the hotels, the transportation, the boats on the lakes, it never could be done. That was my judgment, whether right or wrong."

Park superintendent Anderson, who was supposed to enforce this separate management policy, instead advocated placing the hotels and transportation companies under the same management so that operations could "run more smoothly and there would be less cause of complaint." Anderson spoke before the congressional committee that convened later in the First Session of the 52nd Congress to investigate Noble's decision. In his 1896 superintendent's report to the Interior Department, Lamar noted in his February 7, 1898, brief, Anderson was also opposed to Wylie's permanent camps, advocating the advisability and simplicity of dealing with a single management:

> In 1891 it was determined that the business of keeping hotels, and that of the Yellowstone Park Transportation Company, should not be done by a single corporation. The license to Mr. Wylie, however, has returned to the old methods in the only way in which they were objectionable. I believe that the conduct of all interests in the park should be placed under a single management.[15]

When Secretary of the Interior John W. Noble limited the power of the Northern Pacific in 1891 by ruling that a single corporation could not manage the hotels and transportation, Lamar argued, Noble's sole focus was simply the interdependence between the hotels and transportation and did not include consideration of Wylie's camping operations, which provided both accommodation and transport for his guests, because at that time camping concessions were not required to be licensed. Lamar stated that Captain Anderson based his case against the Wylie Camping Company on an Interior Department policy that advocated separate concessioners to provide for the lodging and transport of tourists, which Anderson did not support. Anderson then went on to argue "in favor of the combination," which would place the Yellowstone Park Association, the Yellowstone National Park Transportation Company, and all other hotel and transportation companies under a single management.

Lamar believed that the notion of single management in favor of the Yellowstone Park Association and the Yellowstone National Park Transportation Company evolved into the official record, the record consulted by Superintendent S. B. M. Young when he recommended that the companies "be required to meet the demand for camping accommodations." Young asserted that if the Hotel–Transportation Companies were prevented from providing their services as a single corporation, then the Wylie Camping Company must be held to the same policy. In conclusion, Lamar asked the judge to consider both sides of the controversy and to grant Wylie's lease.

> Confidently trusting that your Honor will recognize the designing handiwork of this park combination, eliminate the result of its nefarious influences in the premises, view all sides of the controversy, and grant the lease sought.[16]

Wylie's first appointment with Thomas Ryan, assistant secretary of the Department of the Interior, was set for February 8, 1898, at 9:30 A.M. The two men's relationship dated back to 1885, the year Ryan toured the Park with the congressional Holman Select Committee. It was during this trip that Wylie fought accusations that he improperly doused a campfire. During the 1896 tourist season, Assistant Secretary Ryan returned to the Park on a tour with his wife and secretary.

Wylie wrote that he hoped that after the meeting he could "report some encouragement," but that he could "hardly expect it."

Ryan said he would issue Wylie a license, but he proposed issuing one to the Yellowstone National Park Transportation Company as well, for the identical route. Although Lamar knew that Wylie had cultivated Ryan as a loyal Wylie Camping Company friend, Lamar also felt the assistant secretary favored the Yellowstone National Park Transportation Company but was afraid to shut out Wylie. Lamar and Wylie were terribly anxious and discouraged at this point, so Wylie called in reinforcement from his New York attorney, James Blanchard.

Wylie hoped that the Wylie Camping Company could continue operating in the Park and that the Yellowstone National Park Transportation Company would be denied a permit for the same route, but he knew that he was responsible for proving why the route should be given to him and not the Transportation Company. If Thomas Ryan refused to do that, Wylie wanted tourists delivered to Cinnabar by the Northern Pacific with as much factual information about his business as the Yellowstone National Park Transportation Company's operation. The Transportation Company was able to sell cheaper tickets and Wylie pictured a long line of guests hurrying into their coaches while his stood empty.

On February 9, 1898, Wylie and Lamar met Ryan at his Interior Department office and pleaded their case across the assistant secretary's desk piled high with briefing papers. Wylie's co-counsel, James Blanchard, did not travel from New York City, but instead sent a letter, which Ryan read.

As Wylie argued his case, he illustrated his remarks with maps of the Wylie Camping Company route and diagrams of each camp and lunch station, menus of the meals, accounting ledgers, and patron registers. The three men talked about the Hotel–Transportation Companies' request for permanent camp privileges.

Ryan asked Lamar what objections he thought might surface if the Yellowstone Park Association put rowboats on Yellowstone Lake. Lamar later wrote to E. C. Waters about this discussion.

Three days later, Wylie wrote to Mary Ann about what he termed "discouragements." There was still no word from the Interior Department, so consequently he could see no immediate end to his stay in Washington.

> I can't help feeling that it is right for me to be here. This feeling is strong and braces me up—...I really feel your sympathy and your prayers supporting and encouraging me although you are so far away. I am 'leaning hard' on the Arm of Him who said 'will not the judge of all the Earth do right?' I believe he will. And although what we think is right may not be what He knows is right. May we be able to cheerfully obey and trust Him is my prayer —Goodnight My Dear Mary."[17]

The next morning, more waiting. For Wylie, the dreariness of the wait made Washington's winter days even gloomier. On days he ventured out in the Capital to view the sights and enjoy coffee and doughnuts, his blues lightened. Wylie visited area churches to listen to the preaching of renowned clergymen, watched the Senate from the gallery, visited museums, and attended productions at local theaters and the Grand Opera House.

He also spent innumerable hours reading. He read accounts in the *Washington Post* and the *New York Times* that were sympathetic to Cuba's revolt against Spanish domination. Some editors cried out for a U.S. foreign policy that reflected the American idea of Manifest Destiny as it related to overseas expansion; other opinion page editors cried out against American imperialism. Wylie was of the opinion that war would "help farm prices but may lessen Park travel but think not much." He sent Mary Ann newspapers with extensive articles about the conflict and described the mood in Washington as "intense."

E. C. Waters returned to Washington on February 18, 1898, and gave Wylie something else to worry about: Waters' penchant for loneliness. Rather than allow Waters to spend solitary hours on his bed brooding, Wylie invited him to his room to commiserate. They shared meals together when it was mutually convenient.[18] Sometimes Lamar joined the gentlemen. Wylie looked forward to eating at home once again, promising no complaints about Mary Ann's meals.

On the Sabbath—always a day set aside for family during the Yellowstone off-season—Wylie's heart ached deeply. In his letters, he honored Mary Ann as his "good and noble wife," declaring that he wouldn't know what to do without her. He possessed the burden of making a living, but Mary Ann shouldered the equal weight of stoking the home fires. When a friend wrote him that Mary Ann had been ill, Wylie admonished her to keep him better informed in the future. He was concerned about his family's health and reminded Mary Ann that they must eat large quantities of fruit and vegetables, the fresher the better, to prevent jaundice.

In 1898, while Wylie was trying to establish the future of his camping company, his family was growing up. Daughter Elizabeth graduated from Wellesley in 1897 with a Bachelor of Arts, but she was in ill health. Wylie said that he thought Elizabeth was taking too much medication and suggested that Mary Ann take her to their local doctor for an honest opinion.

The Wylies' third child, Grace, was seventeen years old and nearing the end of public high school. Throughout their childhood, Grace and her younger brother, Clinton, shared their father's love of horses. Grace's pony, Pinto, was an energetic horse that needed to be watched vigilantly. Grace and her cousins had been tossed over Pinto's head on several occasions or taken on the run of their lives. Although eager to take courses at Montana State College in Bozeman, Grace now suffered from extreme fatigue, which greatly concerned her parents. Her health was the antithesis of her youth. Now, in 1898, because of her weariness, her parents were uncertain if she could handle a regular course load.

On February 19, ten days after Wylie's meeting with Ryan, Lamar told Wylie that, based on what he had heard, Wylie could plan on being in the Park for the seasons of 1898 and 1899. This, however, did not do much to alleviate the two gentlemen's anxieties, which hung so heavily on receiving something in writing. At 6:40 P.M. that evening, Wylie wrote hastily to Mary Ann that Ryan had denied permission for permanent camps to the Hotel–Transportation Companies. In a postscript, he told her that "you may tell our friends, but please allow nothing for publication."

In a February 21 letter to Mary Ann, Wylie said that he received a letter from Ryan that offered Wylie a special license for permanent camps instead of a ten-year lease. Wylie and his legal counsel filed a motion for review, which they hoped to present to Secretary of the Interior Cornelius Bliss without delay.

On February 22, however, plans changed. Wylie and George Lamar did not call on Secretary Bliss. The meeting with Bliss was put off until Wednesday, because the members of the Interior Department were celebrating George Washington's birthday. Lamar and Wylie, on the other hand, were anticipating the arrival of co-counsel James Blanchard from New York.

Greatly fatigued, Wylie wrote to Mary Ann of his fear that the Interior Department would grant him a license with so many conditions that his business would be harmed. He also told her that he was disgusted by the Potomac River's dirty water and craved a small town with better water. He desperately wanted to go home, remembering E. C. Waters' past experience of expecting to stay in the Capital ten days but having to stay four months. Nevertheless, homesick as he was, Wylie knew there was more value in staying put so he could learn and do as much as humanly possible to promote the interests of his camping company.

Bliss refused to consider Lamar's motion for review, and instead left the matter to Assistant Secretary Ryan. Wylie and Lamar met face-to-face with Ryan on February 24. Although the assistant secretary refused to put anything in writing because of his demanding schedule, he instructed Wylie to operate the camps as usual. He offered Wylie the option of using larger tents at Upper Basin and at Canyon. Ryan objected to there being no white linens on Wylie Camping Company beds, so Wylie agreed to give guests a choice of linen bedding or cotton blankets.

There would be a license issued, Ryan told him, not a lease. He told Wylie he would instruct the superintendent that "no barrier should be put in the way" of the Wylie Camping Company's service to their patrons. He also specified that Wylie cancel his contract with E. C. Waters and reduce his ticket price to "possibly" thirty-three dollars for the six-and-a-half day tour of Yellowstone. The

Interior Department no longer wanted companies to form business partnerships.

Wylie disliked the idea and knew Mary Ann would also. Nevertheless, he was resigned when he wrote: "Now, Mary, I feel this is a great victory considering the opposition."

In a final letter to Mary Ann posted on Monday, March 1, 1898, Wylie wrote that he would depart Washington at 8:05 P.M. He thought he could get home by Saturday night. Wylie said he would have no papers pertaining to the license, but Ryan assured him that all would be clear to Park officials. Indian affairs consumed Ryan at the moment and he needed a few more days to prepare Wylie's papers. Wylie planned to leave Chicago Thursday night and St. Paul on Friday evening. He added that he would be very glad to get home. Wylie enclosed a copy of his brief, a document that had earned the respect of the Interior Department. He requested that Mary Ann shield it from the public for the time being.

Later that spring, the Northern Pacific Railway began discussions with parties interested in buying the Yellowstone Park Association. Harry W. Child, a Transportation Company stockholder, approached the railroad first, but he lacked the necessary finances. E. C. Waters then pursued the matter with Northern Pacific president C. S. Mellen. In May 1898, Mellen stated the railway's terms: a hefty sum of cash, five notes at five percent, and security—one third of the security to come from seventy-five percent of the Wylie Camping Company stock.[19] In his memoir, Wylie made no mention of the proposal. Perhaps if he'd known, he would have thought less favorably about E. C. Waters. When negotiations reached a standstill, Mellen eventually lost patience and chalked it up to Waters' unreliability.

After negotiations with Waters broke down, the Northern Pacific Railway, hoping to avoid investment in a hotel at the Upper Geyser Basin, chose to sell the Yellowstone Park Association to three men with a controlling interest in the Yellowstone National Park Transportation Company—Harry Child, Edward Bach, and Silas Huntley. F. Jay Haynes, owner of the Monida and Yellowstone Stage Company based at the Park's western entrance and the Park photographer, was concerned that his passengers would receive unsatisfactory service at the hotels, which were now controlled by his competitor. The Department of the Interior viewed the sale as a monopoly and resisted it. Although there is no record of his opinion about the sale in his memoir, it seems likely that Wylie shared Haynes' and the Interior Department's perspective about the sale.

Fearful of being labeled a whiner or unable to "walk his chalk"— otherwise being incapable of making his own way in the world of business—Wylie preferred to keep the details about his own negotiations with the Interior Department private. Obviously, family, close friends, and business associates recognized how precarious his situation was, as the situation for concessioners changed every year. During the 1898 season, Wylie Camping Company guests had at least one opportunity per tour to hear Wylie speak matter-of-factly about the company's desire to continue operations in Yellowstone.

Wylie was in Yellowstone National Park because of his deep commitment to the region and to an economical, informal way of touring—a way that favored accurate information about the "peerless National Park." After his talks, he suggested to his audience that if they supported his company's mission in the Park, they could write to their elected representatives, the Northern Pacific Railway, or the U.S. Department of the Interior. Sometimes Wylie spoke at campfires, sometimes at a lunch station or after dinner at one of the camps. Often he found himself close to used up by the battle, but he kept the faith, optimistic he would prevail in the end and be regarded as a dependable, honest, hardworking businessman.

Will and Mary Ann proudly hauled several hundred of their private mailing cards to sell at their camps in the Park. Adorned with a color-tinted photograph of Yellowstone Lake on the front, the backside was reserved "exclusively for the address" and a one-cent stamp, the mailing rate approved by an Act of Congress on May 19, 1898. The cards were also available at numerous Gallatin Valley businesses as well as vendors operating outside the railroad stations in Bozeman, Livingston, and Cinnabar.

Shortly after Christmas 1898, the photographer Henry Bird Calfee and Wylie left Bozeman on a second "Yellowstone Park exhibition
and lecturing tour" under the management of the Slayton Lyceum
Bureau in Chicago, Illinois. The two believed that if they toured to a
number of large cities, they could stay busy through April.

A three-by-five-inch brochure featured a photograph of Wylie,
now in his fiftieth year, in a dark suit with a starched, white shirt, his
beard trimmed, his spectacles on his nose, his hair combed neatly
back, lips pursed, and eyes twinkling. "Prof. W.W. Wylie and Bird
Calfee," heralded the brochure, "can hardly fail in deeply interesting
any intelligent and appreciative audience in the intensely attractive
subject they have in hand…Mr. Wylie will lecture, and Bird, in connection therewith, will add to the entertainment with stereopticon
views of 'Wonderland.'"[20]

The brochure included "opinions of the press and of individuals"
from Bozeman, Montana, to Omaha, Nebraska. The text was inter-
spersed with Bird's lush black-and-white photographs of Yellowstone
National Park and the Wylie Camping Company: Golden Gate, Mammoth Geyser Basin, a striped compartment tent, two tourists proudly
holding up a large trout they had caught, an enormous spouting geyser, and a bridge near one of the Wylie camps. The introduction's
final paragraph said that Professor Wylie "expects to have with him
in the Park this season of 1899 an artist of superior skill who will take
views for the Moving Picture machine, thus enabling him to add to
his already attractive exhibition the marvel of the Geysers and the
Great Falls of the Yellowstone in actual motion."[21]

During the 1899 season the Wylie Camping Company had an
increased number of guests. Wylie ascribed the growth to the
Park's increasing popularity and the publicity he had gained from
his lectures—or some combination of the two. He decided, because
of this, to free up his time by nullifying his upcoming lecture contract with the Slayton Lyceum Bureau. Wylie followed through on
the bureau's request that he write each scheduled customer and
request a release without embarrassing the bureau. After Wylie spent

hours corresponding with prospective lecture clients, he and Mary Ann focused their efforts on a response to the increase in company business.

Although Wylie credited the increase in Wylie Camping Company business to Yellowstone's rising popularity—a likely assumption—it is important to delve deeper into the trend that began in 1890 when the census confirmed the disappearance of the American frontier. One historian noted that "the scarcity theory of value began to work on behalf of wilderness. Americans were becoming civilized enough to appreciate wilderness…as an asset rather than as an adversary."[22] As the middle class acquired the financial means, more time to travel, and a comfort level with packing a trunk or bag, boarding a train, and heading off west, the country "became more self-assured, less conscious of inferiority to the Old World."[23] During the last decade of the 19th century, the country "found itself with the beginnings of a national park *system*…led by Yellowstone, Yosemite, Sequoia, and General Grant national parks."[24] This development was not "the old Europe," but rather, it was "a new product" that was "American."[25] For Yellowstone tourists and Park concessioners, such as the Wylie Camping Company, who looked forward to an authentic experience in a "natural, unaltered landscape or the last vestiges of the western frontier, entering a national park was almost like stepping back in time" and was a source of "national pride…spirituality and beauty."[26] Western tourism had become a fact of American life.

∾

During Iowa congressman John F. Lacey's tour with the Wylie Camping Company, Lacey asked Wylie to call at his home when Wylie arrived in Washington, D.C., the following March 1900. Wylie dropped in on Lacey, chairman of the Committee on Public Lands, who was active in the nation's conservation movement and had sponsored H.R. 6442, the 1894 National Park Protective Act (Lacey Act), which protected birds and animals in Yellowstone National Park and set penalties for violations.

Wylie continued to lobby for a ten-year lease in the Park. To maintain his superior customer service, he submitted a written request to the Department of the Interior for permission to keep a telegraph or telephone connection between Gardiner, Mammoth Springs, and the Willow Park camp. If more patrons than anticipated needed transportation from Gardiner, Wylie could wire or telephone company contacts in Mammoth Springs or Willow Park for additional conveyances. Wylie also requested permission from the Interior Department to keep up to twenty milk cows that would be distributed between his four overnight stations.

Congressman Lacey proposed that they visit with Interior Secretary Ethan Hitchcock, who had been appointed on February 20, 1899. He wondered if there was anyone else in Washington that could be invited along. Senator Mark Hanna—a wealthy Cleveland industrialist and ally of President McKinley's, and former patron of the Wylie camps—came to Wylie's mind. Lacey thought Hanna was an excellent choice.

Accustomed to waiting for an appointment to speak to the Secretary of the Interior, it was strange for Wylie to be in the company of men who simply waltzed past Hitchcock's staff and into the interior secretary's office. According to Wylie, Senator Hanna marched into Hitchcock's office, walked around the secretary's desk, and placed his hand on the gentleman's shoulder. "Hitchcock, my girls and I were out at Yellowstone last summer and we know all about the Wylie Camps," said Hanna. "They are all right and I think we had better let them alone."

Wylie knew that was all that needed to be said, and that he could leave Washington immediately. By April 7, 1900, Wylie received a license to operate in the Park for another season from Superintendent Captain Oscar J. Brown.

Officials in Washington exerted influence over another matter as well. The Northern Pacific Railway contacted Wylie, requesting that he come to their St. Paul office to discuss company policy about railroad and Yellowstone National Park ticket sales. For several years George Lamar had complained about the Northern Pacific Railway's discrimination against the Wylie Camping Company regarding ticket sales.[27] The Railway offered a combination railroad transportation and Park ticket wherever Northern Pacific tickets were sold, but denied the Wylie Camping Company the same opportunity. Wylie Camping Company patrons were able to purchase a round-trip rail ticket from the Northern Pacific Railway, but their Park tickets waited for them at Yellowstone.

Wylie and Lamar also analyzed the cost of a Park visit hosted by the Northern Pacific Railway–National Park Transportation Company–Yellowstone Park Association in comparison to a tour with the Wylie Camping Company. The Northern Pacific Railway's July 1899 Circular No. 227-1899 concerning Yellowstone National Park rates featured a $92.00 round-trip ticket from St. Paul or Duluth, Minnesota, to Mammoth Springs, Montana, which included rail and stage transportation plus hotel accommodations; $47.50 of that rate covered rail fare that also permitted, in the fine print, a return trip via Billings and the Burlington and Missouri River Railway to the points of Omaha, Council Bluffs, Atchison, St. Joseph, and Kansas City along the great Missouri waterway. Wylie Camping Company patrons paid $47.50 for their rail fare as well, plus $35.00 for a Park tour, for a total cost of $82.50.

Patrons who traveled from one of the terminals located along or east of the Missouri River,[28] however, paid less for the Northern Pacific's rail and Park ticket, including transportation and hotel services, than Wylie patrons paid for a rail ticket and local purchase of Wylie Camping Company services. Wylie and Lamar concluded that those Northern Pacific Railway patrons received a reduced rail fare. If the Park portion was reduced, Interior Department rules would be violated, resulting in franchise forfeiture. The rail reduction was a violation of Interstate Commerce laws.

George Lamar wanted to argue the case quickly, but Wylie was indecisive. Although he does not indicate his state of mind in his letters and memoir, one wonders if perhaps he felt that a suit before the Interstate Commerce Commission might bring on more troubles with the Department of the Interior. He might lose the forest for the trees: if he won the suit, he could be denied a permit.

The Wylie Camping Company had yet to turn a profit for the Wylies, yet Wylie was averse to risking his relationship with Yellowstone, having gained immeasurably from the hours spent with the wonders of the beautiful and unique Park—sharing it with Mary Ann, their children, and their extended Park family.

Wylie met with President Charles Mellen of the Northern Pacific Railway, Vice President Jule Murat Hannaford, and General Passenger Agent A. M. Cleland. After discussing Washington's demands for the Northern Pacific Railway to make a reasonable provision, Mellen left the meeting. The three remaining gentlemen moved into the officers' room, Hannaford and Cleland saying they wished to talk with Wylie further. As he sat down, alone, the other gentlemen leaned in to ask him direct and probing questions about his business in the Park.

> "Now, Mr. Wylie, we would like to know how it is that you hold on in the Yellowstone, when we have tried every way under heaven to get you out?" asked Mr. Hannaford.
>
> I replied, "You will not be interested in learning how or what I do to combat your purposes and designs to ruin my business and reputation."
>
> "Oh yes, we will, and if there is not time enough today, we will come back here tonight. We want you to understand that we have no malice against you personally, but only as your business interferes with what we call our rights in the Yellowstone."[29]

Wylie told Mr. Hannaford and Mr. Cleland that he countered potentially damaging distortions of his business practices by filing data and testimonials with the Interior Department. He went on to give specifics relating to Senator Mark Hanna.

That was it for Vice President Hannaford, who slammed his fist on the table, stating that if he were W.W. Wylie, damned if he'd have done the same thing.

The tone of the conversation relaxed at once. When the meeting ended, Hannaford retired to his office and Cleland invited Wylie into his office. The conversation turned to a horrible accident the previous summer involving two ladies from New England, guests of Wylie's company. The ladies were gravely injured.

The accident happened on the first day out from Cinnabar and involved the first visitors of the season. A bolt in a singletree, the wooden bar at the center of a wagon, had loosened during the off-season, malfunctioned, and sent the weighty piece onto a lead horse's heels. One of Wylie's most dependable drivers held the reins and still the horses ran wildly, causing the coach to overturn.

Wylie covered all expenses. Two doctors and a nurse attended the two women, who were sisters, for three months in a hotel in Cinnabar. When they recovered in mid-September, one sister and a nurse toured the Park in a surrey, followed by the other in a private Pullman that was sent anonymously to Yellowstone. Wylie paid for their tickets home. And, as he discovered at that moment in the Northern Pacific offices, the women were Cleland's cousins.

Mr. Cleland and his wife met the women in St. Paul and traveled to New England with them. "Now," he said to Wylie, who sat across from him in stunned silence, "no one can say aught against you or Mrs. Wylie in my presence without hearing a most earnest protest, because those women think you and Mrs. Wylie are the most wonderful people in the world. I wanted you to know this, Mr. Wylie, and to have you know that no business reason can ever have any weight with me in marring the high esteem I have for both you and Mrs. Wylie."[30]

Years later, Wylie recalled that Mr. Cleland's words brought him both "surprise and great comfort."

7

Indian Captives to Cattalos

B Y THE TURN OF THE TWENTIETH CENTURY, William Wallace
Wylie was caught in the wheels of bureaucracy, try as he might
to simply pursue his camping business in beautiful Yellowstone. His
overseer, like it or not, was always the federal government, and with
that came a multitude of bosses as well as regulations. By early 1900,
despite Senator Mark Hanna's recommendation to Secretary of the
Interior Ethan Hitchcock that the Interior Department leave Wylie
alone, the department increased its oversight. The 1900 operating
license was issued in quintuplicate—two more copies than in 1894—
in addition to a written demand by Hitchcock to Park superintendent Captain Oscar Brown that Wylie post a $5,000 bond "for the
faithful performance of the license."[1]

Secretary Ethan Hitchcock—who succeeded Cornelius Bliss and
served from 1899 to 1907 under Presidents William McKinley and
Theodore Roosevelt—denied Wylie's request for a ten-year lease as
well as his request to construct and operate an independent telephone
line. He recommended, instead, that Wylie work out an agreement to
use the Yellowstone Park Association's telephone and telegraph lines.

Hitchcock also felt there was no evidence to show that tourists
desired fresh milk in camp, although he did allow Superintendent
Brown to approve "a sufficient number of cows" in the Wylie camps.
Hitchcock did so with the understanding that Wylie's cows had to be
kept from running amok, destroying trees, and dropping "feces" near
the Park's waters. The cows were not to gather in "unsightly masses"[2]
or in such a way that endangered the health of Park visitors. Hitchcock chose not to tackle the question, however, of how one might
prevent the cows from gathering in "unsightly masses."

By the next year Wylie's permit to operate in the Park from June
15 to October 1, 1901, cost $150 plus a $5,000 bond based on an
estimated need for thirty wagons and rigs. Once again Secretary

7

Hitchcock expressed concerns about the Wylie Camping Company's milk cows, but left the final decision to new Superintendent Captain George Goode. The cows were expected to be on their best behavior or their days in Yellowstone National Park would be hastily cut short.

The heavy hand of Interior Department regulation that accompanied industrial tourism, "the only way to move large numbers of people through Yellowstone," could be considered one of "the now-regretted" practices put in place by the Park's early overseers—like the "aggressive promotion" and the "trivialization of a spectacular natural area's real beauty and power through the standardization or 'packaging' of the visit" that Paul Schullery described. Schullery took the perspective of Park visitors, "who yearned for whatever combination of its features they found rewarding." For visitors, "the promotion of Yellowstone must have seemed entirely good and appropriate." If Park tour packages had been unavailable, it is "hard to imagine how else public use of Yellowstone might have proceeded." The same could be said for the federal government's role in the "development of a recognized Yellowstone experience." While the federal process was, at times, disagreeable and fraught with frustration, it "did serve to protect 'vast natural areas of the park' from random and uninhibited use until attitudes relating to those areas matured to the point that managers understood the risks and how to handle the problems."[3]

Will Wylie remained firm in his commitment to provide his patrons with a satisfying Yellowstone experience. In a section of the Wylie Camping Company's brochure titled "Important Information for the Season of 1900," Wylie wrote that he chose four-horse coach-style carriages to travel from the Cinnabar railroad station to the first stop at Willow Park. From Willow Park on, travelers would be taken in carriages made by the Racine Wagon & Carriage company of Racine, Wisconsin—carriages set on springs, topped with canopies, and drawn by two horses instead of four, in an effort to keep dust down. For a round-trip ticket, a patron could bring twenty-five pounds of luggage, and he or she had to pay an extra ten cents per pound for any excess luggage. The Wylies were "obliged to adopt this rule in justice to the majority of tourists, who do not carry baggage to exceed this free allowance."[4] The travelers could store their trunks, if they brought them, at Cinnabar's train depot.

The brochure reminded patrons that the Wylie Camping Company furnished double beds, but noted that if camps were full, travelers should be prepared to double up.

With the Wylie Camping Company, children under twelve traveled for half fare. Full fare was $35.00 and still included the boat trip across Yellowstone Lake on E. C. Waters' *Zillah*.

The Wylies encouraged fishing enthusiasts to bring their own tackle. At all stops, except those at Yellowstone Lake, the Wylies were allowed by the terms in their license to offer their guests a pole, fishing line, and artificial flies. They insisted this service was not profitable—the twenty-five-cent charge for tackle and ten-cent charge for lost or damaged flies only covered their costs. At the lake, however, only E. C. Waters' boat company had the privilege to provide tackle.

The brochure provided travelers with detailed information, more than provided in the small box in the upper left-hand corner of Wylie's letterhead that continued to advertise "A New Method of Caring for Tourists." It may have been a necessary response to guests' demands and criticisms, or an answer to the common questions posed by potential Park visitors.

∾

Wylie prospered, along with the rest of the country, reaping the rewards of all his hard work. Over the years he increased the Wylie Land and Livestock holdings. He also hired several excellent employees who helped him and Mary Ann adjust to an increase in responsibilities.

As of 1900, Wylie Land and Livestock held 600 acres on Middle Creek (Middle Fork of Pole Creek), where Wylie now stored most of his camping company equipment; 7,040 acres (eleven sections) on Cherry Creek, which included several sections of leased state and school land; 1,000 acres on Spanish Creek; and 640 acres (one section) of pasture on Elk Creek, west of Bozeman.

Eventually, Wylie purchased 5,120 acres (eight sections) in the Spanish Creek area, south of Bozeman, that once belonged to homesteaders who bought up land in 160-acre parcels in the late 1800s. When many of the settlers proved up and moved away, Wylie bought them out, accumulating more land with each passing year.

Wylie used the Spanish Creek land to winter the nearly three thousand horses that were used to draw the wagons and carriages of the Wylie Camping Company. Wylie's Spanish Creek ranch was administered by Belle Wylie Lockhart, Wylie's sister, and her sons, Wylie, seventeen, and Eaton, fifteen. Cowboys on the ranch broke in young stock to work in the harnesses of the company wagons or rigs and for use in carrying tourists on trail rides. Sheep grazed other portions of the property.

Many people in Gallatin County, Wylie included, supported the development of a road up Gallatin Canyon. Work began in spring 1898, but uncooperative weather delayed its completion until August of that year. When the road through the Gallatin Canyon opened at last, it was ten feet wide and featured two bridges—one over the West Fork of the Gallatin River (near the entrance of present-day Big Sky) and the other about one mile south of the West Fork bridge. Although the road stopped at Taylor Fork, about four miles shy of the Park's northwestern corner, Wylie directed his wranglers to continue the tradition of driving horses through the Gallatin Valley and on to Yellowstone.

Clearly, a road needed to be built from Taylor Fork into Yellowstone National Park. People had varied opinions about which was the best route to the Park: the Bannock Indian Trail route east over Big Horn Pass to Mammoth or the Grayling Creek route south from Gallatin Canyon to the Union Pacific railhead at West Yellowstone, which the U. S. Park Service proposed in 1907. The cost estimate for the road was approximately $100,000, and many people wagered on the final decision.

In May 1910 the Gallatin County Commissioners finally chose the Grayling Creek route, south from Gallatin Canyon's Taylor Fork. The commissioners obtained permission from the Secretary of the Interior to survey and build the road, because it cut through the northwest corner of Yellowstone National Park. This final section of road was built primarily on a marsh, and required fifty culverts and pole bridges to keep vehicles from being mired in muck. The Grayling Creek road halved the distance between Bozeman and West Yellowstone, placating the increasing numbers of automobile owners.

ॐ

From 1896 to 1905, Wylie depended heavily on three company employees: Margaret McCartney, Tom Richardson, and Ed Moorman. All worked for Wylie during the off-season and became close to the Wylie family.

Wylie hired Margaret McCartney, a single woman, to work as the manager of camp employees. She traveled from camp to camp for the entire Park season acting as a mobile human resources supervisor. As the Wylie Camping Company business grew, she ultimately put down roots in the large Grand Canyon Camp. In the winter, McCartney worked in the company's Livingston office. A fair-minded, cool-headed supervisor, McCartney, or "Lady Mac" as she was known, was highly regarded and loved by the Wylies and their employees.

Tom Richardson, a widower with two children, was Wylie's Grand Canyon Camp manager beginning in 1896 and worked for Wylie in Bozeman during the off-season. As the weather warmed in 1899, he helped the Wylies' son, Fred, fence pasture at the Wylies' Elk Creek property. The men packed spools of barbed wire and dug post holes in steep, rocky terrain. He also helped a carpenter construct a small house there. Once that work was completed in May, the younger Wylie and Richardson plowed fields at the Wylies' ranch on Middle Creek.

During spring 1899 Ed Moorman arrived on the Wylies' Bozeman doorstep, a young man fresh from Cincinnati with eight dollars in his pocket and a letter of recommendation from an old family friend, Dr. H. H. Hoppe. Hoppe, a recent patron of the Wylie Camping Company, had advised Moorman to look up Wylie when he arrived West. Even though Moorman had never lifted a pick or a shovel, Wylie immediately employed him as a general laborer. While Fred Wylie and Richardson fenced pasture, Moorman dug a basement for the small house at Elk Creek. Working without gloves, his hands were soon very blistered. He also helped the carpenter as needed and assisted Fred Wylie and Richardson with the pasture fence. Moorman took to horseback riding, often riding without a saddle. He genuinely liked horses and took their care seriously.

When the fencing was complete, Fred Wylie, Richardson, and Moorman traveled to Middle Creek. The three men lived in a tent with limited cooking and sanitary facilities. Fred Wylie and Richardson explained to Moorman that it was "always customary for a pilgrim"[5] or newcomer to do the cooking, a responsibility Moorman accepted.

When Moorman told Will Wylie that he was interested in working for the Wylie Camping Company through the summer, Wylie turned him down because he wanted Moorman to remain at Elk Creek. He needed Moorman to ride fences and keep stray animals out of the property, thereby ensuring decent pasture for the Park horses when they returned the following fall.

Mary Ann, however, had the last word. She insisted that Moorman would be the perfect candidate for the job of "camp man" at Willow Park. The Wylie Camping Company needed an employee with the flexibility, stamina, and initiative to build fires, boil water, pack baggage, fill and haul barrels of water, gather wood, rake the grounds, shake and air bedding, dispose of dead flies, and keep bears away at night, then rise each morning at 4:30 A.M. and do it all again. Moorman, she concluded, was up to the job. Moorman accepted Wylie's offer of twenty dollars per month. He left for the Park on the first of June 1899 with his hound, "Uncle Tom" Richardson, Fred Whitney, and forty milk cows. He slept in Willow Park's commissary tent, a storehouse for the camp's food, rising eight to ten times a night to chase off bears.

For the first time in years, Wylie slept blissfully through several consecutive nights because he had a dependable employee to scare off the bears for him. In the middle of one dank and rainy night, however, Wylie awoke to the sounds of snorts, wood splintering, and loud crashes. Reluctantly, he left the warmth of his bed with Mary Ann and stood in the doorway of his tent. A bear sat on the roof of the kitchen, a twelve-by sixteen-foot building constructed entirely of log slabs. The bear, determined to get inside the kitchen, pulled off the roof slabs with ease. Wylie picked up a handful of kindling and threw it up at the bear as he shouted, "Moorman! Moorman! Wake up!" Dressed only in his nightshirt, he then made his way across puddles and mud to the commissary to alert Moorman.

Ed raised his head from his bed in the commissary. "Mr. Wylie, what are you doing?" he said, his voice heavy with sleep. Wylie told him that he was trying to drive a bear away.

Moorman sprang from his bed. "I apologize, Mr. Wylie," he said, scrambling to help Wylie. "I've been up a dozen times already and just finished burying my dog. Damn bear near ate it." When he told the story in the years that followed, Moorman confessed that he nearly left the Park that night. He ventured out from Cincinnati intending to work hard in the out-of-doors and he realized that he ended up in the right place, but that night, after being woken by the bear twelve times—the last time to bury his dog—was almost too much for him. Nevertheless, Moorman stayed on at Willow Park from 1899 to 1902, performing the same kinds of tasks. He also helped open other camps before the first day of tourist season on June 15 and returned to help close up the camps on the final day of the season on September 20.

Richardson and Moorman were responsible for getting the milk cows across the Yellowstone River, likely in the calmer waters near the Upper Falls. Richardson rowed a boat across the river, leading one cow. Moorman, on horseback, drove the others across. At first the herd balked at crossing the river and needed a great deal of "coaxing," but once they were across, the cows were happy because of the good grazing.

Richardson also continued to operate his guiding business in the Canyon area. During the preseason, Richardson and Moorman worked together to stretch a safety rope across the river below Richardson's rowboat crossing near the Upper Falls. Richardson rowed the boat while Moorman held the heavy rope in the boat's stern. Moorman recalled that he fell into the Yellowstone River's fast, springtime current many times.

The two men also improved Richardson's path, still known today as "Uncle Tom's Trail," to the foot of the Lower Falls on the Artist Point side of the Yellowstone River. Richardson built, at his own expense and with Moorman's help, wooden stairs down the trail's steepest portions. During the tourist season, Richardson, described by Wylie as "a very strong, active man," frequently carried "timid women over the most difficult parts of the trail." Wylie commented on another challenge faced by most traveling women of that era, regardless of their personality: "Women did not dress then as they do now for tourist climbing. Hence, Tom carried plenty of safety pins which ladies used to make their costumes into imitation divided skirts."[6]

In the words of Cindy S. Aron—during a camping vacation, "fashion could not hold sway…plain clothes and the wholesomeness of nature" replaced "elaborate attire and attention to etiquette."[7] This western custom was an appealing part of the Yellowstone experience.

For guiding tourists down Uncle Tom's Trail to the Lower Falls during the 1899 season, Richardson, Moorman recalled, charged fifty cents. The charge included a campfire supper or lunch and hot coffee. Richardson made an average of $1,000 per season; however, he loved to play cards in Bozeman during the off-season and usually needed a loan from Moorman until the following summer. Moorman stated that "he always paid me back with good interest."[8]

In 1901 the Interior Department agreed to terms related to the sale of the Yellowstone Park Association. Harry Child, Edward Bach, and Silas Huntley of the Yellowstone National Park Transportation Company were each permitted to hold one-third of the Association's stock. The stock transfer occurred on April 4, 1901.

After Huntley's death, later in 1901, a series of stock transfers took place over the next few years that underscored the cooperative relationship between the Northern Pacific Railway, the Yellowstone Park Association, and the Yellowstone National Park Transportation Company. Huntley's one-third stake in each company passed to a Railway subsidiary, the Northwest Improvement Company. Edward Bach sold his interests in both companies to the same subsidiary. Harry Child lacked the financial means to continue with plans to build a hotel at the Upper Geyser Basin, so he approached the Northern Pacific Railway for capital. Once again, the Northern Pacific was a primary stockholder in not only the Yellowstone Park Association, but the Transportation Company as well.[9]

By the end of 1903 the Northwest Improvement Company, the railway's subsidiary, committed itself to a smaller financial presence in the Park when it sold 50 percent of its stock in the Yellowstone Park Association and the Yellowstone National Park Transportation Company. Because of the capricious nature of these stock transfers and the revolving door of company names associated with the Northern Pacific Railway, Park concessioners and their attorneys, Park superintendents, government officials, and tourists developed their own way of communicating about the Northern Pacific's Park interests and continued to make casual reference to the Yellowstone Park Association and the Yellowstone National Park Transportation Company as "the Hotel–Transportation Company," "the Park Association," "the Hotel Company," or "the Transportation Company," depending on the topic of discussion or who was involved in the discourse.

On his Park tours, Wylie tried to forget about the ever-changing dynamics of Park business, instead reserving his enthusiasm for Park wildlife. Like his Yellowstone guests, Wylie enjoyed viewing animals as much as taking in the Park's picturesque landscape and unusual wonders.[10] Over the years he collected wonderful stories about cow elk, deer, and bears that he observed on his trips through the Park. During the annual January reunion of Wylie's Park family, his stories about cow elk were a legendary part of the ritual exchange of stories about previous seasons in the Park.

In Wylie's eyes, elk were a most intriguing animal. Patrons often confessed to disbelief that elk grew new antlers each year. Wylie explained it as the way nature provides for the survival of the magnificent species. If bull elk hung around the cows during summer or year-round, calves would be born at any time of year, instead of in June when the grasses are able to support hungry mothers and the weather is warmer.

Bulls shed their antlers in April and early May. Like a child's tooth the new antler presses against the old one in an effort to grow. Seeking relief from the discomfort, the bull strikes his head against the ground or a tree. People reported seeing bulls with one antler; this situation did not last long, just until the bulls could get to the nearest tree.

After the old horns are shed, new ones develop quickly. Throughout the summer, they are covered with a delicate velvet, and are painful to the animals. Because of this, the bulls avoid the cows, corners, and narrow openings. They will fight for a wide trail—never with their antlers—by jumping on an aggressor, battering it with their forefeet.

Wylie generally observed bulls in pairs or triplets, but once, while hunting for lost horses, he came upon a lone bull. They met at the entrance to a small park, and the bull began pawing the ground, stepping this way and that, hinting that Wylie should give up right-of-way. Wylie, who was leading his horse, took to the saddle and allowed the bull passage along the trail. He circled the park, hoping to figure out why the bull stood firm on that particular exit.

Wylie realized that there was no alternative for a bull with tender horns. All other points of departure meant a dance with the protruding limbs of lodgepole pines.

Another of Wylie's favorite anecdotes was the story about the herd of cow elk he came upon after a lengthy and unsuccessful search for two lost teams of horses. The herd was positioned on a gentle slope, complacently chewing their cud. When Wylie tried tallying the numbers, he stopped counting at a thousand.

As he rode on toward Willow Park, he came face to face with a cow elk standing in the middle of a trail at the edge of a forest, the cow's feet planted firmly and her gaze directly on him. Wylie stopped. The cow started for the mother herd and behind her, fifty-one calves followed in single file. Halfway down the line, a second cow darted in and out of the line to keep wanderers with the group. A third and final cow prodded those with a tendency to lag.

Wylie started out again for Willow Park, only to come upon a second group of three cows and forty-three calves. A little farther on, another string of three adults and forty to fifty youngsters marched on with the same orderly sense of purpose. When these strings of calves and cows reached the larger herd, Wylie doubled back to watch the mothers find their calves.

The cow elk in the mother herd that were freed from the care and feeding of calves spent the entire day resting and eating sweet Yellowstone grasses. Once the calves arrived, hungry and tired, supper was ready. The next day, different cows took their turn caring for the young. Cow elk care for their young in the same manner as range cattle. One cow cares for three to six calves, providing protection from wolves and coyotes, but a cow elk is unique in that she only allows her own calf or calves to suckle.

When Wylie or young Clinton escorted tourists to an elk haunt, many of them said they preferred watching the cows and calves over a visit to the geysers.

Wylie did not hunt deer or elk, acknowledging that might be considered strange, especially since he was in the Park years before firearms were prohibited by law. In those early years, parties frequently killed more meat than they could eat, and they would traditionally jerk the meat by hanging it in trees to dry, which, Wylie wrote, "proved a godsend to many a hungry, weary traveler." More than once, Wylie ate the meat of another man's kill, but in all his days in Yellowstone, he "never fired a shot at or toward an elk or deer and was "not ashamed of that record."[11] Wylie stated: "I would as willingly go among a band of horses to shoot and kill as to aid in the killing of elk or deer."[12]

∾

By 1901 Wylie was comfortable enough financially to ease his chronic back pain by taking a trip to Mexico—in a new role as a tourist in search of the country's personality—with his brother, John. During the winter of 1902, Will and John traveled from Bozeman to south-central Mexico.[13] John invested in coffee plantations: one near Atoyac, northeast of Acapulco in the Sierra Madre del Sur, and the other at La Pearle. The only mention of Will in John's record of the trip suggests that he was a curious and enthusiastic companion, probably seeking warm-weather relief of the severe pain in his lower back, buttocks, and legs due to an injury or compression of the sciatic nerve.[14]

The men began their journey on January 29, 1902, traveling through Colorado to El Paso, Texas, where they boarded the Mexican Central Railway to Mexico City.

From the rail station in Atoyac, the brothers rode donkeys behind the American plantation manager, Mr. Nutting, to the plantation "in the clouds" at 9,049 feet, where they learned about day-to-day operations of the plantation. It rained daily, but the air was warm and filled with birdsong. At La Pearle, bananas hung on trees right outside the bedroom window.

Their next stop was Orizaba, a coffee, cotton, and manufacturing town in Vera Cruz with a population of forty thousand, electric lights, and mule-drawn street cars. A four-dollar room at the Hotel de France included breakfast in an open courtyard. Will and John spent many sunny hours in Orizaba's myriad of parks enjoying flowers, orange trees, fountains, and the views of Mount Orizaba—Mexico's highest peak—and its surrounding snowcapped mountains. They toured several of the town's fifteen cathedrals.

On February 17, 1902, Mr. Nutting arrived from Atoyac with mail from Will and John's families. Later that same day, the men journeyed to Puebla, then continued to Oaxaca the next day. From Oaxaca, the party journeyed about twenty-eight miles southeast to Mitla on saddle horses, seeing only two-wheeled carts drawn by horses sporting oxen yokes, which the men thought was a brutal custom. John also commented on the great numbers of women with bundles or babies strapped to their backs. They started back for Oaxaca at 3 A.M. The trip took seven and a half hours, owing to the pitiable condition of the horses.

After the trip to Oaxaca, they traveled to Vera Cruz and enjoyed a "first-class supper" with Nutting at the Mexican Hotel, then went to the wharf to inspect the "ocean vessels" anchored there. Vera Cruz also boasted electric lights and a sewage system in the works.

February 22, 1902, was spent in Puebla. The two brothers marked the holiday, Washington's birthday, by purchasing onyx stones and opals. In his journal, John noted that each town in Mexico "makes a specialty of some one thing," crafted by man or nature.

On Sunday, February 23, Will and John attended church services in Mexico City. The services were available in English, Spanish, and Gefman. Bishop Hamilton, John wrote, preached to an English congregation and later that evening, he spoke to a Spanish audience with an interpreter. There was more shopping and wonderful food to be had in Mexico City.

Five days later, the two brothers had worked their way north to Los Angeles via El Paso, Texas, on the Southern Pacific Railway. They reserved a Pullman sleeper, arriving on March 1. During their time in California, the brothers rode an electric car to Altadena and Pasadena, a lovely residential city of orange and lemon groves in the foothills of the San Gabriel Mountains. Later that week, they took a boat to Catalina Island, but the seas were rough and many of the passengers became seasick. They also devoted several days to visiting Los Angeles area friends and swimming at the beach in Santa Monica. They headed north for home, via San Jose and San Francisco, where they stayed at the Ramona, visited the Cliff House baths, and Golden Gate and Sutro Parks, made side trips to Alameda, Oakland, and Berkeley, and toured Stanford University.[15]

Although John's diary ends on March 18, 1902, when the brothers arrived in Portland, Oregon, John's son, Paul Wylie, estimated that the two brothers arrived home in Bozeman on March 21, 1902.

While Wylie was in Mexico, Interior Secretary Ethan Hitchcock and Yellowstone Park's Superintendent Captain John Pitcher, who served from May 1901 to July 1907, corresponded about the Wylie Camping Company license for the 1902 season. Wylie's license gave permission to use forty wagons or carriages at a total cost of $200 and the customary bond of $5,000. In a letter to Pitcher dated January 28, 1902, Secretary Hitchcock focused on the clause in the license that restricted Wylie to forty conveyances—a regulation that was designed to restrict companies from using more carriages or wagons than they paid for. This meant that if Wylie met more patrons than he had anticipated at the Cinnabar railway station, he could not under any circumstances contract with other Park licensees to use their transportation. If he did so, he would risk losing his license.

The Department of the Interior also stipulated any company that provided transportation had to clearly describe the services they offered. Hitchcock suggested in his letter of January 28 that "Wylie Permanent Camps" be "indicated in plain lettering not less than two inches high" on large cards that could be attached to the side of a company carriage or hung on the horses' harness. The Wylie Camping Company also informally adopted the name Wylie Permanent Camps.

Hitchcock also required the Park concessioners to provide tourists with a schedule of charges—an itemized list for specific services. Once this was approved by the Interior Department, Wylie, his family, and Wylie Camping Company employees had to abide by the prices—they could not ask for or accept payment for impromptu services of any kind.

The cows still concerned Hitchcock. On March 10, 1902, Hitchcock wrote Pitcher that he had reservations about Wylie's cows, but he felt that the final decision rested with Pitcher. He mentioned Wylie's schedule of charges, telling Pitcher that "further action" on the matter could wait until Wylie returned from Mexico and "his physical condition is such as to warrant the matter being taken up." In a May 19, 1902, letter to Pitcher, Hitchcock approved Pitcher's decision to allow Wylie the privilege of up to five milk cows at four permanent camps and twelve saddle horses for use by camp patrons.

On June 7, 1902, Thomas Ryan, the Interior Department's acting secretary, sent a telegram to Wylie's son, Fred, granting the department's permission. The telegram stated that Fred Wylie could administer the permanent camps on behalf of his father for "such a period of present season as sickness or disability prevents Mr. Wylie from being in the Park."

On July 14, 1902, a predicament occurred that threw off kilter the delicate balance between federal control of Park events and the concessioners' abilities to respond to the unexpected. Sixteen more patrons arrived at Cinnabar than the Wylies' carriages could accommodate. Because he did not have telephone communication

Wylie Concord coaches, buggies, and drivers in Gardiner. The Wylies' employees were routinely asked by their Yellowstone guests if their repeated tours of the Park grew tiresome, but they insisted that ever-changing park scenery and Park patrons relieved the monotony. The horses sought relief from the monotony by running away. *Courtesy, Yellowstone National Park Photo Archives. YELL 964*

with Mammoth Springs or Willow Park, Wylie was unable to send for more coaches. He encouraged the extra guests to ride with the Hotel–Transportation Company, but they were not interested. In addition Wylie was unable to talk to Superintendent John Pitcher on the telephone, so he sent Mr. Stiff, his superintendent of transportation, to the Park with an explanation for Pitcher. Wylie then sent an employee to a nearby ranch belonging to George Wakefield, former Master of Transportation for the Yellowstone National Park Transportation Company, reasoning that he would still be abiding by the stipulations of his license if he used only twenty-six of his allotted forty wagons and carriages as well as three of Wakefield's, who also had a transportation license.

Wakefield's three new four-horse Concord coaches—coaches with the high wheels and carved frame body that was wide enough to handle the rough, rutted roads of the "Wonderland"—nearly saved Wylie's day and that of his patrons. Wylie and his crew were able to take everyone from Cinnabar to Mammoth Springs, but at the Mammoth Springs registering station, they were refused entry and turned back to Gardiner by order of Park superintendent John Pitcher.

Wylie was furious. Anger fired up his insides as he drove back toward Gardiner with twenty-nine wagons of tourists disappointed not to get into the Park, locked out because Wylie had tried to accommodate them apart from the fine print in a license created in Washington. Words to describe his fury failed Wylie when he wrote about the incident years later, but he did recall, without a doubt, taking to bed right afterward with a bout of sciatica.

That evening his daughter Elizabeth recorded a dictated letter to Pitcher. Elizabeth explained that because her father could not sit up to personally respond to Pitcher's order denying entry "we must ask your permission to send a reply early in the morning." At the very least, she added, Pitcher could expect a written explanation of why her father engaged three of George Wakefield's coaches if Wylie's physical condition prevented a personal visit. She expressed great regret about postponing further communication.

The next day Wylie wrote Pitcher and explained his reasons for hiring the coaches. He stated that he "simply adopted what seemed to me the quickest and most satisfactory way of accommodating the people who had come to make the trip through the Park with us." Wylie assured Pitcher that he had "no thought of a subterfuge." He based his interpretation of the events on simple math: Wakefield's three Concord coaches plus his own twenty-six conveyances equaled twenty-nine coaches, which was eleven wagons under the forty-wagon limit.

George Lamar, Wylie's Washington attorney, weighed in with a July 30, 1902, letter to the Secretary of the Interior. He reviewed the basis for Wylie's decision, beginning with an insistence that Wylie had honored the conditions of his license. Lamar also included a passage from a letter Wylie wrote him on July 22, 1902. In that letter, Wylie stated in all honesty that the misunderstanding had to do with his absence from home the previous winter, and that if his son or his wife had been in Gardiner, they would have had the license with them in closer proximity than company headquarters at Willow Park and their understanding of the amended clauses of the license would have prevented the confusion.

Lamar's letter included his client's logic of July 22 based on Wylie's past experience with Park superintendents, from Captain Anderson and Colonel Young to as recently as 1901 with Captain Pitcher. In the past, if he needed extra carriages, Wylie personally discussed the subject with the Park Superintendent, offering to pay the standard five dollars per carriage. Invariably, each superintendent approved Wylie's use of extra rigs with no additional license needed and at no cost to Wylie; the rationale being that the companies Wylie rented rigs from were already licensed. Captain Oscar Brown, Yellowstone National Park superintendent from June 23, 1899, to July 23, 1900, gave Wylie permission to use unlicensed operators, but Wylie declined.

∾

In mid-August 1902, Wylie and his daughter, Elizabeth, greeted some important Park visitors: the "Cowan Party of Five." George Cowan, his wife, Emma Carpenter Cowan, and their three children were visiting Yellowstone National Park to mark the twenty-fifth anniversary of Mr. and Mrs. Cowan's capture by Nez Perce Indians in August 1877.[16]

George Cowan had earlier contacted Wylie to say that, although the Hotel–Transportation Company offered a coach and free hotel accommodations, he and his family preferred touring the Park with the Wylie Permanent Camps at Wylie's standard rates. George and Emma Cowan were enthused about Yellowstone's "wonders" and wished to visit their former camping spots, the location of their capture by the Nez Perce, the site where the council with Chief Joseph of the Nez Perce took place, and the place where George was shot by Nez Perce warriors and left for dead.

In a lengthy 1903 Montana Historical Society publication, Emma wrote an article about their 1877 Park visit that included seven pictures taken in August 1902, specifically one of the traveling party labeled August 18, 1902, near the place the Cowans were captured in 1877. The same photograph is housed in Yellowstone's Heritage and Research Center and mistakenly identifies Elizabeth as Mrs. Wylie. In the article Emma recalled that the summer of 1877 was "exceedingly hot and dry." A grasshopper infestation in the Radersburg area, fifty-three miles southeast of Helena, Montana, forced the Cowans to close up their house during the day to keep the grasshoppers at bay, compounding the summer heat. Emma's brother, Frank Carpenter, invited the Cowans to join him on a trip to the cooler, fresher air of Yellowstone National Park. Emma said "it required but little effort on his part to enthuse us, and we soon began preparations for the trip." George and Emma Cowan, Emma's brother, Frank, and younger sister, Ida Carpenter, and five companions traveled to Three Forks, then down the Madison River valley via Ennis. The party traveled over Targhee Pass, then once again followed the Madison River into the Park, arriving on August 14, 1877.

The background to the events was tragic. Identified in government reports as "Non-treaty Nez Perce," Chiefs Joseph, Looking Glass, and White Bird felt bewildered, "increasingly beleaguered," and vulnerable as a result of the 1863 treaty with the federal government that reduced the bands' large land reservation, created in 1855, to one-tenth of its size.[17] These leaders and their bands wandered their traditional hunting grounds until 1877, when a civil and military commission recommended the treaty's enforcement and insisted the "Non-treaty Nez Perce" abandon the Wallowa Valley in Oregon and the Salmon River Valley in Idaho Territory to settle on reservation lands in the Clearwater Valley of north-central Idaho, near Fort Lapwai.[18] Between June 1877, when Indians avenged an 1876 death of their own by killing twenty white men, women, and children, and July 12, 1877, the Nez Perce and General O. O. Howard's troops fought three brutal battles. After another battle on the Big Hole River with forces led by General John Gibbon, the Indians went south, crossed the Continental Divide, and turned west toward Yellowstone. Howard was close behind. The Nez Perce headed for Targhee Pass, and ended up on Yellowstone's Firehole River on August 23, 1877.[19]

The Cowans, the Carpenters, and their fellow travelers were fast asleep at their camp a short distance away. Several Indians greeted the Cowan party at sunrise the next morning expressing amiability, but the Cowans and their companions decided to skip breakfast, pack their equipment, and head down the Firehole as "though nothing unusual was at hand."[20]

More Nez Perce appeared as the minutes passed. Emma recalled in her article that "the woods seemed full of them." The Cowan party headed down the Firehole for approximately one mile, accompanied by forty to fifty Nez Perce, before the Indians ordered a halt and gave some commands in their native tongue. Forty to fifty more Nez Perce emerged from the woods, including one introduced by another warrior as: "Him Joseph."[21] Now with Chief Joseph in their midst, the Cowans and their companions followed an order to backtrack. After traveling two miles, the party could not make the wagons move further "on account of fallen timber," so they unhitched and mounted their horses.

At the foot of Mary Mountain, the Nez Perce and their captives conferred. Mr. Cowan spoke on behalf of the captives. Lean Elk, or Poker Joe—a half-French, half-Nez Perce warrior with an intimate knowledge of the region—translated for the Indians. The Nez Perce gave freedom to the Cowan party in exchange for their horses, guns, and ammunition. The Indians supplied them with replacement horses and instructions to leave. Two captives dove into the brush and escaped. A half mile west of Mary Mountain, the remaining members of the Cowan party realized to their "dismay" that they were again being followed by Nez Perce, who told them that "the chief wanted to see" them again.[22] They turned around once again and were escorted back toward Mary Lake.

Two Indians suddenly appeared ahead on the trail, and one took aim with his rifle at Mr. Cowan, and fired. Cowan took a bullet through his thigh. He then realized his head was the next target and toppled off his horse. His wife rushed to him, trying to protect him from further attack. An Indian grabbed hold of her, moving her just enough to shoot her husband in the forehead. Other captors threw rocks at Cowan's head. That was thought to be the end of George Cowan.[23]

After spending a night on the east end of Mary Lake, the captives—Emma, Frank, and Ida—were released near the Mud Volcano with advice from Poker Joe to "ride all night, all day, no sleep."[24] On August 26 they came upon a detachment of the 2nd Cavalry near Tower Junction and were escorted to Mammoth Springs. Photographer Bird Calfee offered Emma, Frank, and Ida a ride to the Bottler

The Cowan family with Elizabeth Wylie touring the Middle Basin. This picture, one of seven dated August 18, 1902, accompanied Emma Cowan's "Reminiscences of Pioneer Life" in a 1903 Montana Historical Society publication. In his autobiography, Wylie indicated that Elizabeth (in the middle seat) accompanied him and the Cowans on their Park tour. *Courtesy, Yellowstone National Park Photo Archives. YELL 39025*

Ranch on the Yellowstone River. From there, Emma Cowan and the Carpenters journeyed east to Bozeman, then on to Emma and Ida's home in Radersburg.

During their 1902 anniversary visit, Wylie offered the Cowans a top-notch driver and coach, intending to follow with Elizabeth in a smaller rig. George Cowan insisted he change places with Elizabeth. Wylie called to the horses and the party was off on a tour that Wylie viewed as having great historical pathos—for Indians and whites alike—narrated by none other than George F. Cowan.

Twenty-five years after the attack in 1877, Cowan led his wife, three children, Wylie, and Elizabeth to the spot where the whites bargained with Chief Joseph and the Nez Perce, and to the setting where he took the two bullets and blows to his head by stones.

At the place Emma Cowan identified as where "she was torn away from the then supposed dead body of her husband,"[25] the Cowans, Wylie, and Elizabeth ate a picnic lunch.

Cowan demonstrated for Wylie how, in spite of taking yet another bullet from another Nez Perce warrior when he regained consciousness, he crawled on his hands and knees from where he was wounded to where the Indians had first ordered an exchange of horses. When he reached a stream the following day, he "fairly lay in the water, quenching his thirst. Then with hands and teeth he tore his underwear into bandages and dressed his wounds as best he could."[26]

Emma Cowan had been home in Radersburg for about one week when two friends stopped by with a copy of the *Independent Extra* that announced: "Cowan Alive. He is with General Howard's Command…. Howard was fourteen miles this side of Yellowstone Lake. This news is reliable."[27] Emma recalled that she "learned nothing more…the hours began to drag." A few days later Emma traveled to Helena in hopes that "telegraphic news" of her husband's exact whereabouts would reach her sooner than in more rural Radersburg. A week after her arrival in Helena, Emma received a telegram stating that her husband would be brought to Bozeman the next day.

Emma left immediately for Bozeman, only to discover that her beloved George had "given out" at the Bottler Ranch on the upper Yellowstone River, so she hastened on to meet him there.

After their reunion at the Bottler Ranch, the Cowans left for Bozeman in an army ambulance. The conveyance overturned in a canyon seven miles east of Bozeman, nearly killing Mr. Cowan again. They settled at a hotel in Bozeman to allow George's wounds to heal before journeying on to Radersburg. An endless stream of friends and well-wishers, however, paraded through his room, and one day several men sat on his bed and broke it, reopening his wounds. It was at that point, George jokingly told Wylie, he thought his time had come at last.

George and Emma Cowan's stories told around the campfire during their 1902 Yellowstone tour would stay with Wylie until the end of his days. Cowan showed Wylie a charm that he wore attached to his watch chain: the ball the army surgeon removed from his forehead. He had it encased in gold; perhaps to commemorate "the worst vacation in American history."[28] When recollecting their shared journey and the hours of wonderful stories, Wylie wrote: "Again, let me say I consider it a rare privilege to have taken this three-times-killed man and his family all through the park."[29]

Wylie thought not simply of Cowan but of Chief Joseph's humane treatment of Emma Cowan and Ida Carpenter. A thoughtful, educated gentleman, Wylie apparently shared Mrs. Cowan's enumeration of her blessings detailed in her 1903 article:

> Yet, at this day, knowing something of the circumstances that led to the final outbreak and uprising of these Indians, I wonder that any of us were spared. Truly, a quality of mercy was shown us during our captivity that a Christian might emulate, and at a time when they must have hated the very name of the white race.[30]

∾

In the winter of 1903 the warmer climates of Arizona, California, and Mexico beckoned Will and Mary Ann with daughter Grace, who had spent the previous school year in Natick, Massachusetts. Grace's health was still poor, and perhaps her parents hoped the warmer weather would restore her strength, just as it helped relieve the pain of Wylie's sciatica. In the coming fall, Grace planned to return to school at Ossining-on-the-Hudson in New York.

∾

The highlight of 1903 at Yellowstone National Park was the April visit of President Theodore Roosevelt, who had assumed the office on September 6, 1901, when William McKinley was assassinated. At forty-two years old, Roosevelt was the youngest man to occupy the Oval Office, and had the energy and grit associated with men much younger than himself. At the turn of the century when "appreciation of the wilderness…was becoming a movement,"[31] President Roosevelt's spring visits to Yellowstone, Yosemite, and the Grand Canyon, and his enthusiastic pursuit of outdoor activities, reminded Americans that a trip to the West's parks and forests, was "a voyage of discovery" which "offered the chance to see and know America, to celebrate a united nation, to be an American."[32]

Roosevelt toured Yellowstone National Park for sixteen days. At a camp near Yancy's, the name given to the hostelry and a fishing hole on the Yellowstone River, he had an opportunity to demonstrate his views on game preservation. According to Wylie, Charles Jesse "Buffalo" Jones, Yellowstone's game warden, roped a wolf for the president to shoot. But Roosevelt insisted Jones set the animal free, for he intended to abide by Park regulations. He spent much of his time on horseback with the exception of sleigh rides to Upper Geyser Basin and Grand Canyon.

On the day he was scheduled to depart, Roosevelt and Park superintendent Captain John Pitcher were ushered by a large herd of antelope across a stretch of sagebrush and prickly pear to the dedication of the Yellowstone entrance arch at Gardiner—the terminus for the Northern Pacific Railway line into the Park.

Under a vast blue bowl of sky, the crowd assembled at the Roosevelt Arch clapped exuberantly, for it had been twenty years since President Chester Arthur's sojourn in Yellowstone. During the ceremony, which was planned by Masonic authorities, Roosevelt helped lay the arch's cornerstone and spoke to the crowd of three thousand about the Park.

Will, Mary Ann, and their son Fred traveled with Ed Moorman, now manager of the Wylies' Canyon camp, from Bozeman to Gardiner by train to see the ceremony. All listened intently to the president's message of preservation and conservation of the Park's curiosities, game, and forests "for the benefit and the enjoyment of the people."[33]

Once the Northern Pacific Railway lines reached Gardiner, Wylie decided to join the flurry of building activity there which included W. A. Hall's new store and a $20,000 Northern Pacific Railway depot. In 1903 Wylie purchased land from the Northern Pacific on which to build a hotel to add an accommodation option for his patrons at the beginning or end of their tour, plus provide convenient, comfortable, short-term lodging for himself and family members when needed. The Wylie Hotel opened that same year. A simple two-story structure, the Wylie Hotel featured a covered porch that ran the entire length of the building—a sheltered perch with chairs and benches, where guests could be on the lookout for Wylie Camping Company coaches or watch fellow tourists.

The Wylie Hotel in Gardiner, circa 1905. Wylie purchased land from the Northern Pacific Railway in 1903 when the lines reached Gardiner, and built a hotel that year to accommodate his guests at the beginning or end of their tour. It also offered comfortable and convenient lodging for Wylie family. *Used by permission, Utah State Historical Society, all rights reserved.*

Shortly after the beginning of the 1903 Yellowstone tourist season, things were lively in the Wylie family, with plenty of weddings and children going off to school. Mary Ann Wylie was most likely in Bozeman for much of the summer, busy with preparations. Fred Wylie, twenty-six years of age, married Marguerite Davis on June 24, 1903. His twenty-eight-year-old sister, Elizabeth, planned a September 9, 1903, wedding to Thomas Heron McKee. In addition, Grace made preparations to attend school in the East.

Although his youngest son, nineteen-year-old Clinton, spent the Park season driving and guiding, Wylie also depended on his trusted employees. He counted on Ed Moorman to manage the Canyon camp.

At various times throughout the summer, Moorman watched the construction of the Chittenden Bridge and noted that one of the steel workers survived a fall into the Yellowstone River. The structure spanned the Yellowstone River above the Upper Falls and was named for Hiram M. Chittenden, an officer of the U.S. Army Corps of Engineers who loved Yellowstone National Park and its history. In addition to his work on the bridge project near the Canyon camp, Chittenden also supervised construction of the Roosevelt Arch and miles of road in the Park.

Construction of a bridge over Cascade Creek in 1903–04 caused change at the Wylie Camping Company. Even though Wylie purchased an old road-sprinkling cart, to the relief of the Canyon camp employees who could now fill the cart with water from a government pipe instead of pail by pail by windlass from Cascade Creek, the Canyon camp moved from Cascade Creek to a picturesque setting on a hill near Canyon Junction.

Uncle Tom Richardson's business at Canyon was also altered. Once the Chittenden Bridge was completed across the Yellowstone River, Richardson's boat service became an unnecessary expense for tourists. He moved his tent to the top of Uncle Tom's Trail and continued to offer guided tours to the Lower Falls for one dollar, an increase of fifty cents over previous years.

Wylie's patience with the activities of Yellowstone's game warden, Buffalo Jones, wore thin. Wylie did credit Jones for increasing the number of bison in the Park. In 1902, Congress appropriated $15,000 for Jones to purchase bison from private owners. He obtained about forty animals—including three from Texas and fifteen from Montana. Some of the bison came from Indians living in western Montana. Jones tended the animals in a corral at Mammoth.

However, Jones' antics with wildlife annoyed Mary Ann and Will, particularly his boast that he could rope a bear. Jones would ensnare a bear with a rope, then draw the rope over a tree limb and whip the bear without mercy. True, the Wylies had their own problems with bears that broke into their camp commissaries, but a rope only made the bear angry and even more dangerous. Jones insisted on visiting the Wylie camps regularly, expecting a meal and a bear or two to rope. The Wylies and their patrons were weary of waking to the bears' horrible suffering. Wylie approached Park superintendent

Pitcher and insisted that Jones be told to stay away from bears in or close by all Wylie camps. He informed Pitcher that he was prepared to go elsewhere with his complaint if Jones refused.

Jones' bear patrols ceased.

One day, Buffalo Jones showed up at Willow Park after the patrons departed for the train in Gardiner. He asked to be served lunch. Mary Ann sat down with him to keep him company. As Jones was eating, one of his prized bloodhounds arrived in the dining tent and keeled over at his feet. Jones stood up and, in a mad rage, accused the Wylies of putting poison out with the intent to kill bears. A second dog appeared and dropped dead at Jones' feet. Jones bolted for his buggy, promising to take action against the Wylies.

Mary Ann located a coach driver who was late in starting for Gardiner and gave him a note warning Wylie. Once he read the note, Wylie started out for Superintendent Pitcher's office to have him review its message.

Pitcher expressed regret that Jones did not receive whatever tonic the hounds got. He told Wylie that even though he was required to initiate some sort of investigation, Wylie and Mary Ann were not to worry.[34]

Wylie left for Willow Park, driving the six miles in haste. Shortly after his arrival, an army officer appeared with a Park scout.

Willow Park's housekeeper, Miss Clara Doyle, explained to the men that late in the season the Wylie camps had almost as many mice in the beds chewing up blankets as paying customers needing those blankets for sleep. Miss Doyle's solution? A lethal sandwich of bread, butter, and "Tough on Rats" poison placed under beds in vacant tents.

Jones' bloodhounds had, unfortunately, found those sandwiches to their liking. Miss Doyle accompanied the men into the tents and produced the partially used box of poison.

Nothing more was heard about the bloodhound incident and not long after that, Buffalo Jones left the Park. Wylie contended that the death of Jones' dogs had no impact on his decision to leave.[35]

Before his departure, Jones had sought Wylie out and asked if he was interested in purchasing a cattalo robe. Cattalo, an experimental hybrid between the native male bison and the domestic cow, were bred in an attempt to preserve the bison species, at that point in time primarily a park animal. Furthermore, the experiment's hypothesis raised the question: Could cattalo thrive in conditions inhospitable to cows? Wylie eagerly agreed to buy the robe, feeling it to be of great worth.

In addition to his difficulties with the game warden, Wylie's rapport over the previous two seasons with his stage drivers had become tenuous and required Wylie to devote time and effort during the 1903 season to forging better relations. The enjoyment of his patrons demanded a climate of mutual respect.

The stage drivers and Colonel E. C. Waters were at odds during the 1901 season. Using a large portion of an inheritance belonging to his wife and children, Waters finally commissioned the building of a larger steamer, the *E.C. Waters*. A boat coupon was no longer part of the Wylies' Park ticket, so Waters paid Wylie's drivers fifty cents a person for those delivered to Thumb dock as passengers for his boat. When he nixed that fee, the drivers talked to their passengers about the unsafe nature of the boat, stating that it had been condemned. Business dropped disastrously. Waters soon reversed his policy, but the drivers continued to be suspicious of him.[36]

The 1902 season brought on a strike by Wylie Camping Company drivers. Patrons had complained that drivers pressured them for tips, and a worried Wylie posted signs at each camp, requesting that guests refrain from tipping employees. The drivers refused to work, and many sympathetic young women working in the camps threatened a strike as well.

Moorman sided with Will and Mary Ann. He worked tirelessly to quell the drivers' discontent. Drivers threatened to throw him into Pelican Creek near the Lake camp. Moorman responded by saying that he would fight any one of the drivers. A brawl ensued, with Moorman overpowering the striker.

Moorman had no time to bask in the glow of victory, because he received word that drivers at the Canyon camp were plotting to abandon their passengers and drive the coaches empty. Jumping onto a saddle horse, he reached the camp as drivers readied their teams. He found one of the camp boys and ordered him to ride quickly to the soldier station to ask the sergeant and his men to bring order to the camp.

Moorman stationed himself along the narrow, one-way road out of camp. As the first team passed pulling an empty coach, he caught hold of the leader's bit. The team stopped, thus preventing the other empty rigs from passing. Moorman held the team until the sergeant arrived with his men.

The sergeant ordered the drivers back to camp, insisting that they load up the Wylie Camping Company patrons and haul them to their destination. He honored Moorman's request for an army escort as far as Norris Basin.

Wylie arrived from Bozeman with enough new drivers to replace those unwilling to work under the no-tipping policy. He took down the notices about tipping. From that point on, the company's morale improved.[37]

8

The Wylie Way

THE TWENTIETH CENTURY INTRODUCED a new addition to the country's transportation network and seized Americans' curiosity. The incorporation of the Ford Motor Company in 1903 and subsequent interest in transcontinental automobile travel and races between San Francisco and New York City, and "guided automobile tours" from New York City to the 1904 World's Fair in St. Louis,[1] provided an opportunity for travelers to shed "set schedules and set routes." Gone were the days when tourists were solely "at the mercy of a corporation."[2] A trip by automobile offered "freedom of action" and "direct contact with landscape unknown to passengers of trains and ships." Once again, an experience that began as "a sport among the rich became recreation for the middle class."[3] Anyone who purchased a car and learned to safely drive it might also be master of their own journey to "see and know America,"[4] perhaps discovering the world described by Jack London in his book, *The Call of the Wild*, published and widely admired at that time.[5]

While William Wallace Wylie likely found automobiles very intriguing, his focus, in 1904, was on the success he enjoyed as a Yellowstone concessioner during the three previous tourist seasons, owing in part to horses that pulled coaches and wagons. Wylie was confident that his business would continue to grow. He purchased the entire inventory of coaches, baggage wagons, horses, bedding, and tents from George Wakefield, former Master of Transportation for the Yellowstone National Park Transportation Company and Park outfitter who wanted to retire in Livingston after his wife died in 1903.

In hopes that wild animals might be lured into the area for the enjoyment of Park visitors, in early spring 1904, Wylie requested and received permission from Yellowstone Park superintendent John Pitcher and engineer Hiram Chittenden to raise alfalfa on a flat south of Gardiner. Nearby were the canals that had been designed by Chittenden. With the canals providing irrigation, Wylie was certain that alfalfa would thrive on the flat and predicted a bounty of two alfalfa crops per year as well as an excellent winter pasture. Wylie's offer included his personal supervision of the alfalfa experiment. He was quite familiar with the crop from his years in the Gallatin Valley and planned to see the alfalfa from seedlings to full-grown crop, irrigation and all. He even purchased ground-breaking machinery and a drill for planting the alfalfa seed.

In his memoir, Wylie reminisced about the hundreds of elk, deer, antelope, and mountain sheep that grazed contentedly on the "fine ricks of alfalfa" growing on that flat south of Gardiner. He recalled: "As a result of this fine winter treatment many of these animals return in the summer, making this one part of the park where wild game can be seen the year round."[6]

Wylie wondered if anyone would remember his contribution after Chittenden departed and Pitcher transferred elsewhere. "Maybe in that future state which a noble but almost extinct race, like the buffalo, call the 'Happy Hunting Grounds' some of these animals may come to me and say 'Thank you, Mr. Wylie, for helping us through many a hard winter.' For in that country all languages will be understood."[7]

Wylie's optimism about the future, however, was not borne out by the Wylie Camping Company's reservations. On approximately June 15, opening day of the 1904 season, fewer than ten people were booked to arrive in Gardiner. When Wylie made inquiries at the Yellowstone Park Association, he was told their hotels were either booked solid or had very few openings.

The decline in Wylie Camping Company business in June 1904 was overshadowed by personal tragedy in the Wylie family. Two months earlier, while she was at Ossining School for Girls, located near New York City, the Wylies' daughter Grace became ill. She then spent approximately seven weeks trying to regain enough strength to return home. When she did return, on about June 21, Grace was accompanied on the train trip by her close friend from school, Elsie Wright of Worcester, Massachusetts.

The day after the girls arrived, Grace grew weaker. Mary Ann felt uneasy about her daughter's condition and summoned medical help. Over the next few days, Grace developed an abscess and worsened. Will, Elizabeth, Fred, and Clinton were summoned from Yellowstone National Park.

Doctors decided that the best course of action to help Grace recover was to drain the site of her infection. Once the doctors had lanced and drained the infection, on June 28, 1904, she improved significantly. Then, early the following morning, Grace relapsed. After a few hours of struggle she died at 8:30 A.M., surrounded by her parents and siblings Elizabeth, Fred, and Clinton. Grace's death not only devastated her family, but also young Elsie, who had wished to spend the summer with her dear friend.

In the obituary for the twenty-three-year-old Miss Wylie, Bozeman's *Avant Courier* announced that death plucked "a Fair Flower from the Gardens of Bozeman," noting her "strong Christian character" and that her "unusual cheery disposition shed rays of sunshine wherever she went."[8]

Will and Mary Ann opened their home the next afternoon to grieving relatives, family friends, Grace's friends from school in Bozeman, members of the YWCA where she volunteered and served as president, as well as members of her chorale group, the Treble Clef Club.

After Grace's service, Wylie returned to Yellowstone. In their memoirs, both Wylie and Moorman noted that, during the 1904 season, the Wylie Camping Company was feeling the adverse effects of the Northern Pacific Railway's policies that related to the promotion and discount of railroad tickets. On days scattered here and there throughout the season, the Wylies' guests numbered less than six. On the whole, the Wylies' 1904 season averaged about fourteen tourists per day, as opposed to the thriving years of 1902 and 1903, when nearly eighteen tourists a day cycled through the Wylies' stations. In contrast, "Uncle Tom" Richardson, the Wylies' former manager at the Canyon camp, guided 1,147 tourists to the Lower Falls of the Yellowstone River.

At the 1904 World's Fair in St. Louis, celebrating the hundredth anniversary of the Louisiana Purchase, the Northern Pacific Railway advertised and promoted their services, including a combination railroad transportation-Yellowstone Park ticket, at one of the many pavilions that decorated the fairgrounds. Wylie understood that the Northern Pacific Railway could promote its rates day and night, but since his patrons also purchased Northern Pacific Railway tickets, he wanted the railway to inform interested travelers that the Wylie Camping Company also offered an attractive option for Park accommodations.

In addition, Northern Pacific Railway passengers traveling to Yellowstone National Park from points along or east of the Missouri River could purchase a combination railroad and Park ticket, which included hotel accommodations, for less than it cost Wylie's guests to pay rail fare plus purchase a Wylie Camping Company Park tour on arrival.

If the Northern Pacific Railway violated an agreement with the Interior Department about hotel fees, then the company risked the wrath of Interior Secretary Ethan Hitchcock, who might deny the Yellowstone Park Association a permit to provide accommodations in the Park. Wylie believed that patrons of the Northern Pacific Railway received reduced rail fare, a violation of Interstate Commerce laws. Wylie decided to act on the advice of his attorney, George Lamar, and filed suit before the Interstate Commerce Commission.

Late in March 1905, the commission convened in Washington, D.C., to consider Wylie's allegations about the Northern Pacific Railway rates. All five members of the commission, chaired by Martin Knapp, participated in the hearing.

The 1905 hearing opened with Wylie's attorney, George Lamar, requesting that Jule Murat Hannaford, vice president of the Northern Pacific Railway, be sworn as a Wylie Camping Company witness.

Mr. Hannaford and his attorney, Mr. C. W. Bunn, exchanged confused glances.

Bunn, Wylie recalled, asked if Lamar expected to call Hannaford as his witness. Lamar replied that was his intent. The vice president, Wylie wrote, took an oath. After he answered a few questions from

Lamar, Hannaford stated to those present that if they would allow him to talk without being questioned, he was sure he could save time, although he agreed to additional questioning when he was finished.

Chairman Knapp permitted this.

Hannaford began by stating that he wished the commission, Wylie, and Lamar to understand that the Northern Pacific Railway had no ill feeling toward Mr. Wylie, that in fact they held him "in very high regard." However, they had invested millions in Yellowstone National Park under the impression that they were to have a lease with exclusive rights to care for all Park visitors, except, possibly, those who used their own private tents and teams.

Hannaford went on to state that he had visited the Wylie camps in disguise. He had eaten at the Wylies' tables, slept in the camp beds, and ridden in the camp coaches. Hannaford told the commission that Wylie furnished accommodations that were in every way as good as the Northern Pacific's, except perhaps in a matter of style. Wylie, Hannaford argued, catered to and always obtained the educated class of tourists, who, after all, were the largest proportion of Yellowstone visitors. Hannaford concluded by saying "that if he is permitted to go on with his park business he will simply bankrupt us."[9]

At Lamar's request, William Wallace Wylie was then sworn in. Lamar asked him about the Wylie Camping Company's rate structure. Wylie explained his company's rates, then concluded by stating that patrons living along the Missouri and points east paid, in 1904, $11.25 extra to travel with the Wylies, as opposed to traveling with the Northern Pacific Railway and staying in Yellowstone Park Association hotels.

One member of the Interstate Commerce Commission asked him how much this amounted to over the course of one season.

Lamar had prepared his client thoroughly. Earlier, Wylie had looked back over his annual registers—which identified the home addresses of all Wylie Camping Company patrons—and ventured to say that during an average season that difference amounted to $16,855.

Chairman Knapp was aghast. He inquired of Hannaford if the estimate meant that those Yellowstone Park patrons paid more than

$16,000 extra to travel with the Wylies when they could have made reservations with the Northern Pacific Railway and stayed in swank accommodations for less money.

Hannaford said he believed Wylie's estimate was accurate. He went on to say that the Northern Pacific Railway's combined ticket cost less because of a reduction in rail fares, which, he acknowledged, was a policy in violation of Interstate Commerce laws.

After hearing two days of testimony and arguments, the commission ruled in favor of the Wylie Camping Company.[10] The ruling stipulated that the Northern Pacific must sell Wylie Camping Company tickets wherever Northern Pacific Railway tickets were sold or the railway had to sell only their Park ticket at the same Park entrance where Wylie sold his camping company ticket.

At the conclusion of the hearing, Wylie received a document that detailed the commission's ruling. Stamped with the seal of the United States of America and adorned with a bright-colored ribbon, Wylie valued the deed as one of his most important Yellowstone treasures.

After the commission ruling, the Northern Pacific Railway, still intent on protecting their investment in Yellowstone National Park, changed their strategy of coping with the Wylies. Wylie noted that the commission's decision resulted in an overture by the Northern Pacific to buy him out, "since they found all other devices to get rid of me had failed."[11]

By 1905 the Northern Pacific Railway's subsidiary, the Northwest Improvement Company, and Harry Child had equal ownership in the Yellowstone Park Association and the Yellowstone National Park Transportation Company—the relationship that Wylie and other Park concessioners referred to as the Hotel–Transportation Companies.

According to Wylie's right-hand man, Ed Moorman, during the summer of 1905 Will and Mary Ann Wylie signed preliminary papers transferring ownership of the Wylie Camping Company to a partnership that included Livingston businessman Arthur W. Miles, owner of a "large, profitable dry goods establishment" and "grocery store." Miles, "Wylie's main supplier…extended generous credit to the camping company for many years." By "calling in Wylie's outstanding bill for supplies," Miles held one-third interest in the company. A.L. Smith, an officer at Helena's State Bank of Montana, purchased the remaining two-thirds interest on behalf of a silent partner, Harry Child.[12] The two gentlemen paid the Wylies the total sum of $15,000 for the Wylie Camping Company, and Miles' lively son, Dan, was hired to work at the Wylies' Willow Park camp.

No one, recalled Ed Moorman, had as much zest for Yellowstone National Park as Arthur W. Miles. Confident that business would grow and with the pluck to follow through, Miles planned to improve the camps with financial backing from Harry Child, who was in turn managing lodging and transportation for the Yellowstone Park Association and the Yellowstone National Park Transportation Company. Wylie, on the other hand, still struggled with the discomforts of sciatica and had different plans.

Then fifty-seven years old, Wylie wanted to retire because of age, the nervous strain brought on by fighting for his lease every year, the difficulties of enduring the weather and high altitude as an older man, and the heart-breaking death of Grace. In addition, over the past several years, the Wylies had put company profits back into the equipment necessary to care for an increase in guests, leaving them with a meager company coffer.

Perhaps, too, he wanted to sell while he and Mary Ann still controlled the company's vision and mission; while he still felt a sense of wonder, not bitterness, about the Park. By selling the Wylie Camping Company, Will and Mary Ann avoided the necessary capital infusion to expand their business or the need to take on a financial partner who might not share their values, past experience with government agencies, or vision for the future.

Because of the unpredictable nature of their ongoing struggle with the federal government, Will and Mary Ann never knew from year to year the exact value of their company or what truly belonged to them long-term, free and clear. If the Interior Department decided to deny the Wylies a permit one cold, dark winter day, then their company's worth would rest strictly on the intangibles of an authentic and personal experience, the opportunity to act as a resource and build a community for fellow Yellowstone admirers, and the capability to breathe life into their dreams—intangibles that would likely be meaningful only to the Wylies and their family, intangibles that would be difficult for a buyer to quantify.

Perhaps Will and Mary Ann wanted to sell while there were winters ahead to spend together, somewhere warm where sciatica couldn't find Will. Whatever their reasons, the 1905 tourist season would be the Wylies' last season as concessioners in Yellowstone National Park.

The 1905 season promised to be busy. The completion of the Grand Loop road, the appeal of the Old Faithful Inn at the Upper Geyser Basin,[13] and an increased number of advance bookings ensured a lucrative year. A number of travelers heading west for the 1905 Lewis and Clark Exposition in Portland, Oregon, were expected to stop over at Yellowstone National Park.

Wylie managed the camps in the summer of 1905 as a $125 per month salaried employee of what the new owners now called the Wylie Permanent Camping Company. Ed Moorman, whom Wylie had hired as a greenhorn from Cincinnati with eight dollars in his pocket, planned to stay on as superintendent of transportation. On June 8 Wylie wrote to Superintendent Pitcher seeking permission to bring one hundred loose horses and sixteen cows into Yellowstone on June 10, 11, or 12, 1905. Wylie hoped to be in Gardiner by June 10.

Will and Mary Ann arrived in the Park that year to unusually deep snows between the geyser basins and Yellowstone Lake. Hiram Chittenden assigned men to shovel roads, but the season opening was moved back several days. News of Interior Secretary Hitchcock's decision to grant the Wylie Permanent Camping Company a ten-year lease likely gave the waiting men and women something to talk about.[14]

On June 22, 1905, the Wylies and a company employee set out from Upper Basin to scout the situation and determine if it would be safe to send company coaches, loaded with the first tourists of the season, on the Upper Basin–Lake stretch on the following day. Because telephone lines were down, the employee followed them in a two-wheeled cart, intending to return to Old Faithful to tell the others of the Wylies' decision.

The Wylies and their scout found big openings cut through the valleys and snow-drifts piled to a height equal to the top of Will and Mary Ann's rig. The day was mild, however, so the snow was melting rapidly. The Wylies sent their companion back with word that the coaches could indeed proceed to Lake camp on June 23, 1905. However, the next morning when Will went to the Yellowstone Lake corral to ready his two horses for the pull to Canyon, the younger of his team was lame from wading through the deep snow.

When Will and Mary Ann arrived at Canyon, drivers for the Yellowstone National Park Transportation Company and the Monida and Yellowstone Stage Company voiced their displeasure. They demanded an explanation for why the Wylies had allowed their patrons to be driven over the Upper Basin–Lake road, when they did not drive their guests along that section of road because they believed such a trip should have been delayed a day or two. The irate drivers took their patrons back to Norris and crossed over to Canyon from there, but visitors were angry. Wylie patrons got to see Yellowstone Lake and they wanted to as well.

During the summer of 1905, nearly 26,000 visitors toured Yellowstone National Park. Approximately 4,000 were patrons of the Wylie Permanent Camps, and 2,248 visitors paid "Uncle Tom" Richardson one dollar to escort them down his trail into the Yellowstone River canyon, ensuring that he started the fall and winter card-playing season in Bozeman with plenty of betting money. It was the first season that the Wylies' former company turned a large profit amounting to approximately $60,000. Because they were no longer the owners of the company, Mary Ann and Wylie did not share in the season's earnings.

Wylie closed the season by requesting a permit from Yellowstone Park superintendent Pitcher to drive about forty horses over Big Horn Pass and down the Gallatin sometime between September 10 and 20, 1905. On September 26, 1905, he again wrote Pitcher notifying him, his scouts, and soldiers to be on the lookout for several Wylie horses, most notably a sorrel with a white face and the Wylie 5Y brand on its left shoulder, that might be in the Upper Basin area. In addition, he mentioned that a band of seven horses that went missing on June

14, 1905, from Willow Park, were last seen wandering of their own accord near the Gardner River.

Will and Mary Ann left the Park with plans to spend part of the year in the warmer climate of southern California. Return trips would be confined to Bozeman or Cherry Creek. Before they acted on those plans, on December 28, 1905, Wylie signed a final agreement with the Wylie Permanent Camping Company in Helena, Montana, transferring his goodwill with the sale of his company and promising not to go into business in Yellowstone National Park. In an article in the *Butte Inter Mountain*, published on December 20, 1905, Wylie commented that he had made peace with his decision to sell his company. He stated "I am through with it. I was offered a large salary to take charge of the business I recently sold out, but had I desired to remain in it to that extent, I would not have disposed of the company."[15]

He also agreed to assist the Wylie Permanent Camping Company for as long as company business reflected what Wylie termed the "Wylie spirit." For these services and any further service for the company's good health, Wylie expected $1,500 per year, paid semi-annually beginning January 1, 1906.

Ed Moorman, Wylie's employee for six years, remembered talking with Wylie about the particulars of the sale of the Wylie Camping Company, including the $15,000 payment that Wylie received from Livingston businessman Arthur W. Miles and his silent partner, Harry Child. Prior to the sale, Moorman noted, Wylie owed Miles a considerable sum of money for equipment purchased from Miles' company. Moorman thought he recalled hearing that Miles held Wylie Camping Company stock as collateral, but he wrote that, "Of this, I am not sure."[16]

The final agreement would be in effect as long as it "was mutually agreeable to both parties concerned."[17] It was an agreement that focused on the transfer of goodwill, rife with open-ended language that was ready for interpretation on both sides; a document very typical of legal documents of the time. Moorman continued to work at the Wylie Permanent Camping Company and later wrote in his memoir: "Wylie was an intelligent man and he knew as well as Child and Miles that the agreement would not last for long."[18]

At Miles' request, Moorman made out a final check to Wylie in August 1907. Miles sent Wylie the check along with a note notifying him that the agreement signed in December 1905 was canceled. Despite Moorman's opinion about the agreement, Wylie was appalled by Miles' behavior. In a letter dated September 1, 1907, Wylie told Miles he found the sudden end of the agreement unacceptable. He reiterated the terms of the contract and argued that his salary was for "good will of business."

During this time, Will devoted his retirement to the Wylie Land and Livestock Company. In 1906, he and his sister, Belle, established an overnight camp at the Wylie Ranch at Spanish Creek. Campers were picked up at the train station in Bozeman and taken by a four-horse Concord wagon to Spanish Creek. Will and Belle charged three dollars each way for transport, and twelve dollars per week (two dollars per day) for room, board, and horse.

The summer of 1906 Will hired his nephews—John and Lawrence Wylie—the sons of his brother, John and his wife, Minnie, to work at his Spanish Creek ranch. John's job was to pack food to sheepherders who tended flocks in mountainous terrain in the Lower Gallatin Canyon about four miles from the ranch. That summer, the herder up Squaw Creek counted his sheep and came up two hundred short. John noticed the animals hoofing their way along Castle Rock, a half mile south of Squaw Creek, and headed back to the ranch, intending to collect his Uncle Will, now the "Chaser of Lost Sheep." Will and John mounted their favorite saddle horses, and with a pack horse on a lead, they rode to Castle Rock, where they camped for the night. The next morning, they picked their way through the logs and downed timber that covered the mountainside.

As they climbed the steep terrain, the men dismounted and walked, leading their horses by the reins. Will's horse—a high-spirited, flighty, young bay—pranced this way and that, prompting him to tie its reins together and loop his arm through the reins. Suddenly a branch from a fallen tree poked the horse in the flank. The horse reared, lost her footing, and rolled, Will in tow. Thirty feet down the mountainside, Will freed himself from the reins. He stood up, shook himself. He escaped with cuts, bruises, and a pair of broken glasses. The horse, however, continued to bounce down the mountain, then flew up in the air, spun about, and hit the ground with a thud, wedged in fallen timber. Will ordered John down the mountain with his six-shooter, knowing that his nephew would find the bay severely wounded, with a broken back, certainly broken legs. He gave his nephew permission to shoot the young bay.

Later in life, John recounted the story to his son. He recalled the horror of watching the horse's terrible fall. As he picked his way down the perilous slopes of Castle Rock, his teeth chattered and his knees knocked. When he came to the horse, he found the bay gasping for her last breaths. Standing directly in front of the dying animal, he aimed the six-shooter, fired, and shot her between the ears. Missing his mark entirely, he aimed again, this time hitting the horse in the forehead and killing it. Will and John located the horse's saddle and bridle on the timber-covered hillside, but some valuable field glasses that were attached to the saddle remained lost on Castle Rock. They resumed searching for the lost sheep with one saddle horse and the pack animal. When they had located the two hundred sheep—a challenge that required two more nights under the stars—they herded them back to the mother flock.

∾

Although the Wylie dude ranching operation closed after one year, Will's Spanish Creek ranch remained a natural respite from the road in Gallatin Canyon, where travelers often stopped for a meal or overnight stay. In 1907 Wylie sold his ranch at Cherry Creek to Harry Child, although he continued to run sheep, horses, and cattle on his properties at Spanish Creek, Elk Creek, and Middle Creek. In 1908, Wylie sold 1,250 head of Aberdeen Angus at $80 a head, making a tidy sum of $100,000.

Soon after Wylie sold his Cherry Creek ranch to Harry Child in 1907, one of his cattle ranching neighbors, Charles Anceney Jr., the son of French immigrants, needed cash. Anceney offered to winter Child's one thousand Yellowstone Park horses on his land at Spanish Creek. Anceney returned healthy horses to Child the following spring, and their relationship flourished for the next several years.

In 1912, believing that horse transportation was outdated in Yellowstone National Park and travel by automobile and bus was the future of transportation in the Park, Anceney and Child ceased their horse ranching operations and turned solely to raising cattle at Spanish Creek. In 1913 and 1914 the men formed a partnership and bought up all the land they could in the Spanish Creek area, a large portion of it from Will Wylie. The two gentlemen called their ranch the Flying D.[19]

∾

After the Wylies left Yellowstone, spending more time in Pasadena, California, the Wylie Permanent Camping Company endured, but it was a very different company. Miles shut down or renovated camps, opened another in the Camp Roosevelt area, and purchased a great deal of new equipment and furnishings that enhanced the travel accommodations. He expanded and rearranged the capacity of all camps to handle tour groups—both small and large (upwards of one hundred guests)—in contrast to the Willow Park camp of seasons past with its ability to accommodate sixty guests. Guests chose from four-room, two-room, or single-bed tent configurations.

The inaugural See America First conference in January 1906 focused on a "western booster campaign" that encouraged Americans who "spent more than $150 million touring Europe during the 1904–5 touring season" to become "better citizens" by learning about their "own land."[20] The following spring Miles dismantled the Willow Park camp—a favorite mosquito haunt where Wylie and Moorman were kept awake nights by bears. Miles created a new camp at Swan Lake, located north of Willow Park and closer to Mammoth Springs, where he showcased a number of new tents that featured wainscoting from the floorboards four feet up the walls. Builders also constructed a new kitchen with modern stoves, wash basins, and cooking gadgets. The dining tent featured new tables, benches, linens, china, and utensils. Miles also installed flush toilets at the camp and purchased new Concord coaches as well as harnesses and stage horses.

Under Miles' guidance, Gardiner's Wylie Hotel received a new addition, plus new kitchen equipment and furnishings.

A hungry, enthusiastic crowd make their way to a Wylie Camping Company dining tent in 1905. Wylie recalled that of the many wonders in the Park, one of the greatest the tourist meets is "his or her own appetite." *Courtesy, Yellowstone National Park Photo Archives. YELL 43686*

Several of Wylie's former employees were retained by A. W. Miles and helped him efficiently run and develop his business for years. Ed Moorman worked in a variety of positions, from company warehouse manager to company auditor. Eventually he became the company's general manager. After an absence of several years, Margaret "Lady Mac" McCartney returned to the Park and was hired as the company's "general matron," likely supervising women employees such as dining tent staff and housekeepers. She went on to manage Canyon Lodge, retiring from that position in 1934.

"Uncle Tom" Richardson did not fare as well as Moorman and McCartney. Late in 1905 the federal government constructed wooden steps on a portion of his trail into the Canyon of the Yellowstone River. Richardson worried that the new steps would make it easier for tourists to hike along his Canyon trail without need for his guiding services. In addition, before approving Richardson's permit for the 1906 season, Secretary of the Interior Ethan Hitchcock insisted that he reduce his rate from one dollar to fifty cents per person. Although Richardson received a permit for 1906, "no more letters from him reporting tourist numbers or other relevant sources have been found."[21] Both Wylie and Moorman recalled in their memoirs that "Uncle Tom's" livelihood suffered as a result of this intervention by the federal government. Moorman remembered that Richardson tried, without success, to obtain a permit for several years following 1906.

In 1906, Arthur W. Miles hired the remarkable Howard H. Hays as his assistant. An enthusiastic advocate of camping in Yellowstone from the beginning, Hays was an advocate of not just any camping, but of camping the "Wylie Way." "In reality the well known slogan, 'Wylie Way' owes its origin to Mr. Hays," Wylie wrote in his memoirs. "He so thoroughly worked this into the minds of the general public that it is hard to separate it from the fine permanent structures which today [1926] have taken the place of canvas abodes for guests."[22]

The Wylie Permanent Camping Company held the only lease for permanent camps until 1913, when the Shaw and Powell Camping Company received permission from the Interior Department to set up permanent camps at Willow Park, Old Faithful, Bridge Bay, and Canyon. Headquartered in Livingston, Montana, Amos Shaw and John Powell had operated movable camps since 1898, but were encouraged by the Wylies' success with permanent stations throughout the Park.

∾

Across the country, from Wyoming to Washington, D.C., there were rumblings of dissatisfaction with Yellowstone Park's military guardians around the turn of the twentieth century. Most soldiers stationed at the Park were inexperienced outdoorsmen who were poorly paid, and trained by the military to think in a top-down, military fashion, while the bulk of the matters in the Park were civilian in nature.[23] In addition, the federal government paid handsomely to finance the U.S.

Army's management of Yellowstone National Park. President Theodore Roosevelt asked Superintendent S. B. M. Young, who served a second stint in the Park from May 1907 to October 1908, to study alternatives to army management of the Park, such as a civilian guard.

Young responded that costs could be slashed from $150,000 to $50,000 if civilians, specifically a Yellowstone National Park Guard, assumed the duties of the military troops. Young expressed a great deal of concern about the army's lack of selection criteria for meeting the demands of a Park assignment in his 1907 Annual Report to the Secretary of the Interior. This practice, Young stated, was "an injustice to the Park."[24] Young was worried because military regiments and squadrons were divided into small groups, separated due of the nature of their duties by time and space, often without the consistent guidance of an officer. He suggested a Yellowstone National Park Guard of twenty men be established and administered by an assistant inspector.

President Roosevelt read the report but hesitated. At his Conservation Conference of Governors at the White House, May 13–15, 1908, he spoke very little about the national parks.

J. Horace McFarland of the American Civic Association, an observer of the battle for Yosemite's Hetch Hetchy Valley, pressured Interior Secretary Richard A. Ballinger to lobby for a bureau of national parks and resorts that had an able administrator and qualified superintendents. Ballinger recommended the idea in his annual report of 1910. As a result of McFarland's unwavering advocacy for a single government bureau and Ballinger's support for that idea, all national park superintendents gathered for six days in Yellowstone, beginning on September 10, 1911, to examine the national park problem and to advocate for a bureau of national parks.[25]

On February 2, 1912, President Taft articulated his support for a bureau in a special address to Congress, stating:

> Such legislation is essential to the proper management of these wonderful manifestations of nature, so startling and so beautiful that everyone recognizes the obligations of the government to preserve them for the edification and recreation of the people. The Yellowstone Park, the Yosemite, the Grand Canyon of the Colorado, the

Glacier National Park, and the Mount Rainier National Park and others furnish appropriate instances.[26]

While various congressional committees and hearings considered the implementation of new management over the next several years, the Department of the Interior started an ad hoc park service in the hectic office of a department attorney who was assisted by a clerk with full-time responsibilities for other department matters.

In March 1915 Stephen T. Mather, newly appointed as First Assistant to the Secretary of the Interior, launched an aggressive campaign for the National Park Service. At a conference housed at the University of California at Berkeley, Mather gathered together and initiated a dialogue among park superintendents, officials from the Interior and War Departments, concessioners, conservationists, park supporters, and members of Congress. The timing of the conference coincided with a flurry of activity taking place across the bay in San Francisco's Marina District—the enthusiastic marketing of domestic travel as a safe alternative to European destinations during World War I.

For the better part of 1915, San Francisco hosted over eighteen million visitors to the Panama-Pacific International Exposition. Once again, the sun shone on the See America First crusade. American railroads enthusiastically promoted the country's national parks. On four and a half acres and at a cost of "half a million dollars," the Union Pacific Railroad created a "best of Yellowstone" exhibit, including a replica of Old Faithful. The Santa Fe Railroad countered with their creation of the Grand Canyon on six acres. The Great Northern Railway focused on Glacier National Park; the Southern Pacific on Yosemite and its marvelous sequoias. A "ritual of citizenship" included a stopover at "one or more" of the country's national parks before returning home; an opportunity to discover "America's greatest achievement—and destination."[27]

Alfred Runte wrote that "no individual inspired the National Park Service...it came entirely from American culture." Representative William Kent of California, a high-ranking conservationist, sponsored legislation, H.R. 15522, supporting the creation of a national park service and the House of Representatives passed the legislation on July 1, 1916. Then, Senator Reed Smoot of Utah introduced a similar bill in the Senate, where it passed on August 5, 1916. While Kent and Smoot's pull plus the determination of Mather's energetic assistant, Horace Albright, combined to help passage of the National Park Service Act, Runte states that by "asking the American public to believe in parks...all could take credit for the breakthrough that came on August 25, 1916,"[28] the day the act was signed into law by President Woodrow Wilson.

In the fall of 1916, National Park Service director Stephen T. Mather invited all Yellowstone concessioners to a conference in Washington, D.C. In Wylie's opinion, the increasing number of Park leases caused the federal government to question the role of competition in Yellowstone National Park. The federal government now wondered if this increase in Park competition was a good thing—creating lower prices and more selection—or as Wylie wondered, if this trend simply confused the public. Mather informed the conference participants that his goal was to allow one hotel company, one transportation company, and one permanent camping company to operate in Yellowstone. The Yellowstone Park Hotel Company continued to manage the hotels. The Yellowstone National Park Transportation Company took on sole responsibility for transportation as it made the switch from horses to motorbuses. F. Jay Haynes devoted his energies to his photography enterprise. Finally, the Wylie Permanent Camping Company merged with the Shaw and Powell Camping Company. A. W. Miles remained president of the company (known as the Wylie Permanent Camping Company until 1917). He (and silent partner Child) held 51 percent of the stock, while the Shaw and Powell Camping Company held 49 percent. Wylie maintained that most participants left the conference feeling that Mather achieved his goal in a fair and honest manner. He wrote in his memoir: "Long may the new system of parks control last."[29]

In 1916, "the new system of parks control" was not the only remnant of Will and Mary Ann's years in Yellowstone National Park being discussed at their now-permanent residence in Pasadena, California. With Elizabeth, Fred, Clinton, and their families close at hand in other Los Angeles neighborhoods, the Wylies expressed their frustration with the Wylie Permanent Camping Company's failure to respect the parties' agreement of December 28, 1905. This agreement outlined regular payments for Will's goodwill, support, and his promise not to carry out business in the Park.

Will filed suit in Bozeman, Gallatin County, against the Wylie Permanent Camping Company. His brother, John M. Wylie, was also listed as a plaintiff, as their relationship was most likely financial as well as familial. Yellowstone National Park historians have yet to reach a conclusion about the timing of Will and John's lawsuit, some eight years after Miles discontinued the agreement in August 1907.[30]

Tom McKee, who was married to Elizabeth, Will and Mary Ann's daughter, and George Y. Patten represented Will and John. Judge Ben B. Law, a former stage driver in Yellowstone during the 1905 season when Moorman acted as the company's superintendent of transportation, presided over the trial. A. W. Miles also attended the trial.

Will alleged that the Wylie Permanent Camping Company failed to honor its agreement with him, specifically that they were unwilling and refused to pay the July 1, 1908, installment of $750 plus each subsequent installment for his goodwill, assistance, and promise not to conduct business in Yellowstone National Park. The plaintiffs, Will and John Wylie, asked for a judgment of $12,000 with 8 percent interest and costs. Ed Moorman concluded that the request amounted to approximately $40,000.

Moorman received a letter from Will before the trial. In the letter, Will stated that he depended on Ed's support as his "star witness." Mary Ann traveled to Gardiner to discuss the suit with Moorman. Moorman discouraged the Wylies from pursuing legal action, but they disregarded his advice. Moorman was subpoenaed as a witness and attended the trial. When he told Tom McKee that he felt obligated to disclose Will's letter, he was "relieved by the plaintiff."[31]

In their response to Will and John's request for a judgment of $12,000 plus 8 percent interest and costs, the Wylie Permanent Camping Company denied not honoring their agreement with Wylie, declaring that their agreement with Will of December 28, 1905, was "in so far as it purported to be a sale of the goodwill of the business was without consideration and void."[32]

During the trial, Will testified about the development of his Yellowstone National Park business from 1883 to 1905, the year of its sale. From 1905 to 1916, he went on to state, he and Mary Ann received letters from tourists asking for travel suggestions, and they always encouraged Yellowstone enthusiasts to travel with the Wylie Permanent Camping Company. Will acknowledged that, after August 1907, neither the company nor its officers asked him for his services. At the point of sale, however, there was no mention of transferring his goodwill, license, or anything similar. Will recalled Miles' letter of August 29, 1907. A final check accompanied Miles' notice that Will's services were no longer needed. Will remembered his own letter of September 1, 1907. He reminded Miles that "You will see by reading the contract for yearly salary that it was made for goodwill of business." He protested "that he could 'not be cut off in this abrupt manner.'"[33]

Judge Law overruled a motion for a non-suit. Officers of the Wylie Permanent Camping Company refused an opportunity to testify, believing that only questions of law and a verdict remained.

After deliberations, the jury returned with "a verdict in the sum of $16,480," and a judgment was "entered for that amount with interest."[34] Judge Law overruled the defendant's motion for a new trial.

Nevertheless, the Wylies' opinion that Wylie Permanent Camping Company payments were for goodwill and the reinforcement of that position in the Gallatin County courtroom placed the Wylies in legal peril. In the long run, they might have been better off legally if they had tied the payments to their support of the Wylie Permanent Camping Company. For example, the Wylies could have asked for a referral fee for recommending the company to potential Yellowstone tourists or for compensation for the time it took them to respond to tourists' letters.

Will Wylie did not discuss the financial details related to the sale of his company, his understanding of the laws pertaining to goodwill, or the 1916 Gallatin County trial in his memoir; therefore, the basis of the family's perception about goodwill did not come to light until four years later when the 1916 judgment and denial of a new trial resulted in arguments before the Montana Supreme Court in Helena, case number 4047 dated January 14, 1920—*Wylie et al., Respondents, v. Wylie Permanent Camping Co., Appellant.*

On the train to Helena, Ed Moorman discussed the case with Tom McKee and George Patten, who once again acted as Will and John Wylie's legal representatives. When Will sold his company, Moorman argued with Patten, he sold his goodwill and his name as well. Edward C. Day and Thomas Mapes, legal counsel for the Wylie Permanent Camping Company, shared Moorman's position, arguing that it violated the Revised Code of Montana of 1907, expressly sections 5057 and 5058, which basically state that Wylie had no goodwill that he could sell, therefore the suit in Gallatin County "was void for lack of consideration."[35]

The contract, the appellant argued, could be terminated by either party. Miles' letter of August 29, 1907, to Will Wylie was cited as an end to the agreement. The Wylie Permanent Camping Company also asserted that legal action by the respondents exceeded the statute of limitations and failed to provide enough evidence to support the judgment.

Associate Justice Charles H. Cooper delivered the Montana Supreme Court's opinion. He avowed that the court's decision must consider the basic truth about a stockholder's sale of stock: "the goodwill of the business goes with it, leaving nothing tangible or of substance upon which to found another consideration touching any part of the same subject-matter. If that be so, all other questions law and fact here presented are subordinate to, and controlled completely by, that issue."[36]

Justice Cooper conceded some merit in Wylie et al.'s insistence that "the goodwill of a business is the expectation of continued patronage (Rev. Code, sec. 4566); is property subject to ownership and capable of being transferred (sec. 4567)."[37] Justice Cooper also noted that there may be agreement between parties stipulating that the seller will not operate "a similar business within a specified territory" while the buyer "or any other person deriving title to the goodwill from him, carries on a like business therein (sec. 5058)."[38] However, he wrote that when Wylie sold the contract and his shares in the Wylie Camping Company, "he separated himself from and parted with the goodwill and delivered himself of all he had to transfer. Goodwill is not a thing apart, but an incident to and inherent in the thing itself—the business."[39]

As evidence of Wylie's single-mindedness about goodwill, Justice Cooper pointed to Wylie's letter of September 1, 1907, in which Wylie tied his yearly salary to the goodwill of the business, and Wylie's testimony during the Gallatin County trial:

> I asked Mr. Child what he expected of me in the nature of duties. He said repeatedly, 'I expect no services from you; I do not care if you don't turn a hand over—if you and Mrs. Wylie would like to go up and ride around the Park once in a while, we would be glad to have you do it; but otherwise, all that we want is your goodwill and that you stay out of the business—' that is the object of this writing. At the close of the conversation I took my copy of the contract and left. * * * But my understanding all the time of the value they were getting was for me keeping out of the Park and for the goodwill and use they were making of my name. * * *
>
> Q. The services which you rendered in forwarding these letters to people telling or suggesting to them how they should go or how to arrange parties and things of that kind—those services were comparatively insignificant?
>
> A. Not insignificant, but not what I bring this suit for.
>
> Q. You don't mean to tell this jury that your services in forwarding letters and recommending people visit Yellowstone Park, by the Wylie way, is worth $1,500 a year, do you?
>
> A. Hardly that.[40]

Justice Cooper concluded that Wylie viewed the sale of goodwill as the "essential element of the contract sued on."[41] After citing several cases, he reasoned that Wylie's goodwill was "incidental to the corporate business and accompanied the transfer to Messrs. Child and Miles of this contract with, and his stock in, the Wylie Camping Company. Upon this ground alone the action loses its foundation and must fail."[42] Justice Copper reversed the judgment and order, "with directions to dismiss the action."[43]

Chief Justice Theodore Brantly and Associate Justices William Holloway, John Matthews, and John Hurly concurred.

Ed Moorman remembered that Wylie's award amounted to one dollar.

On March 3, 1920, the Montana Supreme Court denied a request for rehearing.

∾

With the union of camping businesses as the Yellowstone Park Camping Company and the introduction of motor vehicles into the Park,[44] many of the old camps and stations became a fond memory. Wylie camps at Swan Lake, Old Faithful, and Canyon plus lunch stations on the Gibbon, at Thumb, and at Riverside (near the Park's western entrance) were abandoned, as were the Shaw and Powell Camping Company camps at Willow Park and Bridge Bay. Five permanent camps remained: a new site at Mammoth, a former Shaw and Powell site near Old Faithful, the longtime site (now the lodge locale) of Wylie's Lake camp, a Shaw and Powell site at Canyon, and a Wylie locale near Tower (now Camp Roosevelt).

Howard H. Hays assumed ownership and the titles of company president and manager in 1920. He modified the company name slightly to Yellowstone Park Camps Company. Hays' reputation as tourist expert extraordinaire was known the world over, not just among national park concessioners, but by railroad companies, too.[45] Under his guidance, the Yellowstone Park Camps Company increased in popularity and efficiency.[46] By 1924, Hays' health forced him to retire. He sold the company to Vernon Goodwin of California, a businessman with close ties to that state's hospitality industry, and Billie Nichols, Harry Child's "second-in-command"; with the "omnipresent A.L. Smith, Child's Helena banker and front man," named as secretary and treasurer. The new purchase was christened Yellowstone Park Lodge and Camps Company,[47] with Ed Moorman as general manager. Many old-timers, Will Wylie included, still referred to the business as the Yellowstone Camps.

∾

In 1917, Will and Mary Ann accepted an invitation from the Union Pacific Railroad to establish "Wylie Way" camps in Zion Canyon at Utah's Mukuntuweap National Monument[48] and at Bright Angel Point on the north rim of the Grand Canyon. Earlier that same year, President Wilson signed a war resolution and the country formally entered World War I. Will was all too aware of the war as a mighty obstacle to tourist travel anywhere,[49] but he, Mary Ann, and Clinton persevered with assistance from Margaret "Lady Mac" McCartney, who had worked with them for many years in Yellowstone. On a 1917 tour of "a new world of parks" that include a stopover in Zion, National Park Service advocate Horace Albright was introduced to "an old man, W.W. Wylie." Albright recalled:

> Well, I was amazed. I had never met him before but knew all about him, as he had originated the permanent camp system in Yellowstone, selling out there years before. His so-called Wylie Way was so efficient and popular that it was copied by the Currys in Yosemite. I knew of his integrity, honesty, and knowledge of national park standards…The Interior Department had already granted him a five-year lease for the camp and added the transportation franchise too…I trusted Wylie's experience in Yellowstone and felt he would make a valuable contribution to solving concession problems.[50]

The Wylies operated their Zion camp for seven years, even after Clinton's death in 1922. Elizabeth Wylie McKee managed the Grand Canyon camp for ten years with the assistance of her husband, Tom, and their son, Robert.

Because Zion's climate allows a longer tourist season than Yellowstone's, the Union Pacific considered the need for a big hotel. At seventy-six years of age, Wylie could not imagine investing in such a venture. As a result, he and Mary Ann agreed to the railroad's offer to buy them out in 1924. Full ownership of the Grand Canyon camp belonged to Elizabeth for the next three years until the Union Pacific invested millions in developing the Grand Canyon Lodge complex, and the railroad's subsidiary, the Utah Parks Company, bought her out as well.

Until the Wylies established camps in Zion, the Mormon locals failed to see the national monument as attractive to the touring public. The local bishop told Wylie that area residents looked upon the Great White Throne and the Court of Patriarchs with irritation; the natural wonders took up more than their fair share of space— ground that could be used for pasture. However, the bishop stated, as people discovered that others thought the national monument worth a look, attitudes changed.

The Wylies found that tourists expressed as much interest in the conscientious Mormons as in Zion itself. They wanted to know about the Mormon religion. Why do they haul every tenth load of alfalfa to the tithing barns? Why does one-tenth of their pay end up at the bishop's home?

The Wylies purchased vegetables, fruit, eggs, and butter from the Mormons. A large variety of top-quality fruit was readily available from throughout the county. Wylie maintained that many of the fine kinds of melons grown in California's Imperial Valley thrived in the region around Zion with better results.

He recommended: "When you visit Zion Park stay long enough to meet and know these fine Mormon people. We count them among our best friends." He went on to add: "Could you have seen the reception they gave Mrs. Wylie and me in the fall of 1925, while we visited them and the park, you would understand why I speak thus of them."[51]

Prior to the stop in Zion, Will and Mary Ann were the guests of Vernon Goodwin during Yellowstone's 1925 tourist season, the first time the Wylies had stepped foot in the Park since 1905. Wylie struggled for words to convey the pleasure and surprise he experienced on the tour—pleasure due to the consideration shown to them at all stations as countless times people heralded them as the innovators of the Yellowstone Camps method of touring, and surprise at the vast numbers of tourists and comforts offered. Once again, the Park's wonders amazed the Wylies with their awe-inspiring beauty and originality. Wylie expressed satisfaction that, regardless of life's unexpected turns, the wonders remained the same as when he, Mary Ann, and their family and friends lived, labored, loved, and laughed among them. He marveled at the improved roads,[52] the quick and cushy transport in yellow buses, the well-mannered drivers (their cussing cut to a bare minimum), and superb dining room service—all of which combined to make the stay in Yellowstone an honest-to-goodness joy.

During this 1925 visit, seventy-seven-year-old Wylie took the opportunity to hike halfway down "Uncle Tom's Trail." He recalled, with great fondness, his relationship with "Uncle Tom" Richardson, who had died several years before:

> When the goodly number of tourists making the trip this day under care of a competent guide, were resting on a landing for the purpose, found I was Mr. Wylie, they at once beset me to tell them the story of Uncle Tom. I know of nothing other than this trip within the bounds of Yellowstone Park that will give so much genuine satisfaction for the energy expended, as does this trip to the foot of the Great Falls of the Yellowstone River. I urge all who have sound hearts, to "Do" it. Uncle Tom hardly dreamed, while so often crossing and recrossing the Yellowstone River with his boat loads of jolly visitors, that he would so early be called to cross that dark river over which the boat goes but one way. I feel sure that the severe exertion he so cheerfully forced his strong body to endure in this trail climbing, hastened the ending of his life.[53]

The next time the Wylies rendezvoused with their extended Park family would be in the future state, the "Happy Hunting Grounds… that country [where] all languages will be understood."[54]

After their Yellowstone tour, Will and Mary Ann continued on to Zion and from there to their Emerson Street home in Pasadena. At the urging of many who knew them during their Wylie Camping Company years—among them college presidents, former Park superintendents, educators, and friends—Will wrote of his experiences, not simply of his twenty-five years of service in Yellowstone but also of his knowledge of change in the Park—change wrought by man, change wrought by nature—and of his interest in the Park's "wildlife," both man and beast. Details of the 1916 lawsuit and subsequent appeal were conspicuously absent.

Organized thematically by anecdote, William Wallace Wylie's unpublished manuscript was completed in 1926. In 1966, Paul R. Wylie of Bozeman, fifth child of John and Minnie Wylie, obtained the manuscript from his cousin and Fred's daughter, Mary Lou Wylie Wardle of Los Angeles. Paul Wylie donated his uncle's recollections to the historical manuscripts section (Burlingame Special Collections) of Montana State University with the understanding that the original copy be forwarded to the William W. Wylie collection at the Yellowstone National Park Museum in Mammoth. The reminiscence of Edward H. Moorman, Park loyalist 1899–1936, found its way to Paul via Margaret McCartney's niece. It was also included. At approximately the same time, other surviving family members received copies of Wylie's manuscript.[55]

∾

Mary Ann Wilson Wylie died at home on February 6, 1928, from multiple spinal sclerosis complicated by pernicious anemia. She and Wylie would have celebrated their fifty-fourth wedding anniversary on April 2.

William Wallace Wylie lived the last twenty-five years of his life sciatica-free. An operation on February 6, 1930, to remove a cancer from his lower lip and chin resulted in his death the following day at the Los Angeles County General Hospital.

Elizabeth Wylie McKee and Fred Wilson Wylie continued to live with their respective families in California.

∾

During Yellowstone's stagecoach era from 1878 to 1916, the Wylie Camping Company became the equal of all that is good about the balance between frugality and safety, informality, down-to-earth employees, relaxation around campfires, and fascinating interpretation about the Park's natural wonders. The company attracted thousands of the growing number of middle-class tourists seeking to expand their opportunities through knowledge and adventure, as well as countless guests with wealth who tired of hotel formalities. Wylie Camping Company guests arrived in the Park in search of a genuine, democratic, and personal experience—an experience that exposed Yellowstone's personality and its accompanying peerless, natural beauty.

The Wylie Camping Company's practice of hiring sincere, energetic college students and teachers established a standard for concessions in Yellowstone and other parks around the nation—it encouraged and satisfied guests' curiosity about the Park's wonders in a patient, kind, and humorous manner. Wylie held fast to his inclination for teaching: he appreciated the value of accurate commentary as a way to change his guests' perceptions about nature and science, in hopes of encouraging an authentic Park visit. His effort to bring guiding to a notch above "bell hop and/or guide" challenged the hotels to improve their own tourism services. The National Park Service's post-World War I endorsement of the "educational use of the parks" and the work of former Yellowstone Park Association employee Milton P. Skinner, at an information office opened at Mammoth in 1920 and his championship of a government educational service, were tributes to Wylie's legacy of factual park tours.[56]

During the 1930s—on a train from Bozeman to Los Angeles—the conductor scrutinized a ticket belonging to John and Minnie Wylie's oldest child, Mary, and inquired if she was related to Will Wylie. Mary replied that she was his niece.

The conductor explained that for many years he'd "been on the run" between Livingston and Gardiner and was very well acquainted with her uncle. "Those were the good old days. Nobody ever enjoys any trip now the way the tourists enjoyed that trip through Yellowstone 'The Wylie Way.'"[57]

Notes

Introduction

1. Hal K. Rothman, *Devil's Bargains: Tourism in the Twentieth-Century American West* (Lawrence, KS: University of Kansas Press, 1998), 23, 38.
2. Cindy S. Aron, *Working At Play: A History of Vacations in the United States* (New York, NY: Oxford University Press, 1999), 4, 128.
3. Elizabeth Ann Watry, "More Than Mere Camps and Coaches: The Wylie Camping Company and the Development of a Middle-Class Leisure Ethic in Yellowstone National Park, 1883-1916" (master's thesis, Montana State University, 2010), v, 2; John A. Jakle, *The Tourist: Travel in Twentieth-Century North America* (Lincoln, NE: University of Nebraska Press, 1985), 1.
4. Aron, *Working at Play*, 4.
5. David M. Wrobel, "Introduction: Tourists, Tourism, and the Toured Upon," in *Seeing and Being Seen, Tourism in the American West*, ed. by David M. Wrobel and Patrick T. Long (University Press of Kansas, 2001), 1, 3.
6. Aron, *Working at Play*, 131
7. John F. Sears, *Sacred Places: American Tourist Attractions in the Nineteenth Century* (Amherst, MA: University of Massachusetts Press, 1998), 3.
8. W.W. Wylie to Mary Ann Wilson Wylie, March 1, 1898, Collection 1326, Burlingame Special Collections, Montana State University, Bozeman, MT.
9. Paul Schullery, *Searching for Yellowstone: Ecology and Wonder in the Last Wilderness* (Helena, MT: Montana Historical Society Press, 2004), 103.
10. Sears, *Sacred Places*, 165.
11. Jakle, *The Tourist*, 7.
12. Sears, *Sacred Places*, 8, 179.
13. Lee H. Whittlesey, *Storytelling in Yellowstone: Horse and Buggy Tour Guides* (Albuquerque, NM: University of New Mexico Press, 2007), 265.
14. Aron, *Working at Play*, 43, 111, 128.
15. Ibid., 4, 162, 172.
16. Jakle, *The Tourist*, 4.
17. Lee H. Whittlesey, ed., *Lost in Yellowstone: Truman Everts's "Thirty-Seven Days of Peril"* (Salt Lake City, UT: The University of Utah Press, 1995), xxiii.
18. William Wallace Wylie, "Autobiography, 1926," Collection 343, Burlingame Special Collections, Montana State University, Bozeman, MT, 1.
19. Lee H. Whittlesey, *Storytelling in Yellowstone*, 1.
20. Patricia Nelson Limerick, "Seeing and Being Seen: Tourism in the American West," in *Seeing and Being Seen*, ed. by Wrobel and Long, 55.
21. Mark David Spence, *Dispossessing the Wilderness: Indian Removal and the Making of the National Parks* (New York, NY: Oxford University Press, 1999), 59.
22. Wylie, "Autobiography, 1926," Foreword.
23. Ibid.

Chapter One: Fully Reimbursed for Any Hardships

1. Wylie, "Autobiography, 1926," 2.
2. Ibid.
3. Earl Pomeroy, *In Search of the Golden West: The Tourist in Western America* (Lincoln: University of Nebraska Press, 1990), 60.
4. Roderick Frazier Nash, *Wilderness & The American Mind* (New Haven: Yale University Press, 2001), xii, xiii, 28, 29; Pomeroy, *In Search of the Golden West*, 72.
5. Spence, *Dispossessing the Wilderness*, 30, 31; Elliot West, *The Last Indian War: The Nez Perce Story* (New York: Oxford University Press, 2009), 177.
6. West, *The Last Indian War*, 177.
7. Ibid., 218–23.
8. "What Did Things Cost in 1872?" www.choosingvoluntarysimplicity.com/what-did-things-cost-in-1872/, accessed June 1, 2010. Eggs cost 30 cents/dozen, milk cost 8 cents/quart, and salt pork, 11 cents/pound.
9. Thomas J. Schlereth, *Victorian American: Transformations in Everyday Life 1876–1915* (New York: Harper Collins Publishing, 1991), 91.
10. Veris A. Wessel, "A Brief History of the Bozeman Schools," Collection 2245, Merrill G. Burlingame Papers 1880–1990, Box 9, folder 23, Montana State University, Bozeman, MT, circa 1963, 14 and addendum.
11. Wylie, "Autobiography, 1926," 3.
12. Carlos A. Schwantes, "No Aid and No Comfort: Early Transportation and the Origins of Tourism in the Northern West," in *Seeing and Being Seen,* ed. by Wrobel and Long, 128.
13. Ibid., 129.
14. Wylie, "Autobiography, 1926," 3.
15. Ibid.
16. Ibid., 4.
17. Ibid., 5.
18. Ibid.
19. Ibid., 5-6.
20. West, *The Last Indian War,* 95–96.
21. Ibid., 258–63.
22. Ibid., 226–27 and Wylie, "Autobiography, 1926," 8–9.
23. Wylie, "Autobiography, 1926," 7.
24. Schwantes, "No Aid and No Comfort," 127.
25. Ibid., 130–31; William E. Lass, *Navigating the Missouri: Steamboating on Nature's Highway, 1819-1935,* 236.
26. Wylie, "Autobiography, 1926," 7.
27. Ibid., 8.
28. Ibid.
29. Ibid.
30. Ibid., 9.
31. Schullery, *Searching for Yellowstone,* 90.

32. Schullery, *Searching for Yellowstone*, 24–25 and Spence, *Dispossessing the Wilderness*, 46-47.
33. Wylie, "Autobiography, 1926," 10-11.
34. Schullery, *Searching for Yellowstone*, 89.
35. Wylie, "Autobiography, 1926," 14.
36. Ibid., 15.

Chapter Two: Views of the Wonderland

1. Mark Daniel Barringer, *Selling Yellowstone: Capitalism and the Construction of Nature* (Lawrence, KS: University Press of Kansas, 2002), 18–19; Marguerite S. Shaffer, *See America First: Tourism and National Identity, 1880-1940* (Washington, DC: Smithsonian Books, 2001), 20–21.
2. Lee H. Whittlesey, "Everyone Can Understand a Picture," *Montana: The Magazine of Western History* 49:2 (1999): 6–7; "It's Vastly Different from Trips Made Today," *The Bozeman Daily Chronicle,* August 9, 1964.
3. Wylie, "Autobiography, 1926," 74.
4. "It's Vastly Different from Trips Made Today," *The Bozeman Daily Chronicle,* August 9, 1964.
5. Schullery, *Searching for Yellowstone*, 89.
6. Ibid., 100–101.
7. Wylie, "Autobiography, 1926," 75.
8. Ibid., 75–76; "Capture of the Harlowe Gang Surpasses Fiction," *The Bozeman Daily Chronicle,* August 9, 1964.
9. "Capture of the Harlowe Gang Surpasses Fiction," *The Bozeman Daily Chronicle,* August 9, 1964.
10. Wylie, "Autobiography, 1926," 76.
11. Ibid., 15.
12. Ibid.
13. Ibid.
14. Ibid.
15. When they arrived, Wylie and Calfee asked for the latest news about President James A. Garfield, who had been shot and wounded by Charles A. Guiteau as he was stepping on a train in Washington, D.C. Garfield was fighting for his life.
16. Wylie, "Autobiography, 1926," 16.
17. Alfred Runte, *National Parks: The American Experience* (Lanham, MD: Taylor Trade Publishing, 2010), 20.
18. Rothman, *Devil's Bargains*, 23.
19. Shaffer, *See America First*, 21.
20. Wylie, "Autobiography, 1926," 16.
21. Slayton Lyceum Bureau, *W.W. Wylie*, Burlingame Special Collections, Montana State University, Bozeman, MT, 1898.
22. Wylie, "Autobiography, 1926," 35.
23. Wylie, "Autobiography, 1926," 38. Chris J. Magoc, *Yellowstone: The Creation and Selling of An American Landscape, 1870–1903* (Albuquerque, NM: University of New Mexico Press, 1999), 9–10; Runte, *National Parks*, 32.

24. Wylie, "Autobiography, 1926," 50.
25. Ibid., 51.
26. Shaffer, *See America First*, 5.
27. Aron, *Working At Play*, 5.
28. Ibid., 49.
29. Wylie, "Autobiography, 1926," 17.
30. Runte, *National Parks*, 45.
31. Wylie, "Autobiography, 1926," 98.
32. House Committee on the Public Lands, *The Yellowstone Park*, 42nd Cong., 2nd sess., February 27, 1872, [1].
33. By 1881 there were 153 miles of road and 204 miles of trail in Yellowstone National Park. To reach the Geyser Basins, travelers had to cross Mary Mountain to the Yellowstone River and go south to Yellowstone Lake. The road continued north to Alum Creek, with a bridle path heading for Canyon, Dunraven Pass, and Tower Fall. From Mammoth, another road ventured east to Cooke City across Baronett Bridge. Five years later, the first vehicles rolled along the Norris cut-off road—the road sliced through thick stands of lodgepole pine, an impressive feat of road building—from Norris Geyser Basin to the Grand Canyon. By 1903 most travelers returning home from Canyon and Yellowstone Lake chose the Norris Canyon road rather than the Mary Mountain road.
34. William Wallace Wylie, *Yellowstone National Park; or The Great American Wonderland* (Kansas City, MO: Ramsey, Millet and Hudson, 1882), 10.
35. Ibid.
36. Rothman, *Devil's Bargains*, 23, 41 and Sears, *Sacred Places*, 163.
37. Magoc, *Yellowstone*, 92–93.
38. He also suggested that travelers consider taking along lunch provisions and telegraphing ahead for dinners. The Northern Pacific had built hotels and eating houses along the route, so there were plenty of places for the westbound travelers to stop, eat a fine meal, or rest themselves.
39. Wylie provided a table of distances between principal points in Yellowstone, as well as a summary of the Park's Rules and Regulations. He concluded his book with a variety of advertisements for local vendors: L.S. Willson Dry Goods, Walter Cooper—Rifles, Shotguns, and Revolvers, Bozeman's *Avant Courier*, a livery and feed store, a billiard and saloon, several attorneys, a blacksmith, book store, hardware, a painter, a grocery, a used wagon dealer, and a bank.
40. Schullery, *Searching for Yellowstone*, 20–26; Spence, *Dispossessing the Wilderness*, 57–60.
41. Rudolfo Anaya, "Why I Love Tourists: Confessions of a Dharma Bum," in *Seeing and Being Seen*, ed. by Wrobel and Long, 63.
42. Barringer, *Selling Yellowstone*, 20–21 and Schullery, *Searching for Yellowstone*, 110–11.
43. Aubrey L. Haines, *The Yellowstone Story* (Colorado Associated University Press, 1977), 1:263.
44. John A. Jakle, *The Tourist*, 68 and Spence, *Dispossessing the Wilderness*, 55.
45. Haines, *The Yellowstone Story*, 1:263–64.

46. Barringer, *Selling Yellowstone*, 24–25; Magoc, *Yellowstone*, 54; Schullery, *Searching for Yellowstone*, 92–93.

47. Haines, *The Yellowstone Story:* 1: 264–65.

48. Runte, *National Parks*, 47.

49. Magoc, *Yellowstone*, 69–70.

50. Wylie, "Autobiography, 1926," 37.

Chapter Three: Sagebrushing It

1. Rothman, *Devil's Bargains*, 45; Shaffer, *See America First*, 20–21.

2. Magoc, *Yellowstone*, 29–30, 34–35.

3. Aron, *Working At Play*, 156 –157, 162, 172; Barringer, *Selling Yellowstone*, 41.

4. Janet Cronin and Dorothy Vick, *Montana's Gallatin Canyon* (Missoula, MT: Mountain Press Publishing Company, 1992), 52.

5. Wylie, "Autobiography, 1926," 76.

6. Schullery, *Searching for Yellowstone*, 97–98.

7. Jakle, *The Tourist*, 67–68.

8. Runte, *National Parks*, 43.

9. Jakle, *The Tourist*, 68.

10. Nash, *Wilderness & The American Mind*, 67–69; Sears, *Sacred Places*, 6–7; Runte, *National Parks*, 44–45.

11. "Congressional Acts Pertaining to Yellowstone," http://www.yellowstone-online.com/history/yhfour.html, accessed August 3, 2004.

12. Shaffer, *See America First*, 5.

13. Barringer, *Selling Yellowstone*, 34; Magoc, *Yellowstone*, 22.

14. Schullery, *Searching for Yellowstone*, 91.

15. Ibid., 101.

16. Aron, *Working At Play*, 50–51, 67, 138.

17. Schullery, *Searching for Yellowstone*, 90.

18. Aron, *Working At Play*, 86–91.

19. Schullery, *Searching for Yellowstone*, 92–94.

20. Haines, *The Yellowstone Story*, 1:269.

21. Shaffer, *See America First*, 45.

22. Rothman, *Devil's Bargains*, 45; Runte, *National Parks*, 47–48.

23. Barringer, *Selling Yellowstone*, 26; Magoc, *Yellowstone*, 76–77; Schullery, *Searching for Yellowstone*, 89. See also Grank H. Goodyear III, *A President in Yellowstone: The F. Jay Haynes Photographic Album of Chester Arthur's 1883 Expedition* (Norman: University of Oklahoma Press, 2012).

24. Hiram Martin Chittenden and Richard A. Bartlett, eds., *The Yellowstone National Park* (Norman: University of Oklahoma Press, 1964), 129.

25. Jakle, *The Tourist*, 74.

26. Haines, *The Yellowstone Story*, 1:312.

27. Ibid., 2:36.

28. Ibid., 1:315–16; Magoc, *Yellowstone*, 75; Schullery, *Searching for Yellowstone*, 108.

29. Wylie, "Autobiography, 1926," 78.

30. Shaffer, *See America First*, 45–46.
31. Wylie, "Autobiography, 1926," 4–5.
32. Watry, "More Than Mere Camps and Coaches," 31.
33. Wylie, "Autobiography, 1926," 74.
34. Pomeroy, *In Search of the Golden West*, 122.
35. Aron, *Working At Play*, 85, 99, 140, 155, 157, 165–66.
36. Pomeroy, *In Search of the Golden West*, 122.
37. Rothman, *Devil's Bargains*, 14–15; Shaffer, *See America First*, 7–8; West, *The Last Indian War*, xx.
38. Aron, *Working At Play*, 131.
39. Minnie Stevenson Hughes to Max Goodsill, Collection 1797, Montana Historical Society Research Center, Helena, MT, December 23, 1969.

Chapter Four: Natural and Unnatural Curiosities

1. Watry, "More Than Mere Camps and Coaches," 31.
2. Wylie, "Autobiography, 1926," 19.
3. Nash, *Wilderness & The American Mind*, 8, 96, 143, 147.
4. Shaffer, *See America First*, 3, 52.
5. Schwantes, "No Aid and No Comfort," 135.
6. Schullery, *Searching for Yellowstone*, 104–105.
7. Magoc, *Yellowstone*, 96.
8. Wylie, "Autobiography, 1926," 36.
9. "The Washburn Expedition", http://www.yellowstone-online.com/history/trumbull/trumbill13.html, accessed July 29, 2010.
10. Wylie, "Autobiography, 1926," 80.
11. Ibid., 45.
12. Ibid., 73.
13. James A. Blanchard and George A. Lamar, *Application of William W. Wylie for a Lease in the Yellowstone National Park, with the Privilege of Furnishing Camping Accomodations; Brief in Support of Application*. Filed February 7, 1898 (Washington, D.C.: J.S. Tomlinson & Son, 1898), 8.
14. Ibid., 9.
15. Ibid.
16. Ibid.
17. George S. Anderson, *Report of the Superintendent of the Yellowstone National Park to the Secretary of the Interior* (Washington D.C.: Government Printing Office, 1892), 7.
18. Barringer, *Selling Yellowstone*, 31, 32, 38; Haines, *The Yellowstone Story*, 2:46.
19. Anderson, *Report of the Superintendent of the Yellowstone National Park* (1892), 7.
20. Mary Shivers Culpin, *"For the Benefit and Enjoyment of the People": A History of Concession Development in Yellowstone National Park, 1872–1966* (National Park Service, Yellowstone Center for Resources, Yellowstone National Park, Wyoming, YCR-CR-2003-01), 39.
21. Wylie, "Autobiography, 1926," 25.

22. James A. Blanchard and George A. Lamar, *Application of William W. Wylie for a Lease in the Yellowstone National Park.* Filed June 2, 1897 (Washington, D.C.: J.S. Tomlinson & Son, 1897), 9.
23. Watry, "More Than Mere Camps and Coaches," 40-41.
24. Michael P. Malone, Richard B. Roeder, and William L. Lang, *Montana: A History of Two Centuries*, Revised Edition (Seattle: University of Washington Press, 1991), 362.
25. "A New Elevator," *The Avant Courier*, April 29, 1893.
26. "A Fine Church Edifice," *The Avant Courier*, April 29, 1893.
27. Wylie, "Autobiography, 1926," 92.
28. George S. Anderson, *Report of the Superintendent of the Yellowstone National Park to the Secretary of the Interior* (Washington D.C.: Government Printing Office, 1894), 3.
29. Pomeroy, *In Search of the Golden West,* 134.
30. Chittenden and Bartlett, eds., *The Yellowstone National Park,* 121–22 .
31. Ibid., 121.
32. Haines, *The Yellowstone Story,* 2:62; Magoc, 159.
33. Spence, *Dispossessing the Wilderness,* 65.
34. Magoc, *Yellowstone,* 160.
35 "Congressional Acts Pertaining to Yellowstone," http://www.yellowstone-online.com/history/yhfour.html, p. 6, accessed August 3, 2004.
36. Ibid.
37. George S. Anderson, *Report of the Superintendent of the Yellowstone National Park to the Secretary of the Interior* (Washington D.C.: Government Printing Office, 1895), 3.
38. Ibid., 4.

Chapter Five: A New Way of Caring for Tourists

1. Barringer, *Selling Yellowstone*, 38–39; Shaffer, *See America First*, 45–46.
2. Culpin, *"For the Benefit and Enjoyment of the People,"* 43.
3. Barringer, *Selling Yellowstone*, 49.
4. Ibid., 45 and Schullery, *Searching for Yellowstone*, 92.
5. Wylie, "Autobiography, 1926," 66.
6. W.W. Wylie to Mary Ann Wilson Wylie, March 1, 1898, Collection 1326, Burlingame Special Collections, Montana State University, Bozeman, MT.
7. Aron, *Working At Play*, 147–48 and Watry, "More Than Mere Camps and Coaches," 60–64.
8. Magoc, *Yellowstone*, 115.
9. Schullery, *Searching for Yellowstone*, 115.
10. Watry, "More Than Mere Camps and Coaches," 42–43.
11. W.W. Wylie to Colonel S.B.M. Young, April 4, 1897, Yellowstone National Park Archives, Gardiner, MT. Wylie wrote: "I notice in the dispatches this evening that you are to be transferred to Fort Yellowstone. It has been my privilege to have an acquaintance with all the Army officers who have acted as Superintendents in the Park, and I think I can safely say that never before has a change

been so welcomed by many as in the present instance....Hoping and believing that our acquaintance will be mutually pleasant and agreeable."

12. Schullery, *Searching for Yellowstone*, 90.
13. Pomeroy, *In Search of the Golden West*, 134.
14. B.N. Austin to Edward Swift, approximately early 1897, Yellowstone National Park Archives.
15. Anderson to Edward Swift, approximately early 1897, Yellowstone National Park Archives.
16. Wylie to Chas S. Fee, May 7, 1897, Yellowstone National Park Archives.
17. Ibid.
18. Wylie to Captain George Anderson, May 22, 1897, Yellowstone National Park Archives.
19. Blanchard, James A., and George A. Lamar. *Application of William W. Wylie for a Lease in the Yellowstone National Park*. Filed February 7, 1898 (Washington, D.C.: J.S. Tomlinson & Son, 1898), 2.

Chapter Six: Mr. Wylie Goes to Washington

1. Schullery, *Searching for Yellowstone*, 112–15; Slayton Lyceum Bureau, *W.W. Wylie*, 1898.
2. Watry, "More Than Mere Camps and Coaches," 54-55.
3. Ibid., 55-56.
4. Wylie, "Autobiography, 1926," 28.
5. Watry, "More Than Mere Camps and Coaches," 52–53.
6. S. B. M. Young, *Report of the Acting Superintendent to the Department of the Interior* (Mammoth Hot Springs: Office of the Superintendent Yellowstone National Park, October 26, 1897), 18–20.
7. Ibid.
8. Ibid.
9. Magoc, *Yellowstone*, xiii.
10. Blanchard and Lamar. *Application of William W. Wylie for a Lease in the Yellowstone National Park*. Filed December 11, 1897, 12–13.
11. Wylie, "Autobiography, 1926," 81. Aubrey L. Haines notes in *The Yellowstone Story*, 2:101, that the term "savages" was initially reserved for stagecoach drivers, but eventually widened its appeal to include all employees of Yellowstone concessioners.
12. Rothman, *Devil's Bargains*, 11.
13. James A. Blanchard and George A. Lamar. *Application of William W. Wylie for a Lease in the Yellowstone National Park*. Filed February 7, 1898 (Washington, D.C.: J.S. Tomlinson & Son, 1898), 2, 6, 7, 19, 22–25.
14. Watry, "More Than Mere Camps and Coaches," 56–58.
15. Blanchard and Lamar. *Application of William W. Wylie for a Lease in the Yellowstone National Park*. Filed February 7, 1898, 24.
16. Ibid., 25.
17. W.W. Wylie to Mary Ann Wilson Wylie, February 12, 1898, Collection 1326, Burlingame Special Collections, Montana State University, Bozeman, MT.

18. Wylie paid eighteen cents for their lunch one day, Wylie wrote; Waters paid twenty-three cents on another occasion.
19. Haines, *The Yellowstone Story*, 2:48–49.
20. Slayton Lyceum Bureau, *W. W. Wylie.*
21. Ibid.
22. Nash, *Wilderness & The American Mind*, xiv.
23. Pomeroy, *In Search of the Golden West*, 139.
24. Runte, *National Parks*, 57.
25. Nash, *Wilderness & The American Mind*, 146.
26. Barringer, *Selling Yellowstone*, 59; Nash, *Wilderness & The American Mind*, 387.
27. Barringer, *Selling Yellowstone*, 50; Watry, "More Than Mere Camps and Coaches," 76.
28. Wylie, "Autobiography, 1926," 23.
29. Barringer, *Selling Yellowstone*, 50; Wylie, "Autobiography, 1926," 21.
30. Wylie, "Autobiography," 22.

Chapter Seven: Indian Captives to Cattalo

1. E.A. Hitchcock to Captain Oscar J. Brown, February 12, 1900, Yellowstone National Park Archives.
2. Ibid.
3. Schullery, *Searching for Yellowstone*, 100–101.
4. The Wylie Camping Company, *Important Information for the Season of 1900*, Paul R. Wylie Jr. Collection, circa 1900.
5. Edward H. Moorman, "Reminiscence, 1899–1948," Collection 1316, Montana Historical Society Research Center, 1954, 1.
6. Wylie, "Autobiography, 1926," 45–46.
7. Aron, *Working At Play*, 175.
8. Moorman, "Reminiscence, 1899–1948," 5.
9. Barringer, *Selling Yellowstone*, 40; Haines, *The Yellowstone Story*, 2:49–50.
10. Barringer, *Selling Yellowstone*, 43.
11. Wylie, "Autobiography, 1926," 72.
12. Ibid., 57.
13. Jakle, *The Tourist*, 51, 84.
14. Rothman, *Devil's Bargains*, 31.
15. Pomeroy, *In Search of the Golden West*, Photographic illustrations with limited text (preface), Elegant Hotels: Hotel Raymond, Pasadena (1893); By the Sea: Santa Monica Beach (about 1889); and Cliff House, San Francisco.
16. West, *The Last Indian War*, 214–29.
17. Ibid., 94, 99–112.
18. Ibid., 115–20.
19. Ibid., 219.
20. Mrs. George F. (Emma) Cowan, "Reminiscences of Pioneer Life," in *Contributions of the Historical Society of Montana* (Helena, Mont.: Independent Publishing, 1903), 4:167.
21. Ibid., 168.

22. West, *The Last Indian War*, 219.
23. Ibid., 219–20.
24. Ibid., 220.
25. Wylie, "Autobiography, 1926," 70.
26. Cowan, "Reminiscences of Pioneer Life," 185.
27. Ibid., 182.
28. West, *The Last Indian War*, 221.
29. Wylie, "Autobiography, 1926," 71–72.
30. Cowan, "Reminiscences of Pioneer Life," 159.
31. Nash, *Wilderness & The American Mind*, 147, 155–56; Pomeroy, *In Search of the Golden West*, 152.
32. Shaffer, *See America First*, 10.
33. Runte, *National Parks*, 64; House Committee on the Public Lands, *The Yellowstone Park*, [1].
34. Haines, *The Yellowstone Story*, 2:72–74; Wylie, "Autobiography, 1926," 63–64.
35. Haines, *The Yellowstone Story*, 2:74–75; Wylie, "Autobiography, 1926," 64–65.
36. Haines, *The Yellowstone Story*, 2:126–27; Moorman, "Reminiscence, 1899–1948," 6.
37. Moorman, "Reminiscence, 1899–1948," 6.

Chapter Eight: The Wylie Way

1. Shaffer, *See America First*, 133, 135–36.
2. Jakle, *The Tourist*, 100.
3. Ibid., 101.
4. Shaffer, *See America First*, 10.
5. Nash, *Wilderness & The American Mind*, 156.
6. Wylie, "Autobiography, 1926," 52.
7. Ibid., 52–53.
8. "Grace Wylie Passes Away," *The Avant Courier*, July 1, 1904.
9. Wylie, "Autobiography, 1926," 23.
10. Barringer, *Selling Yellowstone*, 50.
11. Wylie, "Autobiography, 1926," 24.
12. Barringer, *Selling Yellowstone*, 50.
13. Haines, *The Yellowstone Story*, 2:119–20; Magoc, *Yellowstone, 1870 -1903*, 118–19; Schullery, *Searching for Yellowstone*, 116.
14. Barringer, *Selling Yellowstone*, 56–57.
15. "How W.W. Wylie Established His Transportation Business," *Butte Inter Mountain*, December 20, 1905.
16. Moorman, "Reminiscence, 1899–1948," 9.
17. Ibid., 8.
18. Ibid., 9.
19. Barringer, *Selling Yellowstone*, 53.
20. Shaffer, *See America First*, 26–30.
21. Lee H. Whittlesey, *Storytelling in Yellowstone*, 240.
22. Barringer, *Selling Yellowstone*, 70; Wylie, "Autobiography, 1926," 47.

23. Runte, *National Parks*, 87.
24. Aubrey L. Haines, *The Yellowstone Story*, 2:283.
25. Runte, *National Parks*, 77, 79–82, 87–88.
26. Haines, *The Yellowstone Story*, 2:284.
27. Runte, *National Parks*, 90–91; Shaffer, *See America First*, 100–101.
28. Runte, *National Parks*, 95; Shaffer, *See America First*, 100–101.
29. Barringer, *Selling Yellowstone*, 64; Wylie, "Autobiography, 1926," 31.
30. Watry, "More Than Mere Camps and Coaches," 79. Watry described the timing as "a quandary."
31. Moorman, "Reminiscence, 1899–1948," 16.
32. *Wylie et al. v. Wylie Permanent Camping Co.*, 57 MT 115 (1920), 117.
33. Ibid.
34. Ibid., 118.
35. Ibid.
36. Ibid.
37. Ibid.
38. Ibid.
39. Ibid.
40. Ibid., 119.
41. Ibid.
42. Ibid., 121.
43. Ibid., 122.
44. Schullery, *Searching for Yellowstone*, 134–35; Shaffer, *See America First*, 137.
45. Shaffer, *See America First*, 109.
46. Barringer, *Selling Yellowstone*, 70–74.
47. Ibid., 74–75.
48. Horace M. Albright and Marian Albright Schenck, *Creating the National Park Service: The Missing Years* (Norman: University of Oklahoma Press, 1999) includes an October 1, 1917, National Park Service map that notes locations of the country's seventeen national parks and twenty-two national monuments. Mukuntuweap National Monument evolved into Zion National Park in November 1919, 244.
49. Shaffer, *See America First*, 108–109.
50. Albright and Schenck, *Creating the National Park Service*, 244.
51. Ibid.; Wylie, "Autobiography, 1926," 96.
52. Jakle, *The Tourist*, 132; Schullery, *Searching for Yellowstone*, 136; Shaffer, *See America First*, 160, 166–68.
53. Wylie, "Autobiography, 1926," 46.
54. Ibid., 52–53.
55. Recipients included the writer's grandmother, Frances Wylie Travis, eighth of John and Minnie Wylie's nine children.
56. Haines, *The Yellowstone Story*, 2:137; Shaffer, *See America First*, 119–22.
57. Mary Grace Wylie's Recollections circa 1940, "5Y: Wylie Family Memorabilia."

Bibliography

Archival Collections

Merrill G. Burlingame and Haynes Special Collections and University Archives, Montana State University, Bozeman, MT.

Wylie Permanent Camping Company and Wylie Transportation Company Papers, Montana Historical Society Research Center, Helena, MT.

W. W. Wylie Papers, Archives and Research Library, Yellowstone National Park Heritage and Research Center, Gardiner, MT.

Government Publications

Anderson, George S. *Report of the Superintendent of the Yellowstone National Park to the Secretary of the Interior.* Washington D.C.: Government Printing Office, 1892, 1894, 1895.

Annual Reports of the Department of the Interior for the Fiscal Year Ended June 30, 1898. 55th Congress: Third Session. Washington, D.C.: Government Printing Office, 1898.

County of Los Angeles: Registrar–Recorder/County Clerk. *Standard Certificate of Death: Mrs. Mary A. Wylie and Wylie, William W.* County of Los Angeles, obtained December 4, 1995.

Culpin, Mary Shivers. *"For the Benefit and Enjoyment of the People": A History of Concession Development in Yellowstone National Park, 1872-1966.* National Park Service, Yellowstone Center for Resources, Yellowstone National Park, Wyoming, YCR-CR-2003-01.

Day, E.C., Commissioner. *The Revised Code of Montana of 1907,* Vol. I. Helena: State Publishing Company, 1908.

Executive Documents of the House of Representatives. 53rd Congress: Second Session. Washington, D.C.: Government Printing Office, 1895.

House Documents. 59th Congress: First Session. Washington, D.C.: Government Printing Office, 1906.

Wylie et al. v. Wylie Permanent Camping Co. 57 MT 117 (1920).

Wylie, W. W. *Seventh Annual Report of the Superintendent of Public Instruction: For the Year 1885.* Helena: Fisk Bros., 1886.

Wylie, W. W. *Eighth Annual Report of the Superintendent of Public Instruction: For the Year 1886.* Helena: Fisk Bros., 1887.

Young, S. B. M. *Report of the Acting Superintendent to the Department of the Interior.* Mammoth Hot Springs: Office of the Superintendent Yellowstone National Park, October 26, 1897.

Books, Pamphlets, and Periodicals

Albright, Horace M., and Marian Albright Schenck. *Creating the National Park Service: The Missing Years.* Norman: University of Oklahoma Press, 1999.

Aron, Cindy S. *Working at Play: A History of Vacations in the United States.* New York: Oxford University Press, 1999.

Barringer, Mark Daniel. *Selling Yellowstone: Capitalism and the Construction of Nature.* Lawrence: University Press of Kansas, 2002.

Blanchard, James A., and George A. Lamar. *Application of William W. Wylie for a Lease in the Yellowstone National Park, with the Privilege of Furnishing Camping Accomodations; Brief in Support of Application.* Filed June 2, 1897. Washington, D.C.: J.S. Tomlinson & Son, 1897.

_____. *Application of William W. Wylie for a Lease in the Yellowstone National Park, with the Privilege of Furnishing Camping Accomodations; Brief in Support of Application.* Filed December 11, 1897. Washington, D.C.: J.S. Tomlinson & Son, 1897.

_____ *Application of William W. Wylie for a Lease in the Yellowstone National Park, with the Privilege of Furnishing Camping Accomodations; Brief in Support of Application.* Filed February 7, 1898. Washington, D.C.: J.S. Tomlinson & Son, 1898.Chittenden, Hiram Martin, and Richard A. Bartlett, eds. *The Yellowstone National Park.* Norman: University of Oklahoma Press, 1964.

Chittenden, Hiram Martin, and Richard A. Bartlett, eds. *The Yellowstone National Park.* Norman: University of Oklahoma Press, 1964.

Cowan, Mrs. George F. "Reminiscences of Pioneer Life," in *Contributions of the Historical Society of Montana.* Helena, Mont.: Independent Publishing, 1903, 4:157-87.

Cronin, Janet, and Dorothy Vick. *Montana's Gallatin Canyon.* Missoula: Mountain Press Publishing Company, 1992.

Haines, Aubrey L. *The Yellowstone Story.* Two volumes. Colorado Associated University Press, 1977.

Hals, Carl J., and A. Rydstrom, Civil Engineers. *Map of the Yellowstone National Park.* Montana State University: Burlingame Special Collections, 1882.

Jakle, John A. *The Tourist: Travel in Twentieth-Century North America.* Lincoln: University of Nebraska Press, 1985.

Lass, William E. *Navigating the Missouri: Steamboating on Nature's Highway, 1819-1935.* Norman: The Arthur H. Clark Co., 2008.

Magoc, Chris J. *Yellowstone: The Creation and Selling of an American Landscape, 1870–1903.* Albuquerque: University of New Mexico Press, 1999.

Malone, Michael P., Richard B. Roeder, and William L. Lang. *Montana: A History of Two Centuries.* Revised Edition. Seattle: University of Washington Press, 1991.

Morris, Roy Jr. *Sheridan: The Life and Wars of General Phil Sheridan.* New York: Crown Publishing Inc., 1992.

Nash, Roderick Frazier. *Wilderness & The American Mind.* New Haven: Yale University, 2001.

Paugh, Minnie. "Wylie Manuscript Adds Pages to Park History," *Billings Gazette,* Montana Historical Society Research Center, November 13, 1966.

Pomeroy, Earl. *In Search of the Golden West: The Tourist in Western America*. Lincoln: University of Nebraska Press, 1990.

Progressive Men of the State of Montana. Chicago: A. W. Bowen & Co., Montana Historical Society, circa 1900.

Rothman, Hal K. *Devil's Bargains: Tourism in the Twentieth-Century American West*. Lawrence: University Press of Kansas, 1998.

Runte, Alfred. *National Parks: The American Experience*. Lanham, MD: Taylor Trade Publishing, 2010.

Schlereth, Thomas J. *Victorian America: Transformations in Everyday Life, 1876–1915*. New York: Harper Collins Publishing, 1991.

Schullery, Paul. *Searching for Yellowstone: Ecology and Wonder in the Last Wilderness*. Helena: Montana Historical Society Press, 2004.

Sears, John F. *Sacred Places: American Tourist Attractions in the Nineteenth Century*. Amherst: University of Massachusetts Press, 1998.

Shaffer, Marguerite S. *See America First: Tourism and National Identity, 1880-1940*. Washington, DC: Smithsonian Books, 2001.

Slayton Lyceum Bureau. *W. W. Wylie*. Montana State University, Burlingame Special Collections, 1898.

Smith, Phyllis, and William Hoy. *The Northern Pacific and Yellowstone National Park*. Gaithersburg, KY: Keystone Press, 2009.

Spence, Mark David. *Dispossessing the Wilderness: Indian Removal and the Making of the National Parks*. New York: Oxford University Press, 1999.

Toole, K. Ross. *Montana: An Uncommon Land*. Norman: University of Oklahoma Press, 1977.

Wells, Fargo & Co. *Stations and Distances from Salt Lake City to Montana and Idaho*. (Montana Historical Society Research Center).

West, Elliot. *The Last Indian War: The Nez Perce Story*. New York: Oxford University Press, 2009.

Whittlesey, Lee H. "Monarch of All These Mighty Wonders: Tourists and Excelsior Geyser, 1881–1890," *Montana The Magazine of Western History* 40, no. 2 (Summer 1990), 2–15.

_____. Editor. *Lost in Yellowstone: Truman Everts's "Thirty–Seven Days Of Peril."* Salt Lake City: The University of Utah Press, 1995.

_____. "Everyone Can Understand a Picture," *Montana The Magazine of Western History* 49, no. 2 (Summer 1999), 2–13.

_____. *Storytelling in Yellowstone: Horse and Buggy Tour Guides*. Albuquerque: University of New Mexico Press, 2007.

Whittlesey, Lee H., and Elizabeth A. Watry. *Images of America: Yellowstone National Park*. Charleston: Arcadia Publishing, 2008.

Wrobel, David M., and Patrick T. Long, Editors. *Seeing and Being Seen, Tourism in the American West*. Lawrence: University Press of Kansas, 2001.

The Wylie Camping Company. *Important Information for the Season of 1900*. Circa 1900.

Wylie Permanent Camping Company. *Map*. 1909.

Wylie Permanent Camps. *Postcard*. Detroit Publishing Company 1899.

Wylie, William Wallace. *Yellowstone National Park; or The Great American Wonderland.* Kansas City, MO: Ramsey, Millet and Hudson, 1882.

Wylie et al. v. Wylie Permanent Camping Co. Pacific Reporter 187, 279.

Unpublished Materials

Anderson, George S. "Letter to Edward Swift." Yellowstone National Park Archives, approximately early 1897.

Austin, B.N. "Letter to Edward Swift." Yellowstone National Park Archives, approximately early 1897.

Hitchcock, E. A. "Letter to Captain Oscar J. Brown." Yellowstone National Park Archives, February 12, 1900.

———. "Letter to Captain George W. Goode." Yellowstone National Park Archives, March 13, 1901.

———. "Letter to Captain John Pitcher." Yellowstone National Park Archives, January 28, 1902.

———. "Letter to Major John Pitcher." Yellowstone National Park Archives, March 10, 1902.

———. "Letter to the Acting Superintendent of the Yellowstone National Park." Yellowstone National Park Archives, May 19, 1902.

———. "Letter to Major John Pitcher." Yellowstone National Park Archives, June 15, 1905.

Lamar, George A. "Letter to Honorable Secretary of the Interior." Yellowstone National Park Archives, July 30, 1902.

Metlen, George R. "Stagecoach Stations: Map of Beaverhead County, Montana." Montana Historical Society Research Center, 1932, corrected 1935.

Miles, Daniel N. "Reminiscence, 1962." Collection 69, Montana Historical Society Research Center, 1962. Photocopy.

Moorman, Edward H. "Reminiscence, 1899–1948." Collection 1316, Montana Historical Society Research Center, 1954. Photocopy.

Ryan, Thos. "Telegram to Acting Supt." Yellowstone National Park Archives, June 7, 1902.

Sims, Wm. H. "Letter to Mr. W.W. Wylie." Yellowstone National Park Archives, May 20, 1896.

Smith, Hoke. "Letter to Capt. George Anderson." Yellowstone National Park Archives, July 24, 1894.

Travis, John W., M.D., and Richard J. Wylie, Editors. "5Y: Wylie Family Memorabilia and Historical Vignettes." Wylie Family Papers, 1992. Photocopy.

Watry, Elizabeth Ann. "More Than Mere Camps and Coaches: The Wylie Camping and the Development of a Middle-Class Leisure Ethic in Yellowstone National Park, 1883-1916." Master's thesis, Montana State University, 2010.

Wessel, Veris A. "A Brief History of Bozeman Schools." Collection 2245, Merrill G. Burlingame Papers 1880–1990, Box 9, folder 23, Montana State University, Bozeman, MT, circa. 1963. Photocopy.

Wylie, Cameron C. "My Story." Wylie Family Papers, 1952. Photocopy.

Wylie, Elizabeth. "Letter to Major John Pitcher." Yellowstone National Park Archives, July 14, 1902.

Wylie, W.W. "Letter to Chas S. Fee." Yellowstone National Park Archives, May 7, 1897.

———. "Letter to Captain George Anderson." Yellowstone National Park Archives, May 22, 1897.

———. "Letters to Mary Ann Wilson Wylie." Collection 1326, Burlingame Special Collections, Montana State University, Bozeman, MT, 1898.

———. "Letter to Major John Pitcher." Yellowstone National Park Archives, July 15, 1902; March 25, 1904; and June 8, September 8, 23, and 26, 1905.

Wylie, William Wallace. "Autobiography, 1926." Collection 343, Burlingame Special Collections, Montana State University, Bozeman, MT.

Personal Communication

Brouillette, Amanda. Letter to the author about Frank Bozeman Wylie's death certificate, August 18, 2010.

Lindemulder, Veniece. Letter to the author about Frank Bozeman Wylie's death Certificate, July 23, 2010.

Sell, Wolfgang. Email communication with author, August 6, 2004.

Shovers, Brian. Email communication with the author, August 9, 2004.

Tarbox, Gary. Northern Pacific Railway Historical Association. Email communication with author, September 27, 2010.

Websites

"American Landscape and Architectural Design: Lantern Slides History." memory.loc.gov/ammem/collections/landscape/lanternhistory.html (accessed October 13, 2014).

"A Brief History of Stereographs and Stereoscopes." nx.org/content/m13784/latest (accessed April 10, 2009).

"Castle Geyser." www.nps.gov/features/yell/tours/oldfaithful/castleg.htm (accessed October 25, 2014).

"Choosing Voluntary Simplicity." www.choosingvoluntarysimplicity.com/what-did-things-cost-in-1872/, accessed June 1, 2010.

"Congressional Acts Pertaining to Yellowstone." www.yellowstone-online.com/history/yhfour.html (accessed August 3, 2004).

"Delaware County Historical Society." www.delawarecountyia.com (accessed October 21, 2003).

"Excelsior Geyser." www.yellowstonenationalpark.com/midway.htm (accessed July 15, 2010).

"Geyser Waters." www.nps.gov/history/history/online_books/yell/weed.sec5.htm (accessed October 26, 2007).

"Guide to the Yellowstone Park Company Records, 1892–1963." nwda-db.wsulibs.wsu.edu/nwda-search/fstyle.aspx?doc=MTGMss181.xml (accessed August 16, 2010).

"Henry Bird Calfee & Nelson (Nelse) Catlin, Bozeman, Montana." www. yellowstonestereoviews.com/publishers/calfee.html (accessed October 10, 2007).

"History of the Stereopticon." bitwise.net/~ken-bill/stereo.htm (accessed August 5, 2004).

"The History of Stereoscopes and Stereographs." www.3dviewmax.com/page71. htm (accessed August 5, 2004).

"In the Senate of the United States. January 5, 1883." archive.org/stream/insenate ofunited1883unit#page/n0/mode/2up (accessed October 21, 2014).

"Material Culture for Overland Emigrants." OregonTrail.blm.gov/wagons (accessed August 4, 2004).

"Montana: Earthquake History." earthquake.usgs.gov/regional/states/montana/ history.php (accessed October 26, 2007).

"Nez Perce National Historical Park." www.nps.gov/archive/nepe/greene/Chap1a and Chap2.htm (accessed August 22, 2010).

"Northern Pacific, August 1, 1898." query.nytimes.com/mem/archive-free/pdf (accessed February 2, 2008).

"Postal Cards, Stamped Cards, and Postcards." www.usps.com/postalhistory/_pdf/ Postal Cards.pdf (accessed August 12, 2010).

"Scribner's Monthly, Volume 0003 Issue 1 (November 1871)." digital.library.cornell. edu (accessed January 26, 2010).

"Thomas Moran Painting of Castle Geyser 1875." www.yellowstone-online.com/ art.html (accessed October 26, 2007).

"The Washburn Yellowstone Expedition Parts 1 and 2 by Walter Trumbull." www. yellowstone-online.com/history/trumbull/trumbull13.html (accessed July 29, 2010).

"Wet Plate Photography." www.pbs.org/wgbh/amex/eastman/sfeature/wetplate.html (accessed July 29, 2010).

"Wylie Way Camps." www.asu.edu/clas/grandcanyonhistory/sites_northrim_wylie waycamps.html (accessed January 4, 2010).

"Yellowstone Science." www.nps.gov/yell/planyourvisit/upload/ys2(3)part1.pdf (accessed February 10, 2009).

Index

and horses, 6, 8, 20, 71, 82–85, 91–92, 104, 114–16, 161, 174, 175–76; and hunting, 149; initial trip to Montana (1878), 12–15; and lawsuit before Interstate Commerce Commission, 135–37, 169–72; lecture tour (1881), 33–38, (1898–99), 133–34; memoir (1926), 8, 9, 75–76, 92, 117, 131, 168, 184, 186, 192–93, 205n55; and Montana Supreme Court lawsuit (1920), 186–89; and park administration, 68, 85–90, 100–102, 107–12, 117, 152–55, 201n11; and new park service regulation, 184; as state superintendent of public instruction, 67, 70, 75; travels to warmer climates, 149–51, 160, 179; visits Yellowstone National Park (1925), 191–93; visits Zion (1925), 191; and the Wylie Hotel, 161–62. *See also* Truman Everts, Wylie Camping Company

Wylie Way, The, 181, 194; camps in Zion Canyon, 190–91; camps at Bright Angel Point (Grand Canyon), 190. *See also* Howard Hays

Wyoming Territory: session law enactment, 60; application of session law, 63; repeal of session law, 68

Yankee Jim, 45, 52
Yankee Jim canyon, 40, 52
Yankee Jim Hill, 45, 52; toll, 52
Yellowstone Lake, 21, 35, 53
Yellowstone National Park, 1–9; Act of Dedication (1872), 54–55; automobiles in, 179, 184, 189; buses in, 191; economic potential of, 55, 68; federal Indian policy applied in, 6, 44, 156, 160; fishing in, 43, 97; military presence in, 21, 69, 97, 113, 119, 181–82; monopoly of leases in, 99, 119, 123, 124, 125–26, 131; promotion of, 32–33, 59; regulations for, 5, 59, 140; road development in, 21, 22, 24, 25, 26, 66, 104, 106, 174, 191, 197n33; as a tourist destination, 1–3, 54, 55, 57, 76, 77, 92, 97–98, 122; as wildlife habitat, 36. *See also* Wyoming Territory and Lacey Act

Yellowstone National Park; or The Great American Wonderland (1882), 39, 40, 51, 71, 76, 79

Yellowstone National Park Transportation Company, 99, 117–18, 122, 129, 184; lack of stopover privileges, 87, 96; lease obtained by, 87. *See also* Northern Pacific Railway

Yellowstone Park Association, 68, 87, 107, 117, 118; camping tours of, 99, 122, 129; hotels, 96–97, 122, 168, 170; lunch stations, 96. *See also* Northern Pacific Railway

Yellowstone Park Camping Company, 189
Yellowstone Park Camps Company, 189, 191
Yellowstone Park Hotel Company, 184
Yellowstone Park Improvement Company, 48–49; financial woes of, 60; National Hotel, 56, 58; tent hotels, 58
Yellowstone Park Lodge and Camps Company, 189
Yellowstone River, 6, 20, 21; Chittenden Bridge, 162–63; Grand Canyon and Great Falls of, 53, 106; Inspiration Point at, 106; Lower Falls of, 16, 106. *See also* H.F. Richardson
Young, Colonel Samuel Baldwin Marks (S.B.M.), 107, 114–16, 117–19, 126, 155, 182

Zillah. *See* Colonel E.C. Waters
Zion National Park, 190–91

The Author

Born and raised in Calgary, Alberta, Canada, Jane Demaray serves on the personal staff of the Montana Secretary of State. A former special education teacher, she has experience in small business as both an owner and a consultant. She is a graduate of the University of Puget Sound, with continuing education at a variety of universities. Her Wylie kinship provided the spark, and personal insight, to the story of camping in Yellowstone during its early years.